THE MODEL
MANUAL

EVERYTHING YOU NEED TO KNOW ABOUT MODELLING

Photographed by Niall McInerney

Photographed by Nick Knight courtesy of © Condé Nast PL - British *Vogue*

THE
MODEL
MANUAL

EVERYTHING YOU NEED TO
KNOW ABOUT MODELLING

Sandra Morris

WEIDENFELD & NICOLSON
LONDON

First published in Great Britain in 1997
by George Weidenfeld & Nicolson Ltd
The Orion Publishing Group
Orion House
5 Upper St Martin's Lane
London WC2H 9EA

Text copyright © Sandra Morris, 1997

The moral right of the author has been asserted
Design and layout copyright © George Weidenfeld & Nicolson Ltd, 1997

All rights reserved. Without limiting the rights under copyright reserved above, no part of this publication may
be reproduced, stored in or introduced into a retrieval system, or transmitted, in any form or by any means
(electronic, mechanical, photocopying, recording, or otherwise), without the prior written permission of both
the copyright holder and the above publisher of this book

A CIP catalogue record for this book is available from the British Library
ISBN 0 297 83585 8

Designed by The Senate
Printed in Italy

*Right: Casting time: while waiting their turn Elite models
check out each others' books and catch up on industry gossip.*

CONTENTS

Photographed by Rod Howe

Photographed by Niall McInerney

Left: Kate Moss parades down the runway for Gucci. Standing only 5'6" in her bare feet, this superstar model was one of the first to defy convention.

INTRODUCTION

Welcome to the kingdom of modelling, where the stars are impossibly beautiful and implausibly rich; where you can date a rock star, become a famous personality, or refuse to get out of bed for less than $10,000 a day.

It was those glamorous icons – the supermodels – who raised the profile of the profession and turned modelling into one of the most desirable occupations of the nineties. Smart, wealthy, famous and, above all, successful – no wonder every schoolgirl dreams of becoming a supermodel! Supermodeldom is, of course, only for the lucky few. But for every Helena, Naomi and Kate, there are tens of thousands of models working in other fields of the model industry. And, as model mania continues, it's not only the pretty young things who are knocking on agents' doors. From kiddies to little old ladies, all types, all sizes and all ages are getting in on the modelling act.

Whether you're a Siberian Eskimo, a Masai tribeswoman or a pale Icelandic blonde, the model industry does not discriminate. Similarly it makes no bones about former skills, qualifications or background. Nor is it classist: from the cities to the provinces, stately homes to trailer parks,

models hail from all walks of life.

There's no question about it, attitudes are changing as the model industry's key players readjust their notion of the mannequin. Preconceptions of any 'ideal' are rapidly being dispelled by the new breed of model who is undeniably stunning, but hardly conventionally beautiful. Enter Stella Tennant, who has a large nose, thin lips and wears a scowl; quirky-faced Guenivere, Iris Palmer and Esther; the not-so-tall Kate Moss who, along with voluptuous size-14 Sophie Dahl, illustrate that the perimeters are definitely shifting.

Sarah Doukas, owner of top model agency Storm, which represents some of the biggest names in the business, including Kate Moss, Eva Herzigova, Elle Macpherson, Iris Palmer and Honor Fraser, has been instrumental in pushing back the boundaries. Her past challenges have included Kate Moss, Guenivere, Iris Palmer and Sophie Dahl, together with Jane Marsh, who, at 5'1", was breaking all the rules! Clearly, Sarah has an undisputed talent for turning what the model industry had previously considered totally unacceptable into the Next Big Thing. 'You shouldn't be restricted,' says Sarah, whose discerning eye hasn't failed her yet. 'When I look at a potential model I always have an open mind, rather than immediately thinking she's too short, too large, or too alternative looking.' With the multiplicity of images filtering through, it looks as though as long as you've got 'it' – an undefinable quality that captures our attention as we turn the pages – *almost* anything goes.

For all you aspiring Kates and Marcuses possessing such God-given attributes as chiselled cheekbones and tall, sylph-like bodies, this book delves into the glittering, yet gruelling, world of high-fashion modelling. But if you're not drop-dead-supermodel-gorgeous, don't despair. Supermodels may be at the forefront of the modelling world, but they are an ultra-thin layer of the market. Look beyond the ranks of international fashion modelling and you'll discover a whole variety of modelling options all featured within this book.

At the mainstream end of the fashion market there's a mountain of work where, for example, you could find yourself being photographed for a mail-order catalogue or modelling clothes in a local department store. Too short to stand up to the tall, fashion-model proportions? Why not toy with the idea of petite or teenage modelling? And, if you're attractive with a lively personality, did you know that promotional work is a field open to you? Perhaps you're blessed with Rubenesque curves. If so, check out the chapter on plus-size modelling (p.58) to see if you qualify. Alternatively, if you're prepared to peel off a layer or two, the daring world of glamour modelling might take your fancy.

Character has become kooky, and many clients are trading in gloss and glamour for real people – warts and all! From the pleasant-looking, family types to oddball characters and misfits, the scope for non-conventional models is greater than ever before. So, if you don't conform to fashion-model ideals, but are still keen to have a bite at the modelling apple, think for a moment of all the ads featuring 'real-looking' models. You may have found your niche!

As the children's clothing and catalogue markets expand, more kids are entering the profession. Parents eager to see their offspring smile cheekily from the billboards can find out more about child modelling on p.46. But it's not only the tiny tots who are in demand. Increasingly, mature models in their thirties, forties and fifties- plus are gaining ground in the fields of advertising, mail-order and the fashion arena, too.

If you don't slot into any of the aforementioned categories, maybe you've a special feature to offer – perfectly manicured hands or a well-shaped pair of feet. If you're a dead ringer for Princess Diana, Elvis, Tina Turner or some other famous person, you could be hired as a lookalike. Failing that, working as an extra is guaranteed to capture you on film. And, for those who do not wish to model but are keen to work in the business, the chapter on alternative careers in the model industry (p. 98) offers you a host of choices, from make-up artist to model-agency booker.

If you've always longed to have supermodel style and beauty – regardless of whether you want to model or not – Part 3 is devoted to the quest for that much-yearned-for model look. With experts' superhints on many aspects of looking good – style, make-up, hair, skin care, body care, fitness and nutrition – the image chapter taps into all the trade secrets.

The Model Manual peers behind the scenes of the modelling world. It takes you to photo shoots, castings and go-sees, inside model agencies, backstage at the shows, and follows a day in the life of a top fashion model. The book also gives you an exclusive insight into the model industry: who's who, the contests, the shows, the training, the agents – including a comprehensive directory to model agencies around the globe.

Lurking beneath the industry's surface is an underworld where thousands of would-be models are exploited by sharks. Read about, and learn from, the victims who fell into their traps. And to avoid the pitfalls, follow the golden rules on p.94.

Covering the entire spectrum of modelling, this book cuts through the glamour and spells out what it takes to make a model: the basic requirements, how to get started, and the perks and pitfalls of a bittersweet career. Meet top models from each field of modelling and find out how they started, their struggles and their success stories.

Whether you want to follow in the footsteps of Cindy Crawford or simply want to find out more about this exciting world ... read on!

Photographed by Niall McInerney

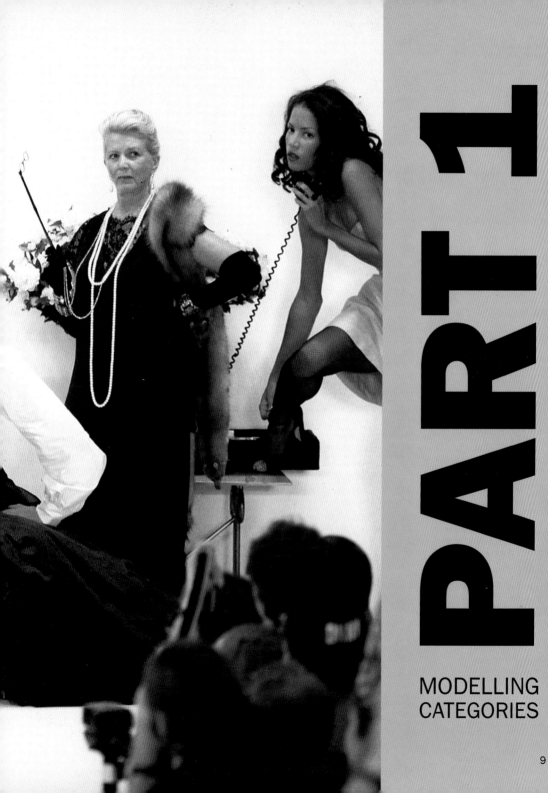

PART 1

MODELLING
CATEGORIES

FASHION MODELLING

Photographed by Jacques Oliver courtesy of © Condé Nast Pl. - British Vogue

Synonymous with the Vogues and Versaces of this world is the fashion end of the model industry.

Since the supermodel exploded onto the scene in 1988, fashion modelling has snowballed into a multi-million-pound global business. Designer frocks, limos, parties and hobnobbing with the rich and famous, it seems a whirlwind of never-ending glamour and fun. International fashion modelling is, undeniably, the most glamorous and exciting area of the profession, with celebrity status and untold millions for those who reach the top. But before you book a Concorde flight or add Inc. to your name, remember – the model's life is tough, highly pressurized and, what's more, the competition is fierce.

Most models who break into this territory have an 'editorial' look: a strong, individual, yet modern image that fits high fashion. Those who are awarded the 'super' prefix have that imperceptible something that separates them from the rest – the 'X' factor, known by the French as *je ne sais quoi*, or what the Germans describe as *ein gewissen Etwas*.

From the perfectly symmetrical Cindy Crawford, to the more quirky-looking Stella Tennant, models' looks are more varied than ever before. The army of off-beat beauties have proved that unconventional looks are as desirable as textbook beauty. However, models' looks go in and out of fashion more quickly than hemlines go up and down, with faces matching high fashion's whimsical demands. You may remember the 'golden girls' as the precursors to the waifs until, more recently, the 'extreme-looking' clan took charge as the 'Next Big Thing'. During their heyday, all these models had what is termed as 'the look of the moment'. But, as superagent Didier Fernandez of Elite Paris, who handles the careers of the supers – Linda Evangelista, Amber Valletta, Nadja Auermann and Karen Mulder – points out: 'Models need staying power and, to ride the tide of fashion, they must possess a chameleon-like quality that enables them to reinvent themselves and present a fresh new image.'

High-fashion modelling is no longer about the capacity to model clothes – it's gone way beyond this. It's about a face, a look, a trend, a mood and – in the case of the supermodels – a name. Once upon a time show models were tall, angular-looking mannequins – a different breed from their photographic counterparts. Times, though, have changed. Nowadays, the top designers want those models currently gracing the pages of the glossies – *Harper's Bazaar, Vogue, W, Elle* and *Marie Claire* – regardless of their height or ability to sashay down a runway.

International fashion modelling is not dissimilar to a game of snakes and ladders. To play, you have to be taken on the books of an editorial fashion agency. Once signed up, you'll be placed on the agency's new faces board and will be required to do the rounds of go-sees, spending every spare moment testing. At this stage, especially if you're

in your early teens, it's likely you'll be booked for teenage fashion magazines to gain experience in front of the camera. This is very much a development time: a new haircut, the right image, and talks on how to cope with castings, rejection and success.

If you're modelling full time, you could spend anything from a few weeks to six months on the new faces board. One lucky new face, 16-year-old Storm model Charlotte Connoley, skipped the go-sees and teeny-magazine stage, and leapt straight onto Storm's main board within a matter of weeks. 'We sent two Polaroids of Charlotte to photographer David Sims, and the next thing we knew, she was confirmed for an ad campaign with Calvin Klein alongside Kate Moss,' says Marie Soulier excitedly. But, as Marie points out, Charlotte is one of the lucky ones: 'Most girls spend at least three months on new faces. And, if a model is still at school, she'll stay on the new faces board until she's ready to model full time – which could mean years!'

According to Karen Long, director of top male agency, Boss Models, guys don't require as much development or grooming as the girls. 'Basically, all a new male model needs is a good haircut, a couple of strong tests, and he's away. Quite often our guys only spend a month on the new faces board.'

Generally, it takes a good couple of years to develop into a fully-fledged model – male or female. During the earlier stages of development, your booker will decide which direction to push you in, i.e. high-fashion editorial or the more commercial route. This is dictated by your particular look. 'You have to be realistic about what you can achieve,' points out Elaine Dugas, who runs IMG's London office. 'If you haven't got a strong, editorial look, you can't expect to get the high-profile editorial bookings.'

At this point you may spend a couple of months in a market such as Milan or London, where it's easier for new models to get magazine tearsheets (a published page from a magazine). 'London is a good place to start,' says Elaine, 'because you have the cutting-edge magazines like *Dazed &*

'It's something of a lottery – a girl may be incredibly beautiful with all the right attributes, but she may not be with the right people in the right place at the right time.'

Confused and *Scene,* who are more likely to use models without tearsheets.' Several of the high-fashion magazines, including *Elle, Marie Claire* and *Vogue* have foreign editions, such as Portuguese *Elle* or Japanese *Marie Claire*, who will more readily book new models than the highly prestigious British, American or French editions. Once a model is armed with published tearsheets, he or she can start casting for a whole variety of fashion work, including runway, point of sale, packaging, catalogues, brochures, music videos, commercials and print advertising, as well as editorial.

Perhaps you have 'the look of the moment' or that 'X' factor that casts you among the rising supermodels. Lucky you! Your dice have obviously landed on six. This could happen at any stage in your modelling career. You might have only joined the new faces board or, like Kate Moss, Stella Tennant and many other supermodels, you could have been modelling for years. 'It's something of a lottery,' says Didier. 'A girl may be incredibly beautiful, with all the right attributes, but she may not be with the right people in the right place at the right time.'

If luck is on your side and you've thrown another high number, New York, Paris or London will beckon, with agencies in one or all of these markets hungry to represent you. Word travels fast in this business. It's quite likely that your booker will be inundated with calls from heavyweight photographers and bookings editors asking to see you, or calling in your book. With prestigious spreads from one or more of the high-profile magazines – *Harper's Bazaar, Vogue, W, Elle* and *Marie Claire* – or the more cutting-edge magazines, such as *The Face, Arena, Dazed & Confused, i-D* and *Details* under you belt, your booker can start hyping you as the Hottest New Thing.'If we think a model's ready, we'll start pushing her,' says Didier. 'But the model needs to have a mature attitude and be a fighter, or she'll crack under the pressure; then all our hard work and effort will be pointless. At the end of the day there's only so much an agent can do.'

It's not necessarily age that determines whether

a model is mature or not. One of fashion's most-wanted models is 16-year-old Caroline Eggert, bought over from the US to Paris by Elite only nine months ago. Within this short space of time, her career has flourished: she's worked for *Harper's Bazaar,* and Italian and French *Vogue*; she's completed her first couture season and, above all, achieved the supermodel prize – a beauty campaign for Yves Saint Laurent. 'It's the fastest ascent I've ever seen,' says Didier. 'I've watched her in action on photo shoots and at the shows – she's a natural who looks like she's been modelling for years. She can also cope in any situation; she really is the most mature 16-year-old I've ever met.'

Once you reach Caroline's level it's all about the right exposure. You have to be seen doing the right shows – Chanel, Galliano, Versace, Gucci, Klein, Prada – be photographed by the big-name photographers and appear in fashion stories and on the covers of the right magazines. It's at this instant that your booker starts strategically plotting your career by picking and choosing whom you work for, and turning down any mainstream work that could jeopardize your high-profile image. One wrong move – in the shape of a second-rate booking – and you could risk sliding back down the snake. A slimline-drink advertiser may be offering a six-figure sum for a world-wide commercial but, as much as it would please your bank manager, if your agent feels it could potentially damage your image, he or she will turn it down. As Elaine explains: 'It's better for a high-fashion model to not work than be seen working for the wrong magazines, photographers or ad campaigns. Once you're labelled as a commercial model, it's almost impossible to change direction. With model of the moment, Angela Linval, we knew she was going to be big, and had to be very careful who she worked for. This meant turning down work until the right job with the right profile came along. Luckily it did. Juergen Teller used her for Italian *Vogue* and she was also booked for the prestigious Miu Miu campaign. Now everyone wants her!'

High-fashion models do, occasionally, step out of the confines of fashion to appear in campaigns

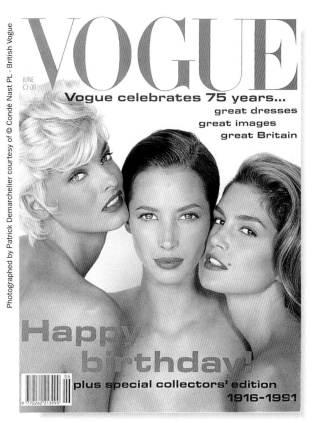

Photographed by Patrick Demarchelier courtesy of © Condé Nast PL – British Vogue

for products like Pepsi. But the profile and the contract must be right. You may recall Cindy and Linda munching pizza in a Pizza Hut commercial, and Kate, Naomi, Linda and Tatjana in the unforgettable 'supermodel' campaign for the Vauxhall Corsa. But remember, these girls had already reached the top.

If you scoop a major fashion or beauty campaign or are booked for the cover of a prestigious magazine, you'll be catapulted to the top of the next ladder. Your day rate will spiral, and other designers and fashion companies will want you in their campaigns. This happened to Stella Tennant when, in one season alone, she dominated the major fashion campaigns, including Versace, Valentino, The Gap and Cerruti. This led to one of modelling's most sought-after contracts: the new face of Chanel.

To be chosen as 'The Face' for a world-wide fragrance or cosmetic campaign is the highest accolade a model can possibly dream of. Some of the models signed to such campaigns include Cindy Crawford, who for many years has been 'The Face' of Revlon; Amber Valletta, the new face of Elizabeth Arden; and Linda Evangelista, who was recently picked by Yardley to update their blue-rinse image. After landing the Obsession campaign, Kate Moss became Calvin Klein's number-one muse. Moss now shares the Klein spotlight with Joel West, the first male supermodel to be signed to such a deal.

Talking of male models, their careers are handled in much the same way as the girls', the only difference being that they have a longer shelf life. 'Apart from the fact that male models spend less time on the new faces board, the strategy is pretty much the same,' explains Boss Models' Karen Long. 'Just like the girls, some male models become overnight sensations, while others take years to crack it. One of our models, German model Norbert, had worked in Paris, Germany, Milan and London for five years and was close to giving up when Juergen Teller booked him for the Eternity campaign. His career has been phenomenal ever since.'

So once you've reached the modelling zenith – what next? Well, it's your booker's job to keep you there and prevent you sliding down the snake. You might explore other career possibilities and spin-offs: publish a book, cut a record, open a restaurant, star in a movie or take a short break from modelling to have a baby. Then again, you might just be a great model and stake your place at the top.

Most models who work in the fashion domain will never pose for *Elle* or sashay down the Paris runways. Nonetheless, they will enjoy rewarding careers in the mainstream areas of fashion. On the whole, these models have a more

Photographed by Niall McInerney

Supermale Marcus Schenkenberg leads the male-model brigade down the runway.

'commercial' image, and are used by clients whose requirements are closer to the so-called girl- or boy-next-door type, rather than the directional editorial look. The term 'commercial' is a by-word for selling a product. Whether the job is for a catalogue or an advertising campaign, commercial-style work is usually photographed in a less creative way than editorial-style photography. Commercial-looking models are booked for catalogue work, in-store display posters, brochures, packaging, all types of consumer print advertising and commercials. These models are still hired for editorial work, but it tends to be for the more mainstream publications, as opposed to prestigious fashion or cutting-edge stuff.

From fashion shows in department stores, boutiques and shopping malls, to garment fittings and showroom seasons, there are an abundance of mainstream opportunities for fashion models. 'Informal' modelling, also known as 'couture-style' (where clothes are modelled without a runway), is another area of live fashion work. For this type of work, models might be hired in-house at a showroom, in-store, on a stand at a fashion trade exhibition, or on a magazine-style television show. Garment fittings, where the model acts as a mannequin while the designer sizes up, pins and tacks the collection, is also an option for fashion models.

Fashion companies and designers who operate as wholesalers have showrooms where they hold a range of samples for retail buyers to order from. Some of these companies hire permanent 'house models', while others may only require models for what is termed a 'season' (those few busy weeks during the buying season). Full-time house models are often expected to take on other roles when they're not actually modelling, such as reception and secretarial work, selling the range to buyers or even making the tea! Mainstream fashion work neither pays the big bucks, nor does it hold the kudos of high-fashion modelling. However, it can earn a model a respectable living.

To work in the international, high-fashion arena, you'll need to be represented by the likes of Elite, IMG, Ford, Storm, Models 1, Women and The Marilyn Agency or other editorial agencies. Most of these agencies are centred in each country's prime modelling markets. Quite often there's a cross-over between editorial and commercial agencies, since editorial agencies also undertake commercial work, and vice versa. Mainstream fashion work is either handled by agencies which represent several model types, or regional agencies based outside the main modelling markets. If you model in the mainstream fashion or commercial field, you can work within a regional market, but if you want to succeed as a high-fashion model, you'll have to travel, be it to studio shoots in Paris, New York and London, on locations, trips, or working the international show circuit.

BASIC REQUIREMENTS

Besides fulfilling the basic requirements of right height, age and vital statistics, you should have clear skin, healthy hair, good teeth and a prominent bone structure. You also need to be photogenic, which means you look even better on film than in the flesh.

Height: Girls should be at least 5'8", although commercial fashion agencies will sometimes relax these restrictions. Agencies who specialize in shows, however, often require their models to be 5'9" and over. Some high-fashion models, including Kate Moss (who stands 5'6" in her bare feet), occasionally break the rules. Men should be between 6' and 6'2".

Vital statistics: Girls should be a size 10 or 12 and have statistics that are more or less 34-24-34. For example, Claudia Schiffer's measurements are 35-24-35, whereas Kirsty Hume's vital statistics are 32-24-34. Men should have a chest size of 38–40, a waist measurement of 30–32 and a suit size 38–42. Marcus Schenkenberg, for example, is suit size 42 and measures 31" around his waist.

Age: Fashion modelling is still primarily a career for young people, so the younger you start the better. Most fashion models begin modelling in their teens – occasionally as young as 12! If a model is still at school or college, she/he can model part time during the school holidays.

Catwalk skills: Firstly, you'll need a strong presence for catwalk work; it will be up to you to make the clothes come alive. You will also need to be able to master that saunter – although this will come with practice. Don't worry if you have got duck feet, it shouldn't prevent an agency from taking you on. For tips on how to walk, see the chapter on training (p.82).

A TYPICAL DAY IN THE LIFE OF A TOP MODEL

International fashion model, Tina Harlow, allowed me to gatecrash her castings, go-sees and photo shoots to join her on a typical working day in London. Originally from LA, this stunning 23–year-old is represented by top agencies around the world including Elite Premier in London, IMG in Paris, as well as her 'mother' agency, Elite LA.

8.00 Alarm goes off When I arrive, Tina is already in the kitchen knocking up a decidedly healthy-looking concoction of scrambled eggs on toast. Having flushed this down with a steaming hot cup of coffee and her daily dose of vitamins, it was time to get ready. 'I always allow plenty of time to shower, wash and blow-dry my hair and, if I'm going on castings, an extra five minutes to put on a little make-up,' she tells me while dabbing on concealer, stroking her long lashes with a mascara wand, and adding a slick of gloss to her poppy-red pout. Now to that impossible task of choosing what to wear. 'I'm not one of these models who feels happy wearing jeans and worn-out sneakers to castings. As a model I think it's part of my job to look good.' Finally, she decides on a black mini and fitted jumper. She flings on her coat, grabs her bag and we're off.

9.15 Travel to casting The traffic is bad so we opt for the tube. A few stops later and we arrive at the offices of *Marie Claire* for her first appointment of the day. 'After working for a while in a city you get to know the best way to travel around, and whether it's quicker to take a cab, walk or catch the tube.'

10.00 Casting for *Marie Claire* In reception Tina spots a model from her agency. They compare books, talk castings and exchange news. 'I always enjoy meeting people, so I don't see castings as a drag; it's also a chance to catch up on industry gossip with other models.' Her colleague is called in. 'Waiting your turn is a bit like being at the dentist's surgery,' jokes Tina, while fingering a pile of magazines. Luckily, it's only a matter of minutes before it's her turn. She's greeted by *Marie Claire*'s bookings editor who flicks through her book and asks what editorial she's done lately. Tina is enthusiastic and friendly, as always. Handing her a composite (a printed model card featuring a selection of her best photos), Tina smiles and thanks the editor for her time. 'I make a point of being as friendly as possible,' she explains. 'I've been in the business long enough to know how important personality and good etiquette is.'

10.30 Drop by her agency, Elite Premier A ten-minute cab ride and we arrive at her agency. One of the bookers greets her with a big hug. 'Everyone at Elite is so friendly. It can be lonely when you're thousands of miles away from home, but these guys make you feel like you're part of a family.' She checks her chart to see if there are any changes to her schedule. There are plenty of additions. London Fashion Week kicks off in a few days and, consequently, she has dozens of show castings to attend. 'I'm working this afternoon so I'm going to miss two of the castings, but it can't be helped.' As she scribbles down the details, Tina's booker waves a foreign edition of *Marie Claire* in front of her. 'Great,' exclaims Tina with excitement, 'I've been dying to see the pictures from this shoot.'

10.45 Appointment with foreign scout The De Boekers agency from The Netherlands is at Elite's offices interviewing models who are interested in being represented in Amsterdam. Tina shows her book to the scout who, admiring each image, offers to represent her. 'De Boekers is one of the best in Amsterdam, so I'm delighted to be on their books.' Yet another name to add to her impressive list of international agencies. Before we go, Tina asks one of her bookers to laser copy certain tearsheets from her book and leave them with the scout. With a smile firmly planted on her face, we head off for the next casting. 'When things go well you feel on top of the world.'

11.15 Juice break Detour to the tube to buy some carrot juice. 'I read that it's great for your skin, so I try to drink a carton of the stuff every day.'

12.00 Show casting The showroom is crammed full of dozens of gorgeous girls from agencies all over town. Unlike her first two castings, this time there's a long wait. Tina remains calm and good-natured, explaining that this is quite normal for a show casting. Eventually, she's handed a couple of samples to try on, which she slips effortlessly into. 'It's always a big plus if the clothes fit you really well. It's amazing how a sample size 10 differs from one designer to another.' After parading up and down the room in each outfit, Tina quickly dresses, then hands the show producer a composite, who says he'll be in contact with her booker later. Sounds promising! Running late, we make a mad dash for the tube.

1.15 Go-see with fashion photographer Rod Howe Three stops and four escalator workouts

Photographed by Cathrine Rowlands

later, we arrive at the studio. Rod is in the full swing of shooting a model, so we settle down on a large leather sofa. As we chat Tina pulls out an item from her bag that goes everywhere with her – water. 'Yes it's true, we models are addicted to the stuff!' Within minutes the crew breaks for lunch and Rod greets us with apologies. Looking through Tina's book (see above pic) he explains that the job is for a lingerie campaign and thinks Tina might be suitable. She looks pleased, but tells me that she's not going to hold her breath over it. 'He still has a dozen or so models to see,' she sighs.

1.30 Go-see at photographers' agents We arrive at Perseverance Works (a large studio complex) in the nick of time. The photographer flicks through

Tina's book, thanks her and we're out of the door quicker than the time it takes to say 'go-see'. Quite justifiably, Tina felt that the meeting wasn't particularly productive, although she admitted that you just never know. 'It's often when you feel you haven't impressed a client you find you've been optioned for the job.'

1.35. A bite to eat Conveniently, Tina is booked for a half-day shoot at another studio in Perseverance Works. We're welcomed by the photographer's assistant who tells us we're just in time for lunch. Tina fills her plate with chicken, new potatoes and heaps of salad from a rather delicious-looking spread. 'I love studio lunches, they're yummy, yet at the same time, healthy.'

2.30 Four-hour booking – catalogue shoot After lunch, Tina is ushered into the make-up room. 'I always enjoy having someone else doing my hair and make-up. It gives you a moment to relax and is the ideal opportunity to swap make-up and hairstyling tips.' While the make-up artist gets to work, Tina sits back and explains that although catalogue work is not considered prestigious, it's enjoyable and pays well. Four outfit changes, and she's through. Tina telephones her agency to tell them we're on our way.

7.15 Back at Elite Tina's mother agency, Elite LA, is in town and is joining Tina, two bookers from Elite London and myself for dinner. 'Because I've been so busy working in Europe and New York,' explains Tina, 'it's been a while since I've seen these guys. They were the first model agency I joined, and are very dear to me.'

8.00 Dinner At the restaurant we chat and catch up on each others' news. Tina chooses a tuna dish accompanied by a glass of dry white wine. When it comes to dessert, she can't resist. 'It's good to watch what you put into your body, but I think it's important to indulge occasionally.' As a heavy schedule lies ahead of her, this dedicated beauty reluctantly tears herself away from the happy crowd to head home for an early night. As we say our goodbyes, a driver from Elite arrives to chauffeur Tina to her apartment.

10.30 Bed Tina falls into bed exhausted.

THE FASHION SHOOT

The shoot is for the fashion pages of the December and January issues of *Cosmopolitan*. The venue: a London studio. The team: *Cosmopolitan*'s fashion editor, Bryony Toogood (who is so pretty I initially mistook her for the model), her assistant Jamie Brogden, a hair stylist and make-up artist, together with fashion photographer Howard Daniels, his assistant and two gorgeous models from Elite. 'When I'm choosing a model,' explains Bryony, 'I look for a girl who has great legs and a fabulous figure that is on the curvaceous side – we don't want to spend hours pinning the samples on her. She must also be photogenic with a lovely smile and good personality.' The whole team arrives at the studio at around 9am, including Rachel Roberts – a tall, staggeringly beautiful, leggy blond who certainly fulfils Bryony's requisite look. Those who don't know each other are introduced, and those who do greet one another with the usual model-industry 'mwah, mwah' on each cheek. Coffee is served. After a few minutes of chit-chat everyone sets to work.

While the make-up artist applies a base to Rachel's scrubbed skin, the fashion team is busy preparing the clothes and accessories she will wear. Bryony has chosen a dazzling selection of winter outfits in rich chocolate browns and deep greens. To complement these shades, the make-up artist applies the season's must-have bronzes and browns. Rachel's hair is kept sleek and simple. Combing her shoulder-length, blonde bob into a side parting, the hair stylist then smoothes it back and fastens it at the nape of her neck. Meanwhile, Howard and his assistant are setting up the lighting, and a prop, in the shape of a pale-beige armchair, is wheeled onto the set. After at least an hour of having her face painted and hair coiffed, Rachel has been transformed from a fresh-faced girl into a glamorous diva. To get her in the mood, Rachel's brought along some of her favourite CDs. She presses 'play' and is ready to go. Positioning herself on the set, she looks simply stunning draped across the chair in an effortlessly elegant but uncontrived pose.

During the usual last-minute preparations, Bryony spots a forgotten tag dangling from Rachel's sleeve and rushes over, armed with a pair of scissors, to snip it off. While Howard's assistant loads the film, the make-up artist and hair stylist do their final check (see right) adding a touch more lip colour with a fine-tipped lip brush, and smoothing stray hairs into place. The lights, which illuminate Rachel's face and pick out the highlights in her hair, are switched on. Howard takes a few meter readings to check the lighting, which he adjusts accordingly. Finally, everyone's ready for action. Rachel immediately springs to life, moving with ease and fluidity. Using her eyes, she flirts with the camera. After several outfit changes and dozens of rolls of film, the team welcomes the opportunity to break for lunch.

In breezes model number two, Lilicoy, a curvaceous brunette from New York. As Howard runs off a few more rolls of film of Rachel, Lilicoy heads off to the make-up room. At about 4pm Rachel is through, and rushes off to catch a flight to Paris for another magazine shoot. Back in the studio, the whole procedure is repeated all over again.

Photographed by Rod Howe

Photographed by Rod Howe

Above: *Behind the scenes – the shots you never get to see. Here Rachel Roberts poses for Howard Daniels' lens.*

Right: *The end result – a published page in Cosmopolitan two months later.*

Photographed by Howard Daniels courtesy of Cosmopolitan

FASHION BY
JAMIE BROGDEN
PHOTOGRAPHS BY
HOWARD DANIELS
STILL LIVES BY
ROBERT WINN
Hair by Matthew
Cross for Nicky
Clarke, using
Hairomatherapy
products
Make-up by Mandy
Winrow at Marina
Jones. Model:
Rachel Roberts
*For where to buy,
see Stockists page*

great
buys

£44.99

Dress, £44.99, Oasis.
Polo-neck jumper, £49.99, The Scotch
House. Tights, £22, Wolford

LISA B

There are models, there are supermodels, then there's Lisa Barbuscia – known to many as Lisa B. This multi-talented model/actress/singer is a compromise between superstar and supermodel – she's 'The Face' of Liz Claiborne's *Curves*, had three hit singles, and starred on the big screen in *Serpents' Lair* and *Edward's & Hunt*. And it's not because she's done the typical supermodel number and turned into a multi-media mogul. On the contrary, Lisa, who modestly describes herself as a jack of all trades, was dancing, singing and acting long before she ever stepped foot on a runway.

Born 27 years ago in New York to a Puerto Rican mother and Italian-Irish father, she has that kind of exotic, mixed-culture beauty that's in constant demand. When I met Lisa, in spite of jet lag, recovering from a bout of flu and having been up half the night at a film premiere party, she still looked ravishing. Talking of premieres, Lisa gets invited to them all. She's reached the enviable stage where, not only does she get to borrow that little Versace dress but, also, as she waltzes into the cinema, both the paparazzi and public – all vying for her attention – shout and yell her name: Lisa B, Lisa Barbuscia or just Lisa. Lisa B was the teenager but Lisa Barbuscia is the woman. 'Lisa B makes me sound like a rap star. I know my full name is a mouthful but they'll get used to it,' insists Lisa, referring to the tabloids who enjoyed turning Lisa B into such headlines as 'Lisa B...haves badly' and 'Lisa Makes a B... line'.

With ambitions to become a Broadway star, Lisa went to ballet school and later joined the New York School of Performing Arts. However, at 15, a quirk of fate led to a diversion in her career path. 'I was in an elevator when I noticed this guy staring at me,' recalls Lisa. 'It turned out that he was a scout from a top New York model agency called Click. He handed me his card and told me I had the makings of a model. I was

so excited I ran all the way home.' Frustratingly, Lisa's father insisted she finished her education before taking up modelling. The Click agency waited patiently, signing her up the moment she left school. A little while later the agency sent her to Europe, where she was represented by both London and Paris agencies. Along with Linda, Naomi, Claudia and Karen, today, Lisa is one of the stars of Elite.

Lisa's debut assignment was a shoot for a teenage magazine – not the most riveting of jobs. But it wasn't long before she left the teeny market behind when she landed an exclusive six-month contract for French *Elle*. While the fashion world was falling for this mysterious beauty, she was falling head over heels in love with Ben Volpeliere, lead singer of top eighties pop group, Curiosity Killed The Cat. 'I was smitten,' she says, with a wistful look in her big, brown eyes. After touring with the band, Lisa's aspirations to perform were revived. Being surrounded by music-industry bods gave her all the connections she needed. A couple of introductions and a few demos later, she signed with Polygram. Although each release was a hit, she soon had enough of touring and living out of location vans, and temporarily shunned the music business for cameras and catwalks.

After spending the best part of a decade in London, Lisa recently moved to the entertainment metropolis, LA, to pursue her acting career. Eight years on from her first modelling assignment, she is booked for major campaigns and only needs to go on the castings she's requested for. 'Trudging to a dozen or so castings each day was the part I hated most about modelling; especially when it was cold or wet and you'd invariably arrive with a bright red nose and your hair looking like rats' tails.' Nonetheless, it was this groundwork that led to Lisa winning some of the choicest assignments around. She was one of the famous Guess? models, has appeared on the covers and in the fashion pages of dozens of glossy magazines, and has sashayed down the runways of every international designer, from Chanel to Versace.

When Lisa first started modelling, the designers overlooked her for the more curvaceous mannequins. 'I guess I was what you'd call the "pre-waif waif",'

'When the Paris shows were in full swing, to get me to each show on time my booker would drive me around on a scooter.'

Photographed by Marco Palumbo for Tatler

need never wear a scrap of make-up, let alone bother with complicated beauty regimes. Juggling several careers at once can be stressful and leaves little time for workouts, so, to keep fit and revive her energy, Lisa practises yoga. Sleep is also high on her agenda of beautifiers. 'I can't go out all night and then work the next day; I just don't know how the others do it,' says Lisa, who'd been partying the previous night with Naomi Campbell and Amber Valletta – neither of whom went to bed at all!

With a wealth of modelling experience behind her, Lisa has plenty of advice for new and aspiring models: 'In a business obsessed with looks, it's important to focus on what's on the inside. And always have hobbies or immerse yourself in interests other than modelling,' she adds. Calling her house the 'Lisa B Motel', she points out how important it is for models to have a permanent base. 'So many models are like strays, turning up on my doorstep with no place to stay, and nowhere to call home.'

From a very young age Lisa worked extremely hard and, although she believes success is

laughs Lisa, who still has a lean, willowy physique. But as soon as the designers started hiring the models dominating the magazines, she became the darling of the runway. 'I was so happy to be doing catwalk work, it was a way of performing and I just loved the immediacy of it all.' It wasn't long before Lisa was doing at least seven shows a day, including fittings. 'When the Paris shows were in full swing, to get me to each show on time my booker would drive me around on a scooter.'

Describing herself as a low-maintenance beauty, Lisa talks skin-care regimes – or lack of them! 'My 80-year-old grandmother, who looks 50, has always moisturized her face with cocoa butter – so I do the same.' With thick, dark lashes that frame her velvety eyes set against a creamy complexion, she

partly down to your face fitting and being in the right place at the right time, she stresses that hard work has a lot to do with it. Of course, the fact that she has the looks of an impishly sexy goddess might just have something to do with it, too!

That American sense of drive and ambition has clearly taken her to the top in the modelling world, and looks set to do the same in the field of acting. Despite her success, there's no 'I'm-too-famous-to-talk-to-you' nonsense with Lisa, she is, in fact, the most charming, friendly person, with her feet firmly planted on the ground. 'I'm not bothered about being on the acting A-list, I just want to do great roles,' says this 27-year-old superwoman, whose appeal – aside from her talent, beauty and charm – is that she has a life elsewhere.

CHARACTER MODELLING

Interesting, attractive, overweight, or ugly with such outstanding features as scars, buck teeth, broken noses and cauliflower ears – character models come in all shapes and sizes.

The next time you're casually flicking through the pages of a magazine or are about to switch off the commercials – stop – take a long, hard look at the models in the non-fashion advertisements. You'll notice 'real people' who don't even remotely resemble supermodels. Admittedly, some are actors, but a considerable number are character models. This is a branch of modelling that most wannabes are unfamiliar with, yet these models are frequently used to promote a wide range of consumer products, including food and drink, cars, insurance, computers, toothpaste or, more recently, fashion. As the industry moves towards an alternative to those high-gloss model types, character models are having a field day.

Top agency Ugly has every imaginable character on its books, from groovy granddads to a 7'6" giant, sumo wrestlers and a whole selection of nerds. Next up are the 'X-Files', a peculiar bunch of pierced, tattooed and odd-looking characters who'd make you quiver with fright. And according to Marc French, Ugly's MD, the weird, wacky and physically extreme characters just can't put a foot wrong at the moment. 'Advertisers are taking more risks than ever before and are using our most way-out models.' Current favourites include Treacle, a 79-year-old gurner, number-one nerd Phil Philmar and the super-ugly-bloke Del. Headed by Del, the Ugly agency has the greatest concentration of crowd-pulling ugly mugs in the world. But as Phil

Philmar points out: 'Whether you're ugly, fat, puny or plain, you'll only be successful if you're completely happy with who you are and the way you look.' Leading photographer, Richard Bradbury, who specializes in photographing character models, echoes this and adds: 'It's also about the ability to act and understand the brief.'

Don't worry if you're not covered in tattoos or built like a sumo wrestler, character agencies also represent models who have much more of a 'normal' look – pleasant-looking, attractive or simply ordinary. Think bank manager, nurse, insurance broker, telephone operator, air hostess, secretary, young mum or businessman. Then think of the suave guy in a car ad, the attractive mother in a washing-powder commercial, or the adolescent munching his way through a packet of Walkers salt-and-vinegar crisps, and you've got the picture. Unlike sumo wrestlers and characters who have a strong, definitive image, the 'normal-looking' characters are generally more versatile and can easily adapt their look to suit almost any role they're hired to play.

The bulk of character work is in print advertising and commercials. However, some character models – especially the oddball types – are breaking all conventions and are being hired by fashion magazines and designers. Buck-toothed character Del, who was recently voted the UK's ugliest bloke, has just completed a Calvin Klein campaign alongside Kate Moss, and 90-year-old supergran

The Turbo engine with the Family Pack.

The Diesel engine with the Business Pack.

The 1.6 engine with the Leather Interior.

VOLVO GIVE THEIR BLESSING TO ALL SORTS OF MARRIAGES.

...omes to marriages Volvo like to put ...d.

..., with the 400 series, we're giving you ...than any other manufacturer. You can ...engine with standard specification

or a smaller engine with the luxury package.
In fact, with a total of five different engine sizes and six different interior packages on offer, you can mix and match as much as you like.'
You could for instance, unite the 1.6 engine with

the Luxury Pack, which features air-conditioning and leather upholstery.
With other manufacturers however, you don't get such a happy coupling. You'll find that the luxury package for example, only comes with the larger engine.

Volvo's approach (which applies to the 440 hatchback and 460 saloon) means you not only get the car that suits your exact needs, but you decide exactly where your money goes.
And you don't have to wait any longer for

delivery of your specially built car. For an information pack call 0800 400 430.
The Volvo 400 series. From $11,175 (white ribbons not included).
THE VOLVO 400 SERIES. A CAR YOU CAN BELIEVE IN

Margot Dillon, was featured in the fashion pages of cutting-edge magazine *Dazed & Confused*. They even get the chance to strut their stuff on the runway. Whether they're meant to look like they were dragged off the street, or are hired as part of a weird and wonderful show cast, you'll spot them stomping down the more eccentric designers' runways. The complete antithesis of fashion models, they always steal the show. Character models are also booked to appear in films and television programmes not just as extras, but also in speaking parts and even star roles.

Fortunately, character models don't have to do the treadmill of go-sees, nor do they have to spend months working for a pittance while building up a book: clients will either hire them directly or request them for a casting on the strength of their pictures in the agency book. It's not unheard of for a character model just to walk in off the street and get picked for a job. Marc at Ugly recalls this happening to one of his models. 'I had just taken on this distinguished-older-gentleman type, who,

although he'd never been on a casting or in front of a camera in his life, was exactly what the client was looking for.' The lucky fellow landed a £20,000 toothpaste commercial! Because character models don't need to spend as much time as fashion models promoting themselves, as long as their line of work is flexible, it's easier for them to continue in part-time or even full-time employment. However, a large percentage get sufficient work to quit the day job.

BASIC REQUIREMENTS
Marc French believes that the perfect character model should have plenty of confidence and an extrovert personality. 'One of the most important credentials is to be completely happy with your particular look. Oh, and a good sense of humour always helps,' adds Marc.

Looks: Strangely proportioned, freakishly ugly, average, attractive or plain – if your face fits you'll get the job.

Photographed by Richard Bradbury

*The weird and wonderful cast of models from the Ugly agency.
From left: Donald Standen, Connie, Phil Philmar, Margot Dillon,
Amica, Amy Lamé, Billy Taylor, Treacle, Joan Wane, Chris Greener,
Mike Edmonds, Del, Chopper and Peter Mastin.*

Camera-friendly: Many models are hired for commercials, television shows and film work – so you can't be camera-shy. Indeed, before agreeing to take you on, some agencies, including Ugly, will screen-test you in order to see how well you react to the camera.

Age: One great advantage for potential character models is the lack of age restrictions. Ugly has models on its books from as young as 16 to the ripe old age of 90!

Special abilities: Some character models can act, but it's an asset rather than a necessity. Indeed, many land acting parts without having ever acted or studied drama before. It also helps if a character model has a special talent. Ugly has jugglers, acrobats, actors, dancers, mime artists and gurners on its books. 'Most of our models have special talents that help advertisers when they're looking for such specialists as a high-wire walker or a competent roller-blader.' So if you can scuba dive, skate, horse ride, ski, play an instrument or have any other hobbies or skills that may come in handy, add them to your modelling résumé.

PHIL PHILMAR

Described as having a 'funny face', top character model Phil Philmar, has played a whole host of characters, including a supernerd, trainspotter, nutty scientist, customs officer, zany pilot and mad hatter. Phil stumbled into modelling by accident. While working as a freelance illustrator he was introduced to photographer John Shaw at a Christmas party. 'Whenever John needed an illustrator he'd call me,' explains Phil. 'Then, on one occasion, he asked if I'd do an advertising job, not as an illustrator but as a model. It sounded like fun, so I agreed.' John later suggested that Phil should approach a character agency to earn some pocket money. 'All I had were these photos of me in a bald wig, but I decided to send them off anyway.' The agency rejected Phil, telling him they didn't need any more baldies. 'When I explained I was wearing a wig and that I did actually have a full head of hair, they apologized and asked me to come in for an interview.'

When Phil started modelling he couldn't believe he was being paid good money for having so much fun: 'I was surprised that most of the work involved hanging around, being made up, and very little time

actually modelling.' But Phil soon discovered that not all jobs were quite so simple. Spending the entire day in a harness 15 feet up in the air, then having to fly like superman, is more than your average day's work. 'To support my weight the harness had to be extremely tight around my hips, and every time I swung forward it was agony,' remembers Phil. The following day, he was dressed in red long johns, cowboy boots and a pink feather boa. 'This isn't a weird hobby of mine,' laughs Phil, 'it was for a French lottery commercial based on the theme of "tarred and feathered".' As if this wasn't ridiculous enough, he was then covered from head to toe in black slime. 'It was supposed to look like tar, but as it wouldn't stick they had to keep pouring bucket loads of the icy stuff all over me. By the end of the day I was shivering uncontrollably.'

Like any model, Phil has to spend hours in the make-up room while he is transformed into character. 'For one job I had to have a false rubber chin and nose built onto my face. It took hours,' explains Phil. 'And just when I thought we were finished, the client decided they wanted warts painted all over my cheeks.' Although Phil doesn't mind sitting while make-up artists paint his face – which has involved as many as four complete make-up changes – it can cause havoc with his skin. 'For years I had some form of eczema which was exacerbated by make-up. I'm no beautiful fashion model, but, being in the public eye I realize I still have to take care of my skin.' After trying homeopathy and Chinese herbal medicine, he eventually found an anti-fungal wash that cleared up the condition. Now he doesn't mind make-up at all. So does the supernerd work out? 'I naturally have plenty of energy that seems to keep me going from one job to the next, so I don't need to exercise.'

After 12 years in the business, at 39 Phil is one of the world's highest-paid and most successful character models; so much so that he is almost on the verge of over-exposure. He has built up an impressive client list: Nintendo, Sega, Levi's, Pepsi, Pioneer, Fosters, Heineken, Sharp, Shreddies, BT and Tetley, to name but a few. After taking the modelling world by storm, Phil is turning his attention to a second career – acting. Nonetheless, he thoroughly enjoys modelling and is not about to throw in the towel. 'I like to think of myself as a performer and, whether it's acting or modelling, I shall continue for as long as the clients want me.'

MARGOT DILLON

In the fashion world she's known as the glam gran, to her friends simply Dolly. At 90, Margot Dillon is up there with the supermodels. She's graced the fashion pages of the glossies, including Italian *Vogue*; been interviewed for television and radio; been featured in newspaper articles; filmed in action and broadcast on television screens from England to Australia. It seems the world just can't get enough of this remarkable woman. Sparked off by her debut appearance in *Dazed & Confused*'s fashion pages, the furore surrounding her continues. But Margot's no recent phenomenon: this veteran – in the true sense of the word – has been modelling for over 23 years. You might think that 67 seems rather late in life to embark on a modelling career,

but for Margot it was the beginning of a wonderful and fulfilling time that has given her a second lease of life.

Prior to her modelling days, Margot worked for 17 years in the exclusive London fashion store, Simpson. Starting out on the fashion floor, she progressed to the position of personal fashion adviser. So how on earth did she become a model? 'My husband Wentworth had a sort of "retired-colonel" look, and modelled part time,' explains Margot. 'So when I finally retired from Simpson, to keep me out of mischief, he introduced me to his agency, Ugly.' Until her husband's death five years ago, the dynamic duo – who were teenage sweethearts – often modelled together. Margot recalls these memories as some of the happiest moments of her life. 'I felt a great loss after his death, but modelling has helped keep me occupied.'

Margot has two grown-up grandchildren who are very proud of their amazing granny. 'Everyone seems to think it's great, except for my sisters, who just can't seem to fathom why on earth I do it.' Nevertheless, her friends are impressed, and look out for her on the television and in the papers; though Margot confesses that until the recent media coverage, none of them knew her age. 'Now they all tease me, telling me I've blown my cover.'

Like many a supermodel, Margot is a prime target for fans. On one occasion she was travelling on the London underground when a couple of Australian tourists asked if they could take her photograph. 'They came up to me and said "you're the lady in the telephone commercial who comes into our living room at least once a night".' Breakdancing for Panasonic was another memorable commercial, which made Margot instantly recognizable. So, too, was an insurance advertisement in which Margot – clad in black

Photographed by Richard Bradbury

leather as a biker gran complete with helmet and goggles – is unloading shopping from the back of a Harley Davidson. 'A chap once stopped me in the street and said "would you like a lift or have you got the bike",' she says with a giggle.

Although Margot sees herself primarily as a character model, she has caused quite a stir in the fashion world, posing for glossy magazines and fashion photographers. Top photographer David Bailey was one of the first greats to spot Margot's potential, hiring her for the much-coveted anti-fur campaign. 'I had to sit in the audience and wear an expression of disgust while models in bloodstained furs walked down the runway,' remembers Margot. In addition to her fashion work she has played every type of granny, from an aristocratic grandmother to a pink-haired punky gran. She's also a regular in pop videos: you can

see her in Pulp's 'Common People', and as a zany dental nurse in Björk's 'Army of Me'. 'I get on very well with young people and modelling gives me the chance to be with them,' she says.

Margot appreciates artistic talent when she sees it. 'Friends of mine thought the *Dazed & Confused* pictures were unflattering. But I loved them. I tried to explain that it's art and, anyway, I'm not supposed to look like some glamorous supermodel.' Margot is, however, extremely glamorous. She may be only 5'2", but she's a delicately framed size 10 who always looks incredibly chic, with pretty features and a peachy complexion. Rankin, who photographed Margot for *Dazed & Confused*, sums her up: 'She's not only aesthetically beautiful, she's proof you can grow old gracefully.'

Currently one of the most in-demand models on the circuit, Margot is chauffeur-driven to every job.

'My agent insists,' says Margot, 'he won't allow me to take the tube.' Even after all the attention that's been lavished on her, she remains one of the sweetest people who certainly enjoys life to the full.

ALEX CAMERON

Take a look at this six-foot, blue-eyed dude and you imagine him suavely striding down the runway of Armani – not pulling comical expressions with his eyebrows in a Ford car commercial, or playing the businessman type for a Post Office ad. But it's precisely this ability to be versatile, coupled with a strong, commercial appeal, that has helped 31-year-old Alex become such a huge success.

After graduating, Alex became a training officer in the travel business, and it was here that he met an agent who said he was an ideal candidate for modelling. 'The agent rang me to ask if I'd like to model in, of all things, a reflexology video,' remembers Alex. 'I ummed and ahhed for a bit, but eventually I agreed.' Alex quickly developed a taste for modelling and decided to chuck in his job and take his new-found vocation seriously. 'It seemed like a far more interesting way to earn a living,' remarks Alex. But after a few sporadic bookings he became fed up and disillusioned. Finding he was spending more time waiting for the phone to ring than actually modelling, after only a short period of working, he set off backpacking around Europe.

When Alex returned to England six months later, he dropped by his agency. No sooner had he walked through the door when a booker asked if he could play football. 'I hesitated at first,' says Alex, 'but like most guys, I just about knew how to kick a ball around, so I said yes.' He attended the casting and, later that day, celebrated a booking for a month's television work where he was to pose as a football manager. This assignment was swiftly followed by a commercial for a national newspaper. From this point on, Alex's modelling career rocketed.

From the young executive type to the father figure, this handsome chap is in no short supply of 'Mr Nice Guy' offers. Besides these roles, he models fashion, has appeared in a steamy Häagen Dazs commercial and has posed as the mysteriously handsome Milk Tray man. Playing different guises has got him into trouble on more than one occasion. Alex recalls one particular shoot where, trying to capture the essence of the archetypal businessman on the move – stepping off the curb and hailing a cab – caused a few problems. 'There was a several hair-raising near misses, and I had to deal with irate taxi drivers who'd stopped to pick me up,' he explains.

A popular choice for the young dad role, Alex is quite used to having a baby thrust in his arms and all the joys that go with it. 'Holding a baby is definitely one of the chief occupational hazards,' says Alex with a chuckle, explaining how he's had to change his shirt on more than one occasion (see picture on opposite page – a shot taken after Alex had put on a clean shirt).

Alex has made the most of opportunities to travel to all corners of the globe. Each year he spends a month modelling in Barcelona and a few months in South Africa. The next modelling market on his agenda is Australia. He also gets booked on trips to warm, sunny climates, but somehow he always manages to jinx the weather. 'Each time I go on a trip I can guarantee it will pour with rain for the first couple of days,' admits Alex. 'It's become a standing joke with photographers.' During his last trip to Greece, violent thunderstorms prevented the team from working for the first four days. 'As it was a six-day trip, we only had two days left to shoot 114 rolls of film,' continues Alex. That's over 4,000 shots!

With three agencies in London and several overseas, Alex is busy every day of the week. 'Because I take on such a wide range of modelling work, I'm represented by more than one agency,' he explains. 'Luckily, this doesn't seem to present problems with work overlapping. I usually accept the first job that comes in, unless, of course, it means turning down a major commercial. All my agents understand this,' says Alex, who treats modelling like a business. 'It's great being self-employed, it gives you freedom and control over your life. But if you want the work, you've got to get out there and promote yourself.'

Having other jobs before modelling helped Alex to appreciate how great a profession modelling is. His advice to aspiring models is to not be taken in by the whole modelling thing. 'Be yourself, keep your feet on the ground, and work hard.' He also warns wannabes against having any inhibitions. 'I often have to get changed on location, which can mean taking everything off – including my boxer shorts,' he says with a knowing smile. Watch out for Alex at a location near you!

LOOKALIKES

Are you always being mistaken for a celebrity, pop star, royal or other famous person? If so, why not actively exploit your similarities and rake in the money by impersonating the real thing?

There is a huge demand for convincing lookalikes. Not surprisingly, the bigger the star, the greater the need for a double. Lookalikes of celebrities such as Tina Turner, Joan Collins, Jack Nicholson, Prince, Madonna, Michael Jackson, Liam Gallagher, The Spice Girls, Rod Stewart and Elton John are some of the most sought after. So, too, are the royal impersonators of figures like Princess Diana, Fergie, Prince Charles, the Queen Mother and, one of the most popular lookalikes – Her Majesty Queen Elizabeth II.

Besides megastars and royalty, other doubles stealing the limelight are legendary icons like Elvis and Marilyn Monroe, politician lookalikes including Bill Clinton and Margaret Thatcher, together with those who mimic the stars who are currently saturating the tabloids.

Susan Scott, who started up the very first lookalike agency in the UK, represents the cream of lookalikes. Susan explains that it's not just about being the spitting image of a person – it's about the whole package: 'As long as there's a glimmer of similarity in the face, the hair, make-up and clothes will do the rest.' But she stresses that lookalikes must dress exactly like the person, complete with all the paraphernalia: wigs, glasses, hats, jewellery or, in the case of the queen, a tiara. Mastering the stars' mannerisms is a must. 'Without executing Princess Di's bashful glances, our two top Dis wouldn't be half as convincing,' remarks Susan. Lookalikes should make a point of finding out as much as possible about the person they are trying to resemble, from their birthplace right down to the shade of lipstick they wear. And it helps if lookalikes sound like the person in question, as they often have to greet people, mingle at a party, or make a speech. 'One

of my John Majors looks identical to Mr Major himself but, unfortunately, his Scottish accent lets down his act,' says Susan. Pop-star lookalikes must be able to sing. Rina Pritchard, for instance, not only looks like Tina Turner but sings just like her, too. 'I can't tell you how many times Rina's been hired to sing "Simply The Best" at award ceremonies.'

Lookalike work involves personal appearances (PAs) at corporate-entertainment and other hospitality events, exhibitions, shop openings, functions, parties and award ceremonies. But it doesn't end with PA work: these artists are also booked for television and film appearances, commercials and print-advertising campaigns. For PA work the fees are approximately £500 – not bad for a few hours' work. 'Our most in-demand lookalikes earn enough money for modelling to be their sole occupation, but for others it's simply a hobby,' explains Susan.

Once an agency has agreed to take you on, all you need is a selection of good photographs. When you become more established, you can consider having a composite or flyer printed. 'As long as lookalikes have one strong image,' says Susan, 'it's all I need to promote them.' Lookalikes do get booked on spec but, like models, they also have to attend castings. In addition to supplying photographs, lookalikes must provide their own outfit, and should also be capable of doing their own hair and make-up.

The good news for would-be lookalikes is that agencies like Susan Scott's recruit a considerable amount of artists: 'We don't limit ourselves to one double of each star; we often have as many as 20.' And there's plenty of work to go round. 'I've supplied 20 Tom Joneses, and have been asked for as many

Princess Dis as possible.' But this doesn't mean that all 20 are equally good. The ranks are similar to any other type of modelling. The difference is that a top lookalike is far easier to define than a top fashion model. Essentially, the stronger the resemblance and impersonating skills, the more popular the lookalike will be. 'When hiring a solo artist, clients want the best, especially when it's for advertising stills or commercials,' insists Susan.

Agencies are swamped with photographs of convincing lookalikes, as well as pictures from those who look nothing like the person they claim to resemble. 'I had one chap who kept reapplying in different guises', says Susan with a smile. 'He tried to impersonate Sean Connery, and even though he was kitted out with a gun, dark suit and receding hairline, he still looked nothing like him. Eventually we agreed to take him on as Batman – a masked role that virtually anyone could play!'

Occasionally, agencies have requests for supermodel lookalikes. 'We've been asked for a Kate Moss and a Claudia Schiffer, but I find that unless the supermodel has really distinctive features, the lookalike could pass for any pretty girl. Clients want people who are instantly recognizable. For example, Pamela Anderson is OK because she has the costume as well as the cleavage!'

Potential lookalikes should bear in mind that they must resemble someone well known, as a semi-famous person would expect to be hired themselves, and could kick up a fuss, particularly for an advertisement. Although it's not illegal, as Susan Scott points out, it can cause problems: 'A few years ago, Barbara Woodhouse [the late infamous dog trainer] was so insulted that she hadn't been asked to appear in the advert, she managed to put a stop to it.' Most celebrities are flattered, but a few, including Woody Allen, have been known to embargo advertising campaigns.

BASIC REQUIREMENTS

Looks: Susan Scott says: 'As long as there is similarity in the face, you're in with a chance. But it's important to get the whole image right.'
Voice: It really helps if the lookalike sounds like the star, especially if they are hired for events where they have to mingle, make a speech, or sing.
Personality: As a lookalike you are essentially an entertainer, so it's important that you are outgoing and confident enough to carry off the act.

NICKY LILLEY

She stays in five-star hotels, is chauffeur-driven in stretch limos, and often has the red carpet rolled out for her, but when 34-year-old Nicky Lilley leaves her Princess Diana role behind, it's back to the joys of motherhood, having to queue at the bus stop, and a never-ending cycle of school runs. 'It's wonderful to be treated like a princess, but when normality hits you, it's down to earth with a bang,' exclaims Nicky.

Ever since a friend showed a picture of Nicky to a photographer three years ago, she's been playing the role of Princess Diana. But long before she started wearing Di-style skirt-suits and little black evening gowns, people would stare, whisper and point; a couple of people even went so far as to ask her if she was the real thing. Her first job as a lookalike – a three-week cruise where she had to greet people aboard a ship – confirmed this uncanny likeness. 'I was amazed that some people thought I really was Diana,' says Nicky, who is often greeted by curtsies, trembling handshakes and tears. 'One woman even kissed my hand and said it was the most memorable moment of her life.'

When a newspaper believed that they had discovered the scoop of the century – a video of Princess Diana and James Hewitt – Nicky became a star in her own right. It all stemmed from a booking by an independent television company for, what her agent was led to believe, was a pilot for a satirical current-affairs programme. Filmed romping around a room with a James Hewitt lookalike, Nicky had no idea that pictures from the video would end up splashed across the front pages of newspapers.

'It was a few months after the job when I noticed stills from the video on the front page of *The Sun* newspaper,' says Nicky, still remembering the shock at seeing herself. In what the press purported to be the biggest coup since the alleged discovery of the Hitler diaries, the story, accompanied by dozens of photographs from the video, hit the headlines from one side of the world to the other. When it was discovered that the video was a hoax, and Princess Di was really a lookalike, Nicky's agent was inundated with bookings and media interviews. 'Whenever Di becomes the focus of the press, it usually results in a flood of bookings, but this was ridiculous – things went completely mental,' says Nicky, admitting that she quite enjoyed all the attention.

EXTRAS WORK

If you want to brush shoulders with famous actors, spot yourself in a commercial, or amuse friends with anecdotes – how about extras work?

You've probably wondered if the people milling around in the background of a commercial, television programme or film are hired actors or real people who just happen to be passing by. Well, in the majority of cases, they are supporting artists, known as extras. Extras work started back in the sixties. Until then, producers would pluck people off the streets or hire friends and acquaintances to fill these roles. There was – and still is – a long line-up of people willing to pay to be close to a famous actor or to get a taste of the world of entertainment. But as the film and media business grew into a thriving industry, a supply of professional supporting artists was needed. 'It's great fun, you get paid, you get fed, and you get to watch the movie stars at work,' says Joan Dewar-Spangler, president of the Look Talent agency in California, which represents extras and 600 actors for shows like *The Phantom of the Opera*, and the entire cast of *Beach Blanket Babylon*.

Extras are hired for commercials, photographic stills, music and corporate videos, television productions and feature films. A commercial producer might be looking for a mixed bunch to push trolleys around a supermarket, while a director might need alien-looking extras to be in the background of a sci-fi film, or twentysomethings to sip Martini cocktails at the bar in a TV soap.

There are two levels of extras work: background work, where you are just one of a crowd, and walk-on parts. Sometimes the walk-on artist will have a line or two to speak – a role that is teetering on acting. Laila Debs, director of leading extras agency, The David Agency, explains the difference between each role: 'Imagine a restaurant scene in a film or commercial. The principal actors – known as the featured artists – are sitting at a table chatting to each other. Then, enter the walk-on in the guise of a waiter. Turning to the featured artist he asks: "How would you like your steak done sir?" Although he has a line to say, his part is still termed as walk-on. Sitting at other tables are the background extras.'

A few model agencies have extras or talent divisions, but the majority of work is booked through specific extras and talent agencies, or via casting directors who book extras direct. Extras agencies usually specialize in either commercials, film and television, or photographic work. These agencies represent all kinds of people: overweight, ordinary and old. But as Laila Debs explains, the last few years have seen a trend towards hiring younger extras. 'Although we take on artists between 16 and 60, the majority of work is for 16 to 35. There's also a greater demand for male extras: for every ten extras hired, six are male and four female.'

On average, you can earn £85 a day for background work, and double that for walk-on parts. Few artists work every day of the week, as most use extras work as a fill-in when they are not acting or modelling. It is possible to earn a livelihood from this type of work, but in order to get regular bookings you would need to be signed to several different types of extras agencies. 'As long as artists stick to agencies that specialize in different areas of work, it shouldn't present any problems for the artists or agents alike,' says Laila. 'For instance, we specialize in commercials and corporate videos, so I suggest our artists also sign up with an agent who handles either film and television, or photographic work.'

When clients are looking for a small group of extras or artists for walk-on parts, they normally hold a casting. However, if they require a mammoth amount of extras they will simply telephone an agency requesting numbers and giving specifications of types they require. 'I often have clients who call me up and say, "find me 200 extras for tomorrow",' says Laila. 'They may ask for all ages, or be more specific.' For a building-society commercial, The David Agency supplied no less than 400 extras each day for three days.

You don't have to be the next Laurence Olivier to break into extras work; nevertheless, agents prefer artists to have some kind of acting experience, be it a drama course, amateur dramatics or full Equity membership. 'I recently took on a girl who had no acting experience whatsoever, but her enthusiasm won me over,' explains Laila. 'In fact, she was so keen she insisted that if getting into extras work meant sleeping on a bench in order to be at the job on time, she'd do it! She followed my advice by taking a course and auditioning for a small part in a play. Meanwhile, she's busy doing extras work for commercials, television and film.'

Starting out as an extra is relatively easy. 'We ask new artists for a couple of professional photographs which show them in at least two different guises, such as a business-like role and a more casual image,' points out Laila. Unlike models, extras don't need a composite, but as clients often choose supporting artists straight from agency books, those who appear within a book stand a far better chance of getting picked. According to Laila, a good wardrobe of clothes, including suits, hats, wellingtons, jeans, briefcases, etc. also increases an extra's chance of working. 'When a client asks for a businessman type, if the extra doesn't possess a suit and briefcase, there's little point in us even bothering to put him up for the job.'

Extras work is a great way to supplement modelling and can be a springboard to more serious acting. Some actors start out as extras, move on to walk-on parts, and eventually become featured artists. And you can progress far quicker than you think. Extras are sometimes upgraded on the day from a background to a walk-on or even principal part. 'On a shoot for a commercial, if the director thinks an extra looks the part they may upgrade them to principal,' explains Joan Dewar-Spangler. 'The role principal is defined by the Screen Actors Guild as anyone holding the product being promoted.' But as Laila Debs points out, there are many extras not lucky enough to progress to walk-on parts even after years – let alone on the day. 'I have one girl who has been with me for eight years and, although she's desperate to act, she's only ever been hired for background work. In contrast, another extra, who joined us without any prior acting experience, has done background, walk-on work and, after only six months, has already landed a part in a play.'

Supporting artists get treated reasonably well, but if your aspirations lie in the leading role, it can be a frustrating and somewhat demeaning position. And this is why extras work is not something professional actors normally highlight on their CV. 'Many actors do extras work to pay the bills, but they keep quiet about it,' admits Joan Dewar-Spangler. There's also a lot of hanging around. You could be waiting all day just to appear for a fraction of a second. And don't always expect to see yourself in the final commercial or film. You may end up on the cutting-room floor. All said, if you've got patience and are fascinated by how the media industry operates, this may be for you. I met a woman whose claim to fame was that she'd been an extra in *Godfather II*. She met Al Pacino, enjoyed a banquet-style lunch, and both she and her seven-year-old son were paid for the day.

BASIC REQUIREMENTS

Looks: You don't have to be attractive or have strong features – you just have to be yourself.
Personality: If you are self-conscious and inhibited, extras work is probably not for you.
Age: From 16 to 60. However, the majority of work is for 16- to 35-year-olds.

Photographed by Stephen Perry

GLAMOUR MODELLING

Nudity has become acceptable; it's no longer perceived as something decent girls never do. Why? Because these days, even the supermodels shed their clothes for the camera.

Wearing little more than a strategically placed leaf or smattering of gold paint, an endless stream of supergirls, including Eva Herzigova and Naomi Campbell, have struck subtle yet provocative poses for the highly revered Pirelli calendars. Cindy Crawford, Stephanie Seymour and Elle Macpherson stripped for *Playboy*, Kate Moss posed naked for *The Face* and, in Calvin Klein's Obsession campaign, she bared her breasts to the world.

Distinction between glamour work and tasteful nudity has become less defined as fashion models have edged in on what was traditionally the domain of the glamour model. Yet, once upon a time, fashion models refused to pose in their underwear – let alone strip for a calendar! Now there's very little they won't do, unless, of course, it's not artfully shot or is too risqué. Although there is still a demand for Page Three types and pin-up girls, the image of glamour modelling is shifting. Nineties glamour models are far less blatantly sexy than the tarty all-cleavage, bottle-blonde who reigned over the last three decades. Back then, glamour models were photographed in a tits-'n'-arse, smutty way, but nowadays the images creeping in are more on a par with fashion photography. One individual who's been instrumental in this movement is fashion photographer Stephen Perry. 'I photograph glamour models in a way that is subtle and sexy – not sexist!'

Since glamour modelling first became prominent, many premier-league glamour girls, Page Three models and *Playboy* playmates – Pamela Anderson Lee, Anna-Nicole Smith, Samantha Fox, Jenny McCarthy, Gina Lee Nolan, Linda Lusardi, Jilly Johnson, Suzanne Mizzi and Kathy Lloyd – have become famous personalities and have gone on to present TV shows or star in television soaps. More recently, however – with the exception of one or two major names – the supermodel clan have eclipsed the glamour stars and have stolen the spotlight. But supermodels take note: the new breed of glamour stars, including Joanne Guest and Melinda Messenger, is hot on your heels! These girls may not be household names but, just like their supermodel counterparts, they have fan clubs, personal calendars and their own model memorabilia.

Doyenne of the glamour world Samantha Bond, who's been running her London agency for 20 years, points out that glamour modelling is not just about getting your kit off. 'Our models are frequently hired – complete with all their clothes – for work

Left: Masters of the ring – glamour agents Samantha Bond and Paul Bozchac with their models, from left: Sam Jessop, Danni Wheeler, Vanessa King, Emma Noble and Belinda Charlton.

ranging from fashion shoots to television shows. Clients come to us because they want girls who are pretty, feminine and sexy – the glamorous babe, rather than the androgynous-looking or off-beat fashion types. And most nude work involves a suggestion of nudity rather than smutty full-frontal images of models completely starkers,' continues Samantha. Sam's models are also booked for calendar work, tabloids and advertisements for products such as shower gels, soaps and deodorants, as well as men's fashion magazines, notably *GQ, Esquire, FHM* and *Loaded*. Evidently, the launch of the new-style men's magazines, including *Loaded, Maxim* and *FHM*, has opened up a whole new market for glamour models.

Although the majority of work is for women, men aren't entirely excluded from the glamour circuit: 'Male glamour models have great torsos and are often prepared to flash a little more flesh than your average fashion model,' says Paul Bozchac of the Samantha Bond agency. Indeed, one of their male glamour models was 'The Body' in the world-wide campaign for Chanel's fragrance, Antaeus.

Like fashion models, glamour models also need to test and do the usual rounds of castings and go-sees. The nature of the work means that, in order to get a job, they must make an effort to look the part: wearing make-up to castings and, to show off their bodies, slipping on a bikini or swimsuit when necessary. Although top glamour models have never had the earning power of their fashion peers, nude work can pay double the average day rate, so the money is not to be sneered at. And, as many calendars are photographed abroad, there's also the opportunity to travel to some of those palm-tree-lined locations.

Glamour modelling attracts many pretty girls who are not quite tall enough for fashion, as well as those who've simply chosen to take the glamour route. Bill Farely, PR of The Playboy Agency in Beverly Hills (owned by the Playboy empire), takes on many girls who have been rejected by fashion agencies. 'One of our top glamour stars, Jenny McCarthy, was turned down by all the fashion agencies in LA. We took her on, she became Playmate of the Year, and is now a presenter for MTV,' he explains. What Bill looks for in a glamour model is symmetry and beauty: a girl with a perfectly proportioned body who has that girl-next-door look but is still sexy.

Once you've become a glamour model it can be difficult to move into fashion modelling and, if you've appeared in top-shelf magazines – forget it! There are always the exceptions, however, like Anna-Nicole Smith, a *Playboy* playmate who was also one of the Guess? models, and has modelled in fashion magazines such as *Marie Claire*.

Let's face it, *Playboy* is big business. And, as Cindy Crawford, Elle Macpherson and many celebrities have proved, it's not all big tits, bums and lusty pouts that grace their centrefolds. 'Once a model has appeared in the centrefold of *Playboy* it leads to other glamour work, including calendar shoots, television appearances and advertising,' explains Bill Farely. 'However, we never allow our models to appear in the pages of any hard-core magazines.' At Samantha Bond, Paul Bozchac was in the throes of tying up a deal for one of their girls to become a *Playboy* playmate. "As *Playboy* has become such a celebrity-led magazine, there's a certain amount of kudos that goes with appearing in it,' points out Paul. 'And if you win Playmate of the Year, there's a cash prize of $100,000.'

Top-shelf magazine work is quite independent from regular glamour modelling and, understandably, genuine glamour agencies like Samantha Bond won't touch this hard-core end of the market. If you wish to pose for the more hard-core men's magazines, be prepared to be draped across a bed or studio in uncompromising positions. The degrees of indecent exposure vary from one magazine to the next. Some may be acceptable to you, whereas you might find others utterly vulgar.

If you are still interested in top-shelf work and have no qualms about the moral issue, it's advisable to approach the magazines direct. Normally, models are paid cash on the day. But at what cost? Modelling for top-shelf magazines and their spin-offs, such as videos and calendars, is *not* to be entered into without serious consideration. Appearing in such a publication could cause repercussions, which might affect your future career prospects, or lead to problems with your family or partner, who might see it as exploiting your dignity, rather than as a job. And, as Samantha Bond points out: 'Many glamour clients refuse even to consider a model if they know she or he has done adult magazine work.'

The field of glamour attracts sharks who are ready to pounce on any hungry wannabe. Therefore, if any so-called photographer approaches you in the street avoid them at all costs; the chances are that they are out to make money by charging for photographs, or, what's worse, to sell the pictures to some seedy publication. If you're keen to give glamour modelling a go, it is vital that you approach a reputable glamour agency or a talent agency which represents glamour models. A good agent will control every booking. 'We make sure the brief is as tight as possible, and always agree to the conditions with the client in advance,' says Paul Bozchac. 'If a model is uneasy about a situation we suggest she or he calls us immediately.'

To avoid falling into the hands of sharks, Samantha Bond and other reputable agencies advise would-be glamour models never to answer photographers' advertisements. 'Just send a couple of snapshots to a reputable agency (a head and full-length shot of you in a bikini) but no nude pictures,' pleads Paul, explaining how ploughing through dozens of not-so-nice nude pics each day puts him right off his morning coffee.

BASIC REQUIREMENTS

Looks: You need to be good looking, with a body that is in proportion to your height. Successful glamour models often have that textbook prettiness, with dreamy blue eyes and a creamy complexion. 'With the girls, I look at the face first, then the body. With guys, it's the other way round,' says Samantha Bond.

Height: Girls should be 5'3" and over; 5'10" and above for men.

Age: Most glamour models are between 16 and 25. Agencies refuse to represent models under 16.

Measurements: 'Glamour models are usually shorter and more curvaceous than fashion models,' says Paul Bozchac, 'so the the measurements tend to be more varied than 34-24-34. It's all about being in proportion.' And, contrary to popular belief, you don't necessarily need to be a double D-cup.

Body: As you are exposing most of your body, you will need to have smooth skin without stretchmarks or blemishes. Scars that cannot be camouflaged with make-up may cause problems. And, as for cellulite, you will have to be one of the small percentage of women whose body is cellulite free. Your breasts must be pert and firm, not droopy. Male glamour models should have a toned, muscular torso.

JOANNE GUEST

It is that mixture of schoolgirl innocence meets girl-next-door that helped Joanne Guest soar straight to the top of the glamour league. Having always longed to be a Page Three glamour girl, she's now the model whom wannabes aspire to be and men want to take home. 'Mum and Dad used to buy *The Sun*, so I'd turn straight to Page Three to see who the model was,' says the girl who started work in a shoe shop and now has her very own calendar and global Internet fan club. With her modest 34B chest, Jo has helped dispel the 'big breasts' myth by proving that you don't need to be a DD cup to pose for Page Three. 'I always assumed you needed to be more than a meagre B cup to make it,' says a straight-talking Jo.

Since she started modelling two years ago, this new-age glamour babe has become quite a celebrity:

Photographed by Stephen Perry for Loaded

she's never out of the tabloids and is constantly being interviewed for various magazines. Indeed, when I met Joanne, she was about to be whisked off by a journalist from *FHM* magazine who was profiling her in a forthcoming issue. Together with presenting the odd television show – although surprisingly for a model she confesses it's not really something she enjoys – Jo's been a guest (pun not intended) on many television shows. It's always when she's clad in a low-cut, slinky number that she's asked to perform her boiled-potatoes joke – a visual joke that, unfortunately, has to be seen in order to grasp the punch line!

A regular pin-up for many tastefully shot calendars, she's also appeared in Blur's 'Country House' video, and has beaten off the supermodels to win fashion company Giant's advertising campaign. Modelling has taken her to the Caribbean and other exotic places yet, curiously, one of her favourite assignments was a studio shoot for the men's lifestyle magazine, *Loaded*. 'When I arrived at the studio there were bags full of beer. It was great!' remarks Jo, who enjoys a pint.

While most girls would do anything to hide it, Joanne is not afraid to come clean and admit that, before she moved into mainstream glamour modelling, she posed for top-shelf magazines. 'A friend introduced me to a photographer who specialized in naughty

Photographed by Stephen Perry

Emma Noble bareback!

magazines,' says Jo unashamedly. 'I had no idea what I was letting myself in for, but cash on the day seemed very appealing at the time, even though £20 an hour for fully clothed and double for naked was a pittance compared to the money I now earn.' But Joanne soon found posing for men's magazines difficult to handle. 'I'd only had one boyfriend, yet there I was revealing my body to the world, and getting flak for doing so.' Fortunately for Joanne, her future career as a glamour model was not jeopardized. 'I realize how lucky I am,' she adds, 'as most of the girls who do that type of work find it very difficult to get on the books of a reputable glamour agency.' Her agent, Samantha Bond, reiterates: 'Most of our top clients wouldn't touch a model who's done the top-shelf magazines, Jo's the only one who's broken the rules.'

Although her persona might appear to be that of a flighty blonde, her agent points out that it's her professionalism and convivial personality that has led her to become one of the top glamour models. Number one in the rankings may be, but Joanne remains modest about her looks, pointing to three spots on her chin to prove that she's not superhuman. 'I generally eat what I like and would never consider giving up chocolate or beer.' Although she's naturally pretty, with a fresh complexion, she insists that she needs to wear make-up to castings. 'Well they just wouldn't book me if I didn't wear a scrap, would they?'

In the midst of her modelling career, Joanne took a part-time course to train as a private investigator. 'I'd always been fascinated by the idea of becoming a PI,' explains Jo, 'and I wanted another interest apart from modelling.' During a television interview she regrettably let this slip. The next day, a story along the lines of 'Glamour Babe Turns Private Eye' hit the tabloids. 'It's taught me to keep my mouth shut in future.' As you can well imagine, Joanne has a huge male following, but at the moment she says she's far too busy with her career to have time for a boyfriend. When she does have a spare moment, you'll find this independent babe chilling out at her local pool hall, enjoying a pint of beer, and wiping the pool table clean.

EMMA NOBLE

From sweeping hair off the floor in the local hairdressing salon to a celebrity who is on the guest list of every important party in town, Emma Noble's career has been something of a modern-day fairy tale. In her early teens, Emma suffered from the ugly-duckling syndrome. 'I was short, with big feet, a funny face and, to top it all, one of those ghastly metal braces,' she admits. But by her 17th birthday a transformation had taken place. Her teeth had straightened out, and she had blossomed into a young woman with dream statistics of 36-24-35 and that so-called chocolate-box prettiness. As if this wasn't enough to make the boys' heads turn, she shot up to a leggy 5'10". But it was that very chocolate-box appeal that made the first fashion agency she approached reject her. After spending an hour scrutinizing her snapshots, they finally decided that her look just wasn't strong enough.

The disappointed 17-year-old and her mum headed off to the next agency on their list – The Samantha Bond model agency. Samantha liked the look of Emma the moment she clapped eyes on her and offered to take her on the books. But Emma was in for a bit of a surprise when she realized that they represented glamour not fashion models. 'I had always been prudish, so the last thing I wanted to do was Page-Three-style modelling.' Emma was about to walk out of the door when Samantha pointed out that just because they specialized in glamour didn't mean that all their models did topless or nude work. Realizing that she didn't have to take the Page-Three route at all, Emma signed up. And her agent was certainly true to her word. Today, Emma is basking in the glory of being chosen as 'The Face' of Jo Bloggs jeans.

Over the years Emma has appeared in dozens of commercials, and has undertaken editorial, show, beauty, fashion and television work. She's done tasteful nude work for calendars as well as body work advertising products such as shavers and hosiery. She's even had to sing an aria from *Carmen* for a pasta commercial. Emma adores being on stage, yet she never really enjoyed runway work. 'I think it was falling off the edge that finished it for me,' remembers Emma. 'This particular show involved a heavily choreographed dance routine and, as we danced down the runway, the girl standing next to me flung out her arm and sent me flying over the side and into the audience.' Luckily, Emma wasn't badly injured. Like a true pro, she managed to clamber back on the runway and even curtsied to the audience who, in turn, clapped and cheered.

Modelling has taken Emma to exotic places including Mauritius, Barbados and (her all-time favourite location) the rainforest of St Kitts. It was on this very island that she shot a commercial for a French cosmetics company. 'Although the scenery was beautiful', remembers Emma, 'I looked a mess.' No sooner had she stepped off the plane when a huge, unsightly pimple appeared smack in the middle of her chin. 'It was so big, that even the make-up artist had difficulty concealing it,' she explains, looking rather embarrassed as she recalls how the producer had to edit it out. But spot or no spot, Emma gets rebooked by the company every year.

Like most successful models, her career's not been without knock-backs. But Emma, who at 23 has spent six years riding the highs and lows, still says modelling is the best thing that ever happened to her. Remembering how disillusioned she was when she first started modelling, Emma explains why she thought it was a horrible business: 'If I wasn't picked for the job, I presumed it was because I was ugly. But it's made me a much stronger person.' Her advice to new models is to not take rejection or criticism personally. But she also believes that if someone pushes you too far, you should stand your ground. And she talks from experience. During one of her first shoots, a female photographer went a little too far with the personal criticism. 'She was tearing me to pieces, saying I had small eyes, thin lips and naff hair. I felt like bursting into tears, but instead, I pulled myself together and asked her how she would feel if I disputed her ability to photograph me. She apologized, and we are now good friends.'

When it comes to looking good, Emma has got it sussed. 'I don't diet, but I do watch what I eat,' says Emma, admitting that she does indulge in the occasional hamburger. And skin care? 'I have dry skin, so I have to make sure I keep it moisturized. Oh, and I always take my make-up off before I go to bed, no matter how late it is.' With the risk of demystifying her blonde image, Emma admits that her gleaming blanket of long, blonde hair is actually from a bottle. 'Brown hair just didn't suit my personality, I wanted something to give me a strong identity. It seemed a bit extreme at first, but now it's very much a part of my character.' To the delight of her agent, her ratings went platinum, too.

Hovering on the brink of stardom has resulted in spin-offs such as personal appearances, media interviews, as well as a flood of invitations to film premieres, launches and other bashes. Consequently, she's busy both day and night. 'Until recently, I was never much of a party girl, but now, you can't keep me in,' says Emma, still somewhat awestruck at her glittering lifestyle.

PROMOTIONAL
WORK

Photographed by Rod Howe

Showgirl: *On the Naturana stand at a lingerie exhibition.*

From greeting winners at motor-racing events to handing out trophies aboard the *Orient Express* – promotions models have fun, meet lots of people and get paid in the process.

You don't need to be extremely young, excessively tall or exceptionally beautiful to qualify. So, if you had your sights fixed on fashion or glamour modelling, but didn't quite make the grade, why not consider promotional work? And, if you're attractive, with a dynamic personality and a sense of adventure – look no further.

Whether it's a new product launch, promotion, conference or corporate-hospitality occasion, an attractive, lively person adds sparkle to any event. Companies showing at a wide variety of trade and consumer exhibitions often require promotions people to work on their stands, which could involve anything from demonstrating a new product, posing on the bonnet of a car, or lounging on a 40-foot yacht at a boat show. Promotions models are also occasionally hired for fashion work, such as modelling clothes on a stand at a trade fair, or showing the latest trends on a magazine-style television show. Hosting sports events, handing out trophies, attending road shows, opening shops, manning reception areas and greeting people at functions, are some of the other roles they are booked for. You can also spot them in supermarkets, department stores, or bars and pubs persuading people to sample everything from the latest designer fragrance to the newest health drink.

Promotional work (also referred to as hostess work) remains firmly in the shadow of the more glorified areas of modelling. Handing out leaflets at an exhibition is neither the most scintillating work, nor is it considered modelling, but, as promotions agent Stevie Walters points out, this is only one section of a diverse area of work. 'Most of the bookings we get are interesting,' enthuses Stevie. 'For example, one of our girls recently spent three days dressed in *haute couture* aboard the *Orient Express* for a Courvoisier promotion. She had a great time and was treated like a true celebrity.' During Stevie's 17 years of running leading London model and promotions agency Models Plus, she has supplied promotions girls and guys to a vast range of clients from Microsoft, Ford, and Louis Vuitton, to Coca Cola, Pepsi and Jim Beam. Her promotions models have, among other things, dressed up as aliens for a sci-fi television channel, been cheer leaders, tequila slammer girls and Jim Beam raiders.

So what makes a successful promotions model? 'A good-looking, bubbly person, who is a consistent worker and, at the end of the day, enjoys the job,' says Stevie. Contrary to popular belief, clients don't just prefer blondes. 'They may ask for a sultry brunette, then again they might want a feisty redhead, it all depends on the job. And some are not fussed about hair colour at all.'

Starting out in promotions is relatively inexpensive compared to regular modelling. Although you will need a selection of photographs and a composite, you don't necessarily need a book. Clients often supply promotions models with T-shirts, dresses or other outfits displaying the company logo, so you'll also save on clothing. Furthermore, as clients generally book direct, you won't need to waste time, energy and money on casting. Quite often, a client will simply request the type of promotions model they want, without even needing to see a composite. It's down to the skill of the agent to supply clients with an attractive, professional person who matches the brief.

Promotional work is not as highly paid as regular modelling. However, as promotions people are often booked for a few days or several weeks at a time, they can earn a decent living. For one day or an evening's work you could expect to earn in the region of £70–£150. There are promotions agencies, as well as model agencies which have promotions divisions. Rather than being centred around a particular city, promotional work is often scattered across the country, so you must be prepared to travel.

Although some fashion, character, glamour and other types of models undertake promotions work to supplement their incomes, it is not a stepping stone to regular modelling. Concerned that it might damage their chances of getting prestigious fashion work or lucrative advertising campaigns, some models are loath to admit that they do promotions work. But their I'd-rather-be-on-a-catwalk-or-stage attitude soon rubs off on the client. Many models, however, will quite happily shoot a commercial one day, and be on an exhibition stand the next.

BASIC REQUIREMENTS

The requirements for promotions models are far less stringent than for fashion or glamour modelling.

Looks: You need to be attractive and presentable with a slim figure. Ideally, women should be 5'4" and above and men at least 5'10", but many promotions agencies will accept those who fall below these heights. Long-haired promotions girls seem to get more work than their shorter-haired contemporaries.

Age: Between 18 and 40. However, if you are in your mid- to late thirties, you must look young.

Personality: A lively, outgoing personality is essential for this kind of work. A permanent smile is also a must. And, as you're dealing with the public, you need to be friendly and helpful.

Stamina: You'll need tons of it. Exhibition and shop hours are long, you could be standing on your feet for eight hours or more.

Selling ability: It helps if you have the ability to sell a product, but this is by no means essential.

NANCY SORRELL

Unlike the rest of her school friends, who all had fixations on the supermodels, Nancy had never harboured ambitions to become a model, even though she had the desired model looks. With her future cut out at the typewriter, at 17 this stunning 5'8" teenager, with a mane of waist-length golden hair and bright-blue eyes, began her career as secretary. Stuck behind a desk, her talent could have quite easily gone unnoticed; a pensions company wasn't the type of place frequented by model scouts. However, fate intervened. Nancy had only been working for a matter of weeks when she caught the eye of a fashion photographer who just happened to be one of her boss's clients. With her boss's permission, a test shoot was arranged. 'I was really surprised that my boss was encouraging; he even agreed to let me take an afternoon off for the shoot,' remembers Nancy.

Delighted with the results, Nancy took the photos to a model agency which handled fashion models. To her amazement, she was taken on. 'The agency told me I had great potential and would soon be getting plenty of work. They even suggested I gave up my job,' she explains. But the harsh reality of starting out as a new model meant that she had to hike to 10 or 12 castings a day – every day – without a booking in sight.

Sensibly, Nancy kept her hand in with temporary secretarial work. When she did finally manage to secure her first modelling assignment, it wasn't anything like she'd imagined. 'I was made up to look like Princess Diana for a book called *How to Look Like a Princess*. The whole thing was a waste of time – the job was unpaid and I'd never dream of putting the pictures in my book,' says Nancy, remembering how quickly she became despondent. 'I had no money coming in, but I knew that in order to get work I would have to persevere with the castings and go-sees. On the days I wasn't casting, I'd just sit at home and wait for the phone to ring. It was so depressing.'

Nancy was seriously thinking about giving it all up when a model friend asked if she could fill in for her at the last minute. 'She told me she'd spoken to her agent, who was more than happy for me to come to the rescue,' Nancy recalls. The job was promotional work, which involved playing the part of a Bond girl for a James Bond theme evening. 'I hadn't done any promotional work before, so I didn't know what to expect. We started off by handing out drinks and greeting people. Then, for the rest of the evening, all we were asked to do was swan around the party looking gorgeous. I thought to myself: "this certainly beats queuing at a casting or hanging around a studio".'

Being multi-talented, Nancy can sing and dance. So, no sooner had a band started to play than she was up on stage singing the classic hit, 'The Greatest Love of All'. The following day, word boomeranged back to her friend's agency, Models Plus, that the client was most impressed. Nancy was officially taken on the agency's books later that day.

From handing out awards at motor-racing events to dressing up as Marilyn Monroe, Nancy's work

Photographed by Martyn Elford

Nancy greets fomer racing driver John Surtees at an Auto Sport event.

and Chris Ewbank. She's also brushed shoulders with other sporting celebrities, including Damon Hill, whom she met while handing out brochures at an *Auto Sport* bash. At a golf event, Nancy was hired to stand on a golf course clad in nothing more than a skimpy swimsuit. But being a true pro, she remained unfazed. 'It was a boiling hot day so I didn't mind.' Later that day Nancy and her colleagues were invited to the golfing dinner. 'I really wanted to go, but all I had to wear were a pair of denim shorts and a minuscule sun top.' The client came to Nancy's rescue and decked her out in the latest golfing fashions – a pair of checked trousers and a polo shirt. 'Well, they always said free clothes was a perk of the job,' says Nancy, with a hint of sarcasm in her voice.

is extremely varied. 'What I love about promotional work is that it's always such fun and, as most clients book you direct, you don't have to go on nearly so many castings.' To the delight of her proud and supportive mum, Nancy has been getting regular television work, from modelling the latest fashions to appearing in some rather more unusual slots. 'For a beauty programme I was in covered in an edible face pack, then told to sit in a bubble bath with a male model who was supposed to look as though he was eating the stuff,' says Nancy with a girlish giggle. For the same television show she took part in a series about dreams; this involved running barefoot around London dressed only in a white, flimsy nightgown pretending she was being chased. 'By the end of the day, the soles of my feet were red raw.'

Sporting events bring in regular work. She's a favourite ring girl at boxing matches, and has been in the ring with such greats as Mike Tyson

It's not only her vivacious personality, but also her dedication and enthusiasm for every job that makes Nancy so popular with her clients. 'No matter what the job is, I give it my all. I want the client to go back to my agent with positive feedback – not complaints. If I don't feel happy about doing a particular job, I will turn it down rather than risk upsetting the client. I've met some promotions models who only want to do fashion modelling and therefore feel they're too superior for promotions work,' she says disapprovingly.

When she's not busy at sports events or being filmed in bubble baths, Nancy works as a dancer and has just cut a record. At only 22, it looks like this talented all-rounder has many more years of fun and excitement ahead of her.

CHILD MODELLING

Nothing makes a mother or father more proud than to see their beautiful, bouncing baby in a television commercial, or their little cherub in the pages of a catalogue looking as though butter wouldn't melt in her mouth.

Children sell. And for years advertisers have capitalized on their irresistible appeal. Promoting every imaginable baby and child product from toys to nappies, fashion, rusks and sweets, they are also popular models in advertisements for food, fabric conditioners, soap and sun-tan lotions, to name but a few. Catalogue advertising is a large area of work for child models, as are fittings and sizings. You'll also find them peering cheekily from the pages of mother-and-baby magazines, and as the ultimate adult accessory in glossy magazines. Fashion shows give kiddies the chance to play at being supermodelettes. As they hop and skip down the runway, they are guaranteed to liven up any show, and are especially cute when dressed from

Courtesy of Advertising Archives

Patterned, striped and plain tops; white pants, shorts, skirts. Cand head to toe in mini versions of Chanel. But don't think they need to be trained mannequins. Quite the contrary. The more natural and childlike they are, the louder the applause.

It can be thrilling seeing your offspring in the public eye. But before you reach for the phone, remember, agencies turn down 95 per cent of kids who apply. It's not every child that has those special qualities – nor indeed, every parent!

Pat Swift, owner of Miami-based agency Swift Kids, has child models on her books who work for such prestigious clients as Calvin Klein, Estée Lauder and Tommy Hilfiger, including three-year-old Charles Hamilton, who raked in $60,000 for three commercials, and 10-year-old Calvin Klein girl Samantha Palmeri. 'Samantha is in such great demand because she looks like your averagely pretty girl next door,' explains Pat. 'She is very

All the colours in the world.

pretty, but she has not got the type of looks that would cause you to stop and say "Wow, what a beautiful child". Samantha also enjoys modelling. I believe kids should see modelling as great fun and really want to model. We are very wary of parents who are paying the mortgage with their kids' earnings and are therefore pressuring and pushing the kids to model.'

Children grow rapidly and, therefore, their looks are constantly changing. As Pat Swift explains, a child who is photogenic at six may not have what it takes, or may lack the sparkle, by the time he or she has reached the age of seven or ten. 'It's strange how, for example, at three years old a model could be in demand, but by the time she reaches four she might get very little work,' explains Pat. 'Then, at seven, the work might pick up again, only to drop off when she hits puberty. There's no set pattern, it just depends on the child.'

When kids start losing their milk teeth problems can occur. Top child photographer Daniel Pangborne, who shoots everything from catalogue to fashion photographs, recalls working with one American girl who had lost a baby front tooth, yet managed to continue modelling. 'To minimize her loss of earnings, her mother had gone to great lengths by taking her model daughter to the dentist to have a false tooth made', says Daniel. 'But I must admit, it looked pretty real.'

Some children start modelling before they're out of nappies and continue well into their teens. But they are the lucky ones. Only the exceptional few, notably Helena Christensen – who began modelling at the tender age of one – go on to become fashion models or, as in Helena's case, a world-famous supermodel.

BABIES AND CHILDREN

It is far more than just a cute smile, head of golden curls or pretty face that makes a successful child model. Good behaviour is vital. A photographer won't be happy if a child plays up, sulks or refuses to move or pose when asked to. It's also important that the child should be at ease when working with strangers. Prospective child models must be easy-going and easy to direct. Temperamental types and tantrum-throwers are a definite no-no. Clients won't risk rebooking a difficult or miserable child in case the end result reflects his or her mood. Babies who respond well to strangers are preferable to ones who cry the moment they leave their parents' arms. Incidentally, prospective child models should be outgoing but not precocious – somewhere between extrovert and shy.

So what makes one particular child get booking after booking? According to top child agent Elizabeth Smith, who's been in the business for over 30 years, it's a combination of a child's personality and the attitude of the parents: 'A well-behaved, lively child, who is supported by a parent with the right approach towards modelling, is the ideal recipe. Success is also down to being available at the right time, being exactly what the client's looking for and – luck!' explains Elizabeth, who, like Pat Swift, also believes that a child should want to model. 'Child models must be serious about modelling yet, paradoxically, they must see it as being fun. It's important that they achieve this healthy balance.'

TEENAGERS

If you are in your teens, but not tall enough to become a fashion model, you may be suitable for a child agency's teenage division. You will need to look extremely young, however. A 15-year-old girl represented by a child agency has a very different look to that of her contemporary who is signed to a fashion-model agency. She's hired because she looks like a typical, fresh-faced schoolkid – not a glamorous babe.

The type of work teenage models undertake ranges from catalogue, book-cover and family work, to advertising such products as soft drinks, crisps, young fashion ranges and spot lotions. As male models generally start their careers later, if a client is looking for a boy in his early teens, the casting director will approach a child agency, as boys this young are not normally found on the books of an adult agency. Thus, there is a greater demand for a child agency's teenage boys than its girls. 'Child agencies bridge the gap between boys and male models,' explains Elizabeth Smith. The downside of teenage modelling is that it's short-lived, unless you successfully move into another branch of modelling, or are one of the lucky few who get signed up by a fashion agency.

GETTING STARTED

To find out whether your child or baby has potential, send off a couple of recent snapshots, along with details of their height, age and weight, to an agency. If your offspring has potential, the agent will invite both parent and child in for an interview. Child-model agencies normally charge a small interview fee that covers the cost of administration and a screen test. This is usual practice in many countries, including the UK. If you are unsure of the procedure, contact a modelling association. Once the parent has agreed, the agent will arrange a photo session. This cost is borne by the parent. It's worth bearing in mind that, as babies and children are continuously changing, your child will require a photo session every six months to a year. Therefore, you will be ploughing some of the child's earnings back into promotion.

PROMOTION

The child-model industry operates quite differently to the adult modelling business. Unlike adult models, children don't need a portfolio of pictures or a composite. Instead, they are promoted via their agency's model book. Most agencies produce a book either once or twice a year, and print circulation charts or headsheets in the interim. Since an agency book is circulated to clients – who often book models directly from its pages – it is essential that every baby and child model appears within it. Because of the cost involved in printing such a book, agencies have to charge a mandatory fee to parents – often before the child has worked. Normally, this fee covers the cost of an initial photo session, together with entry onto the chart or headsheet and/or into the agency book. Although an agency cannot guarantee work, if your child is accepted by a reputable agency, it's usually money well spent.

AUDITIONS

When child models attend auditions (child-modelling speak for castings), unlike adult models they often receive an audition fee – although this varies from country to country. Auditions are tedious at the best of times, as you often have to queue, or hang around waiting your turn; but it's particularly frustrating when your child has taken time off school only to find that he or she hasn't got the job. Most clients do, however, try to arrange auditions out of school hours, and keep the waiting time down to a minimum.

PARENTS

Every agent agrees that parents are instrumental in a child's success. 'I cannot over-emphasize how important a good parent is,' stresses Elizabeth

Photographed by Rod Howe

Little sheriff: *four-year-old Jack Davis strikes a pose for Daniel Pangborne.*

should not be treated any differently to other extra-curricular activities, hobbies or sport,' says Elizabeth Smith. If parents follow Elizabeth's advice, they should have no problems.

Parents also take on the role of chaperone, ferrying their child or baby to and from auditions and assignments. The good news is that for most assignments, chaperones are paid a fee. If it's not possible for you to accompany your child, the agency will engage a professional chaperone. 'As the child always needs to be accompanied, it's not just the child who works,' says Daniel Pangborne. 'Parents must also understand the commitment of going to auditions and jobs all over town.' But as Daniel found out, some parents have a thoroughly good time as chaperones. 'We were on location at this manor house in the country with two children and their parents. I, the crew and the kids headed off to shoot in a nearby field, leaving the parents behind, and telling them to help themselves to anything from the kitchen. We returned to find two very tipsy parents polishing off their fourth bottle of the most expensive vintage wine. The manor house never let us shoot there again!'

EDUCATION

Critics of child models worry that modelling will interfere with their education. You may be comforted to know that, in most countries, children of school age are protected by regulations that prevent them from working more than a certain number of days each year. In order to work above the days stated, parents must apply for a licence, which then needs to be authorized by the head teacher of the child's

Smith. 'They need to be professional, resourceful and reliable – but not too pushy.' Many kids are bulldozed into modelling – often against their will. Whatever your reason: whether hearing of a four-year-old earning a ten-figure sum prompts you to contact an agency, or because you want to be the proud parent of a child model, if you force your child, he or she will invariably be the one who throws tantrums at auditions or sulks on photo shoots. Unless your child is happy and willing – don't even attempt it.

Many parents are afraid that their delightful daughter will turn into a precocious little madam, or that their well-behaved boy will become a cocksure brat – but this is rarely the case. 'Modelling school. As long as schooling comes first and modelling is treated as a hobby – not as a means to bring in as much money as possible – no harm will be done to the child's education. 'We find our child models are generally better students,' says Pat Swift. 'If we hear that a child is not doing well in school, we suggest stopping modelling until he or she get better grades. The last thing we want is for a child's education to suffer.' Children have long school holidays and, if parents so wish, modelling can be restricted to holidays and weekends alone.

BASIC REQUIREMENTS

Babies: Has your baby got large eyes, a well-shaped head, smooth skin and a cute smile? If the answer is 'yes', then he or she might have what it takes to make a model.

Children: It's not only the conventionally pretty children who flourish as models. An ordinary-looking kid with a great smile, expressive face or even sticking-out ears, can do equally well.

Teenagers: As a fresh, natural look is essential, you must look young, not sophisticated.

Height: Girls: 5'–5'10". Boys: 5'–6'.

Age: It is more advantageous if you are in your early teens, as you are bound to look younger and, therefore have a longer career.

GEMMA DUNN

Only nine years old and already a cover girl, Gemma Dunn from Richmond, England, is one of child modelling's success stories. Having appeared in dozens of television commercials, she is, at this very moment, waiting to hear whether she will be booked for a major Cindy-doll advertisement, and – as she gets nearly every job she auditions for – the answer's probably 'yes'!

But it wasn't long ago that Gemma, an only child, was a painfully shy seven-year-old who, when in public, would cling on to her mother's skirt, too embarrassed to speak when she was spoken to. And, because she was afraid to ask questions in class, even her school work was suffering. Then, a friend of Gemma's mother (whose children were both models) suggested that modelling might help boost Gemma's confidence. Taking her advice, Lesley Dunn and her daughter went to see top child

agent, Elizabeth Smith, who, noticing Gemma's potential, signed her up on the spot. Lesley explains that it wasn't long before Gemma came out of her shell and lost her shyness: 'During her first few jobs the photographers made such a fuss of Gemma that she soon gained confidence,' says Lesley. 'Now she tells jokes to the photographers and even has the whole crew in stitches. She's cheeky, but in the nicest possible way.'

Two years later, teachers comment on how Gemma's school work has dramatically improved as a result of her new-found confidence. And she's even joined a drama group. Modelling has also enabled Gemma to pursue two of her favourite hobbies. With the money from her first few assignments she bought a computer which she uses for games – and school work, of course! Gemma's number-one passion has always been horse riding, yet owning a horse was just a dream. However, a few weeks ago, a delighted little girl

Photographed by Darleine Honey

Three supermodelettes skip and hop along the catwalk at the Sonia Rykiel show.

realized that she'd saved enough from her modelling work to be able to buy a pony, which she named Spice.

Lesley, who is not only Gemma's mum but her chaperone, too, explains how much her daughter enjoys modelling: 'She sees it as great fun and always gets on well with people she works for. Luckily, there are no tears or tantrums with Gemma, and she never seems to get fed up or bored. If I know there's going to be a lot of waiting around, I'll take along a few of her favourite books and games to keep her occupied.' Gemma's agent confirms that she is a total little professional. And, as a result, Gemma finds herself being rebooked time and time again.

Not only is she a hit with girls as the face on their Cindy doll boxes, but Gemma is recognized by boys and girls as the famous 'hero girl' in the Milky Way commercial. She also poses for major catalogues, including Littlewoods and, with her wispy blonde hair and Scandinavian colouring, gets regularly booked by German and Swedish companies. One of the highlights of her career was when she was featured on national television demonstrating a day in the life of a child model.

So what next for this budding supermodelette? 'When I grow up I want to become an actress and a show jumper, oh, and carry on modelling, of course,' says Gemma with such enthusiasm that she hardly stops for breath. Lesley is happy for Gemma to model for as long as she wants to. 'The day she stops enjoying it, I'll know it's time to quit but, until then, I am delighted that Gemma is doing so well and will continue to support and chaperone her.' Well, after all, chaperones do get paid as well, you know!

FAMILY MODELLING

A commercial featuring a genuine family happily munching cornflakes around a breakfast table is far more believable than a group of unrelated models or actors who have been picked in an attempt to resemble a family.

The Walshes – two parents, five kids, and an Irish terrier – are a growing band of entire families taking the modelling world by storm. Not only do these genuine families look the part but, being naturally at ease with one another, they come across as considerably more authentic in the final image. For this reason, clients find real families far easier to work with than a bunch of strangers just playing at being families. This is even more evident when working with young children or babies, who respond better to their parents than to any model or actor. Then there's the logistics of hiring a real family. For starters, as the kids are already with their parents, it's immediately more cost-effective for the client than having to pay extra for chaperones. And when a job involves hotel accommodation, the client needs only book one family suite, instead of separate rooms for each adult model, each kid and

each chaperone. It's also far simpler for photographers and casting directors to hire a whole family in one fell swoop, rather than spend long hours casting until they've found a bunch who look like they could *possibly* be related.

There is seemingly an increasing amount of work for family models. 'I think clients have realized you get the true family feeling with a genuine family,' says leading family agent Elizabeth Smith. 'Every time the new model book comes out we have more family entries.' Families are hired for catalogue work, leaflets, brochures, commercials and print advertising for a whole range of products, from holidays to toothpaste, supermarkets to cars. The work can be great fun; often it's just like a family outing. 'I had one family who were booked for a Volvo commercial,' explains Elizabeth. 'They spent a day in the countryside playing games, basking in the sunshine, and enjoying a picnic; they hardly noticed the filming going on all around them.'

Family groups can take the shape of a husband and wife complete with baby, or up to five kids. Mother-and-baby units are also hired. The usual request, however, is for a family unit of parents with two children – preferably a boy and girl. One of the most successful model families in the UK is the Walsh family, a family of seven, plus their dog, who has also been booked for family assignments. Parents Caroline and Mike, along with their youngest, Rosie, 3, Sophie, 7, Laura, 9, Sam, 12, and eldest, 17-year-old Ben, have appeared together in such advertisements as

Eurostar, Rover and Safeway. The Walsh family's agent, Elizabeth Smith, explains the secret of their success: 'They just look like the average family next door. It also helps that Mike Walsh's job entails working shifts, which gives him more free time.'

According to Elizabeth Smith, one of the problems with family modelling is finding a complete family whose lives are flexible enough for all its members to be available at the same time. 'The mother and kids may be free, but if the father is away on business, or cannot get time off work, the rest of the family will lose the job, no matter how suitable they are.'

Because family modelling is a small, specialist category, no agency as yet exclusively handles families. However, most child-model agencies have a family division; often the kids are already signed up as child models. Other agencies which represent families include character and talent agencies, as well as agencies representing the whole spectrum of model types.

Besides real families, model agencies also handle a few, specially assembled families where, for instance, one parent is substituted by an unrelated, yet similar-looking model. This could be due to such reasons as a one-parent family, or a family where a spouse is rarely available for work.

Few people can expect to earn a living from family modelling. However, it's a way of bringing in extra cash, is fun and extremely rewarding. Think of all those wonderful pictures for your family album!

BASIC REQUIREMENTS

Looks: Parents and kids do not necessarily have to be extremely attractive – just average looking. Families of all creeds and colours are wanted.
Age: Parents can be between 25 and 50. The kids can be any age from a new-born baby to late teens.

THE ELLISON FAMILY

Jane and Paul Ellison, together with their three little boys – James, 5, Billy, 3 and Sam, 2, are tailor-made for family modelling. When they're not booked for family assignments, Jane, 30 and Paul, 31, model individually. The couple, who both started modelling in their teens, met while shooting a commercial for Shell oil and married shortly after.

Described by their agent as a young, attractive family, part of the Ellisons' success can be attributed to their professional attitude. 'We try to be very organized,' explains Paul, 'with a separate set of clothes for modelling, and plenty of books and toys to amuse the children.' The Ellisons are often booked for trips abroad. This might sound like a great excuse for a family holiday but, having recently returned from a seven-day catalogue trip

Family modelling is great fun and extremely rewarding. Think of all those wonderful pictures for your family album!

to Portugal, Paul explains why it's hard work: 'Although we only worked three days out of seven, those three days were utter chaos. Trying to get ourselves and three kids ready at the same time was not easy. Next time I'm determined not to leave home without the nanny!'

The family have appeared in many advertisements, including Mercedes and Fiat; in supermarket and store-training videos, and are regularly pictured in mail-order catalogues. Of their many different assignments it's the Fiat shoot that sticks out in Paul's mind. 'Because the weather was so bad, we spent hours in the hotel room playing with the kids. Whenever it stopped raining we'd all pile into the car, strap in the kids and wait for a glimmer of sunshine. This happened several times until, just as the sun was setting, the clouds disappeared. It made a beautiful shot.'

Like all genuine model parents, Paul and Jane know exactly what makes their kids tick. 'They are naturally much happier with us than models, so it's easier to animate them if, for instance, the photographer wants them to smile or pose in a certain way.' Although Paul and Jane model full time, they limit the amount of family assignments so as not to overwork the children. 'It's a great way to earn a living,' enthuses Paul. 'But just because the kids are modelling at the moment doesn't mean I intend to push them into a full-time modelling career. But if they do decide to take this path, I'll be more than happy to support them.'

MATURE MODELLING

Levi's shocked the fashion world when it abandoned the superbabes in favour of a bunch of older folk; Versace featured a grey-haired older woman in a recent advertisement; and many other fashion names, from Donna Karan to Hennes, are turning to mature models to add a dose of sophistication to their shows and ad campaigns.

This is no fleeting trend, nor is it a fashion fetish for the blue-rinse brigade, older models – from 30 years upwards – are now permanent fixtures on the modelling scene. The elegantly cool, 66-year--old Carmen Dell'Orefice is frequently seen gliding down the international runways; Donna Karan featured 53-year-old Italian model Bernedetta Barzini in a recent campaign; and one of Vivienne Westwood's favourite muses is 56-year-old Jibby Beane. And let's not forget all those models who are hired to advertise everything from cruises to incontinence pads.

Gone are the days when models have passed their sell-by date by the time they reach 25. A model's career expectancy and earning span is now considerably longer. Not so long ago fashion-model agents set a cut-off date discarding any girl pushing 20. But that's all changing. Nowadays, agencies sign up new girls of 20 plus. Male models have always had the better end of the deal: they may not start until their late teens, but often continue working into their thirties, forties and fifties plus. Far from becoming has-beens, Cindy, Linda, Elle, Tatjana, and other female thirtysomethings of their ilk, still get as many bookings as any nubile supermodel. And these models have staying power. Linda Evangelista said in an interview with *Vogue* that she'd go down the runway with a walking stick if they'll have her!

Top international fashion agency Models 1 started a mature division five years ago, and now has over 70 of the world's top mature models on its books, including Carmen Dell'Orefice, Bernedetta Barzini, Lesley Lowe, Debbie Carr and Jerry Hall. 'These models are not being booked just because of their age, but because of their look,' says Jane Wood, who runs Models 1's mature division. 'Our models do a variety of work, including the beauty and fashion pages of magazines, brochures, shows, catalogue, commercials and cosmetic campaigns.' Jane represents models in their thirties, forties, fifties and sixties, but stresses that: 'No matter how old a model is, it's important she's happy with her age – wrinkles and all.' So potential mature models needn't rush out and have a face-lift or overdose on AHAs. However, Jane points out that they should have the same desirable attributes as the younger fashion model, notably height, good skin and prominent cheekbones.

Work for – as they are also called – 'classics' and 'sophisticates' is evenly spread across the ages. Many mature fashion models like Jerry Hall, Marie Helvin, Gunilla Lindbald, Lesley Lowe

'It all started to happen again for Carmen when the legendary photographer Norman Parkinson told her she didn't look so bad for an old bag.'

and Lauren Hutton have always modelled, while others, like Bernedetta Barzini and Carmen Dell'Orefice, resumed their modelling careers later on in life. Indeed, Carmen, the great French model, returned to the studios and the runways in 1978. 'It all started to happen again for Carmen when the legendary photographer Norman Parkinson told her she didn't look so bad for an old bag,' laughs Jane Wood, who represents her. 'He then booked her for a shoot for French *Vogue*.' With her highly distinctive, bob-length grey hair and sophisticated beauty, she immediately had

Photographed by Niall McInerney

Sheer elegance: Carmen Dell'Orefice.

all the greats queuing up to photograph her. Unsurprisingly, this spellbinding creature has become the role model for many mature models and older women alike.

Mature models have many different guises. Besides fashion models, there are a variety of 'types', from the mother and father type to the white-haired, pink-cheeked grandmother, or the distinguished older gentleman. Don Rosay, owner of mature-model agency Top Models, who's been in the business since 1968, explains that there's always been a need for older models at the consumer end of the advertising market to promote insurance, cruises, pensions, food and drink, holidays, gifts, etc. 'This type of client wants older models who look believable rather than glamorous, and are of an age their customers can relate to. For example, 62-year-old Vicky Hoskins, with her silvery, ash-blonde hair and pleasant, smiling face is the perfect "credible-looking" older model. She's one of my busiest models, and has played many guises, from mother-of-the-bride and business executive to a Doris Day lookalike,' enthuses Don.

Vicky Hoskins loves every minute of her modelling career: 'I have been to many wonderful locations and met lots of interesting people.' Most mature models like Vicky discover that modelling is great fun but, as Don points out, it's still hard work. 'Models get extremely excited if I tell them they're booked for a ten-day cruise, but they forget that for the majority of time they'll be busy working. They may be on deck for a photo shoot at 8am and find they're still being photographed in the disco well after midnight.'

Don't think that, just because they're older, mature models get handed the cushy jobs. Far from it. One of Don's 75-year-old models had to hold a pose while balancing on top of a 12-foot-high dinosaur. And Vicky Hoskins has worked in extreme conditions from modelling underwear on bitterly cold moors to posing in fur coats in the Sahara desert. You also need to have a sense of humour, especially when, like Vicky, you're asked to jump up and down 80 times for a vitamin advertisement, or have your face covered in stark-white powder to look like you're suffering from angina.

You can break into mature modelling at virtually any age and, indeed, many non-fashion models like 90-year-old Margot Dillon, who started modelling at 67, begin much later on in life. But how does a woman of 45 or a 60-year-old man get into modelling? 'Often their daughters or friends have suggested modelling,' explains Don Rosay. 'We have one male model who used to be a flight captain and another a fireman. As long as they are bubbly, outgoing people, it doesn't matter if they've never modelled before. They'll soon learn the ropes.'

Top mature models like Carmen Dell'Orefice and Lesley Lowe are working almost every day, but others might find that they only get one or two assignments a month and should not, therefore, rely on modelling as their main source of income. Modelling suits those who have flexible jobs, are retired, or at home with children. There are agencies which specialize solely in mature models, and fashion agencies including Models 1, Wilhelmina and Ford, which have mature-model divisions. Potential non-fashion, mature models can approach character agencies or mature-model agencies like Top Models, which represents 'types'.

BASIC REQUIREMENTS

Looks: Fashion agents are looking for older versions of younger fashion models: a beautiful face with good skin and regular features. Non-fashion models should be attractive but believable looking.
Age: A model can be classified as a mature model from as young as 30.
Height: Women: 5'6" and above – taller for fashion. Men: 5'10"–6'3".
Measurements: Mature fashion models should have fashion model proportions and be dress size 10–12 or suit size 38–42. Non-fashion, mature models tend to be on the larger side – usually dress size 12–16 and suit size 38–44.

LESLEY LOWE

For the cover photograph of her composite card, Lesley Lowe refused to have her wrinkles airbrushed out. 'I want clients to know exactly what they're getting,' says the 46-year-old international fashion model candidly. Lesley's exceptionally long career has spanned some 26 years. During this time she's modelled for the world's leading photographers, worked with the fashion luminaries, and shuttled between Europe, Japan and the United States.

It all started back in the seventies, when Lesley fell into modelling by chance while teaching English in Japan. 'I became friendly with a make-up artist who decided to open a model agency in Osaka. There were only two other models and myself, so we had the pick of the work,' says Leslie, explaining how she's seen the industry change dramatically since 1970. 'Things were not what they are today. You often had to do your own hair and make-up and, although there wasn't so much work around, it was far less competitive.'

After a couple of years of engaging the camera, Lesley felt vanity was getting the better of her, and returned home to the USA to run a boutique. But it wasn't long before she tired of expensive frocks and difficult customers, and her urge to travel returned. 'I knew I wanted to see the world, but I also figured I needed to earn money. Then it dawned on me – modelling was the perfect solution.' First stop – Tokyo, then Paris via New York, and on to London, where she met the man she was to marry. 'He was a jeweller and travelled frequently. Modelling gave me the chance to work in different countries and still be with him. It was ideal.'

When Lesley reached her mid-thirties, for the first time in 15 years she was beginning to notice a lull in her career. While other models' careers nose-dived, fortunately for Lesley, she started gaining a bit of weight. 'I was heading towards a size 14, so my agency decided that – with the help of a bit of padding around my hips – they would market me as a plus-size model.' It worked. By the time she was 39, Lesley had slimmed back down to her normal size 10, and was getting regular modelling work.

Since her modest beginnings in Osaka, she has done all kinds of work, from beauty and fashion advertising to editorial for women's magazines, and from in-store packaging for companies such as Marks & Spencer to commercials for products as diverse as Oil of Ulay, Nescafé and Ferrero Rocher chocolates. Lesley earns a good living from modelling. Nevertheless, when she's not working, she endeavours to keep a balance in her life by dabbling in other things. 'I like to think I have a well-rounded life,' says Lesley, 'with many interests apart from modelling.' She helps out in her ex-husband's jewellery shop, does book-keeping, and is currently studying Japanese.

The secret of Lesley's success and commercial longevity is partly down to her chameleon-like quality. One minute she looks glamorous, the next elegant, as well as being able to slip into the sporty or the smart executive image. Couple that with her ability to adapt and update her look, her long-lasting popularity is clear. 'I think I've managed to keep up with the times,' says Lesley. 'Some former models return after a ten-year break and are still in some kind of time warp – wearing the same hairstyle and still doing the "teapot" pose.'

When it comes to holding back the years, Lesley doesn't go in for age-defying creams. Instead, she prefers basic moisturizers like Vaseline and baby oil. Mixing up her own toner, she favours natural products, and also likes to make a home-made facial scrub and body treatment from oatmeal. 'I stick some oatmeal into an old pair of tights and put it in my bath. It really softens your skin.' Oh, and her best-kept beauty secret – she's always used a sun block on her face. Wearing her hair in a short, fashionable style, she does admit to colouring it. 'I'll probably let it go grey when I'm 60 odd,' she says. And to keep her size-10 figure in shape, she energetically runs up and down the stairs several times a day. 'I live on the fourth floor, so I make use of all those stairs.'

Being a mature model has its moments: photographers play around with special lighting and filters, and, as Leslie discovered, you often get mistaken for the client. 'I've been called the stylist, client and photographer – everyone but the model,' admits Lesley. But it also works the other way round. She was sent on a casting for an advertisement for a non-surgical face-lift, but when she arrived she was told she looked too young.

It's very tempting for mature models to lie about their age, and even Lesley confesses to knocking off a few years on one occasion: 'If I hadn't lied I wouldn't have got the job,' she says. 'The casting director was looking for a 'husband' and 'wife' for a commercial. I was 42 at the time, but told him I was 36. I was convinced he wouldn't believe me.' Sure enough, Lesley was hired. By the end of the day the male model, who posed as Leslie's husband, had helped ease her guilty conscience. 'We got chatting, and I discovered that he'd also lied about his age. He was, in fact, 29, not 34! We both giggled at the thought of our 12-year age gap.'

Lesley realizes how lucky she is to be blessed with regular features and a universal look that works as well in Japan as New York. 'I just hope they'll still be booking me for the stair-lift advertisements when I'm 90!' she says optimistically.

PLUS-SIZE MODELLING

Ask the average woman whether she'd prefer to see clothes modelled on a pencil-thin size 8 or Rubenesque curves and, chances are, she'll pick the more realistic option.

The voluptuous models stalking the runways have proved that big is beautiful. Indeed, one of fashion's hottest new finds is Sophie Dahl, the stunningly curvaceous granddaughter of Roald Dahl, who, at size 14 with a 38DD chest is very comfortable with her figure. But Dahl is no plus-size model. Unbelievable as it may seem in the oh-so-slim-world of fashion modelling, not only is she on the books of a top editorial fashion agency, she is being courted by some of the world's hottest snappers and editors of the glossiest magazines. And if Dahl is an indication of the way things are going, skinny might become an anachronism, and big – the ultimate chic!

A shade more believable than the wafer-thin fashion model and – some would say – a touch more politically correct, models from size 12 to 18 are the healthier-looking and more voluptuous option to the spaghetti-thin size-8 brigade. 'Fashion photographers have been wanting to photograph bigger girls for a long time and have been quick off the mark to use Sophie Dahl,' says Storm's Jessica Hallet. Wearing nothing more than a feather, Sophie was photographed by Ellen von Unwerth for Italian *Vogue*. 'Ellen thought she was fantastic', enthuses Jessica, 'as did Nick Knight, David Lachapelle and many other big-name photographers.' But before she signed up with Storm, Sophie was overlooked by many fashion agencies, who either told her she was too big or else sent her away to lose weight. 'Her reaction to this was to go home and indulge in a huge chunk of chocolate cake,' says Jessica approvingly. 'I would never dream of asking her to lose weight. If the clients want her, which they certainly do, they will just have to alter their sample sizes!'

Another agent who doesn't believe that curvaceous models should be discriminated against is Susan Georget, of New York agency Wilhelmina. Susan, who runs the agency's plus-size division, Ten20, has ambitions to amalgamate her models with the main board, as opposed to boxing them into a speciality division. 'These girls are no different to regular models. They have beautiful faces, great bones and flawless skin – they are just more curvaceous and take a larger dress size,' she insists. 'And, just like the main board, we also have models with strong editorial looks and quirky features.' One of her top models is *Vogue* cover girl Kate Dillon who, currently a US size 14, was one of the first larger models to do a regular fashion story in the glossy magazine *Glamour*.

Fuelled by the success of Sophie Dahl, slowly but surely curvaceous models are edging their way into the high-fashion arena. But for those who don't have an editorial look or are larger than a size 14, plus-size is an area of modelling where models from size 12 to 22 are required. Pioneered 19 years ago by Pat Swift, of Miami-based agency Plus Models, plus-size is now well established as a category of modelling. Since Cheryl Hughes, proprietor of plus-size agency Hughes Models, discovered a niche in the UK market, she has seen the plus-size field grow. 'Up until recently, outsize ranges were frumpy, mother-of-the-bride-style clothes,' says Cheryl, 'but since fashion companies have realized larger women want to buy clothes with fashion and flair, they are designing stylish collections in accordance. And, as 50 per cent of women are closer to a size 16, it's about time too,' adds Cheryl emphatically. Designer Anna Scholz, herself a size 24, is one of the few directional designers catering for larger women. 'I believe women who want to dress fashionably shouldn't be discriminated against, so that's why my clothes start at size 10 and go up to size 28,' says Anna, who uses a size-18 model to promote her collection which is now sold world-wide.

Nothing is worth putting yourself through such anguish,' says Simone, who is now a successful plus-size model. 'I soon realized that I'm built this way and, short of sawing two inches off my hips, I just wasn't going to get any slimmer.'

Fuller-figured models may have more generous measurements than their thinner counterparts, but they still have curves in all the right places. 'I look for a larger version of Elle Macpherson, Kate Moss or Cindy Crawford,' says Cheryl Hughes. And just because these models are a size 16 or 18, doesn't mean they are covered from head to toe in lumps, bumps and cellulite. When undressing at shoots or shows in the presence of size 10s, top plus-size model Sarah Paterson is always amused by the looks on their faces when she reveals a body that is as taut and firm as theirs. 'They are so surprised you're not the big round ball

'These girls are no different to regular models. They, too, have beautiful faces, great bones and flawless skin – they just take a larger dress size.'

Former fashion models Kate Dillon, Michelle Griffin, Amy Davies and Sarah Paterson – who struggled to stay unnaturally thin – have successfully moved into plus-size modelling. 'Several of our models crossed over from the main board,' explains Susan. 'Most of these models find they are far happier and more confident with their natural weight, rather than battling with their bodies.' Of course there's also the added bonus of being able to scoff those cream cakes they previously avoided!

You'd be surprised by the vast number of would-be models unaware that plus-size modelling even exists. Traipsing from one fashion agency to another, most give up on the idea of modelling after being told that they are too big. One such wannabe, Simone Ive, struggled relentlessly to break into fashion; she was eventually accepted onto a model course only to be told by tutors that unless she lost weight she wouldn't make a model. By the end of the course she had become so neurotic about her weight that she started taking laxatives and slimming pills. 'I can't believe I was so stupid.

they'd imagined you to be,' says Sarah smugly.

Plus-size, outsize, fuller-figured – Allison Branwell, a former model who started up plus-size agency Excel, admits that she still comes up against clients who don't quite know how to label plus-sizes. She's even been called the woman from the 'fat' agency. 'It's sad that some people think of larger models as "fat models",' remarks Allison, who is quick to add 'but this is one of the reasons why these models must be proud of their size.'

Fuller-figured models are no longer solely being hired to model outsize ranges in catalogues: they are photographed by leading fashion snappers for hot editorial shots. 'Many of our models, like Kate Dillon, have done regular fashion editorial,' says Susan Georget. 'There was a time when plus-size models weren't supposed to move, apart from left hand in pocket and right hand carefully placed beside the mouth. Now they have the flexibility to move with the spontaneity of any fashion model.'

More magazines devoted to the larger woman are being launched. In the USA you can buy *BBW*

(*Big Beautiful Women*), *Mode* and *Real Women*, and in the UK Condé Nast (the company which publishes *Vogue*), in conjunction with outsize store Evans, has launched *Encore*. Along with editorial, fuller-figured models are also hired for catalogue work, advertising and shows – the latter being an area of work that gives both the model and customer mutual satisfaction. Simone Ive explains why she gets a buzz from the appreciation of large women: 'When I'm doing an in-store fashion show, women often come up to me and say how delighted they are to see a model they can relate to. I think women are far more tempted to buy a skirt or jacket if they've seen it modelled on a fuller figure and know it will look good on their shape.'

Although the need for plus-size models is growing, it is still a relatively small category compared to regular fashion modelling. At present, the largest chunk of work for bigger models can be found the USA where even top fashion agents like Ford and Wilhelmina have plus-size divisions. Outsize models can also find work in Canada and some parts of Europe, including the UK, France and Germany. Fashion agencies like Storm are taking girls who are bigger than a size 8 or 10. However, for the moment they are few and far between and must, like Sophie Dahl, be outstanding. And as for guys? 'As yet, there's very little demand for them,' says Cheryl, adding 'but as soon as the market is ready, I can assure you that there will be a long line of bigger guys queuing up to model.'

BASIC REQUIREMENTS

To be considered for plus-size modelling, a girl needs to be at least a size 14 but not plump in the face. Attitude is extremely important. Models will not succeed in plus-size modelling if they're continuously wishing they were pencil thin.

Looks: An attractive face, flawless skin, healthy hair and good teeth. Generally, similar attributes to a fashion model with the exception of size.
Size: Plus-size models start at size 14 and continue up to a size 22. The most requested size is 16–18. Their body weight should be fairly evenly distributed.
Height: Plus-size models need to have the height to carry off the weight. The requirements are 5'7" and above.
Age: 18–45. But the bulk of work is for 18–30-year-olds.

SARAH PATERSON

Former high-fashion model Sarah Paterson (see picture right), is the closest you'll get to a plus-size supermodel. With agencies in London, New York and Germany, this gorgeous 5'10", size-16 model has reached the privileged position of picking and choosing whom she works for. But life wasn't always a bed of roses. At 19 she dropped out of college and, not knowing what career path to follow, she took a stop-gap job as a nanny. Then a friend introduced her to the director of a top high-fashion agency. The good news was that they said they'd be happy to take her on, but then for the bad news: 'As I was close to a size 14, they told me I would need to lose weight,' says Sarah. Determined to crack it, she headed home and spent the next three months carrying out a vigorous fitness programme. 'I certainly didn't starve myself – it was much more a case of toning up,' insists Sarah. 'Mum would wake me at the crack of dawn for my seven-mile run. Then, to get my waist close to the desired 24–25 inches, I literally did hundreds of waist twists every day. Some days I even managed an aerobics class. It was a bit like training for the army – physically gruelling.'

After three months of non-stop preparation, a superfit, superlean teenager waved goodbye to her parents and headed for the bright lights of London. With that fresh-faced, English-rose look that was in huge demand, after a couple of test shoots with good photographers the bookings started pouring in. 'It was great being in such demand but the problem was I was so busy working there was very little time to exercise. Even though I was careful about what I ate, the weight started creeping back on. I knew it wouldn't be long before squeezing into an 8 or 10 was utterly impossible.' Tired of the constant battle with her weight, and faced with the downward spiral of fewer and fewer bookings, Sarah quit modelling and went back to college to study literature and media.

Several months later, however, Sarah had an unexpected call from a booker at the agency, who explained that lingerie company Triumph was looking for a voluptuous girl for a major advertising campaign. 'She asked me if they could put me up for the job as a one-off. As I thought I was in with a good chance, I agreed.' But as soon as she walked into casting, the client pooh-poohed her, explaining that it was a big girl they were looking for. 'I was furious,' says Sarah, 'if I wasn't too big, I was too small.' But all was not lost. In fact, this casting was the turning point of her career. The client told her about a plus-size agency which took on girls from size 14 upwards. Hughes Models signed up Sarah immediately. 'I'll never forget Cheryl's words as I walked out of the agency. "Don't lose any weight – if anything, put it on".'

Today, Sarah is more comfortable and confident about the way her body looks. 'Now that my weight is stable, I feel much happier. I don't have to diet or deprive myself of naughty foods, although my craving for sweet things seems to have gone.' And she's not the only one happy with her size. Men love Sarah's curves, as do clients. The only slight problem she has encountered is finding trendy clothes to fit her. 'Because many of the outsize ranges go up to size 30, the clothes are designed to be loose fitting and baggy. For someone of my size to look stylish, I think it's important to wear tailored garments.' Sarah finds the trick is to shop around. 'A size 16 in one shop can differ considerably from a size 16 in another,' she says. 'A few of the younger ranges do go up to a size 18, but you have to look quite hard to find them. I also find department stores are a good place to buy larger sizes.'

During her three years as a fuller-figured model, Sarah has modelled all over the world, in particular New York, Paris, Spain, Egypt and Germany. Sarah, who has worked for magazines, catalogue companies, television shows, fashion shows and commercials, enjoys all types of modelling, but admits to having a preference. 'Photographic work is my favourite, that is unless I'm left to freeze in a flimsy dress in the middle of winter,' says Sarah, referring to her worst-ever job: a shoot for an outsize fashion range in Paris on a bitterly cold November day. 'We were at the top of a hill, so it made matters worse. I'm not the type to complain but, as my hands were turning blue, and in fear of getting hypothermia, I decided to tell the client how cold I was.' But the

client ignored her comments and carried on regardless, even when the make-up artist explained that, no matter how much make-up she piled on, she couldn't get Sarah to look warm. 'In the end I just burst into tears. Looking back, this was the only hellish job – the rest have been great,' says Sarah, explaining how assignments range from fun and interesting to challenging and outlandish. 'Catalogue and editorial work are fairly straightforward, but for commercials you get asked to do all kinds of things. For a Ford car commercial I was covered in padding, dressed as a buxom farmer's wife, then asked to hula-hoop,' laughs Sarah. 'In this business you just never know what you might get asked to do next!'

Photographed by Derek Lee

PETITE MODELLING

It wasn't long ago that any prospective model with a stunning face – but lacking the requisite height for modelling – was cast aside with the rest of the no-hopers. Now they're in with a chance!

Since the success of Kate Moss – who stands only 5'6" in her bare feet – the height restrictions for high-fashion modelling have become less stringent. These days, even the international designers, who traditionally used tall, willowy models of 5'9" and above, are sending the short brigade down the runway. Teenage modelling sensation Lonneke Engel, and hot new model Devon, both at the lower end of 5'6", are two examples of shorter high-fashion models who have hit the big time. As agents are doing their damnedest to make small become more acceptable, the barriers are slowly coming down. However, it must be pointed out that fashion models under 5'8" are rare creatures, who should be staggeringly beautiful, with that 'X' factor or 'look of the moment', to enable them to compete with their taller counterparts.

An increasing number of fashion companies are, at long last, beginning to appreciate that the average woman is closer to 5'4", not the 6' supermodel proportions. And, thanks to designers like Calvin Klein, Donna Karan, Anne Klein and Liz Claiborne, petite women can now buy directly off the peg, rather than going to the expense of having their clothes tailor-made or altered. The launch of petite fashion ranges has opened up a market – albeit a limited one – for petite models of heights of 5'2" and upwards.

You might equal Kate Moss in height, but if you're signed to an agency's petite division don't expect to cast for the type of high-fashion jobs assigned to girls on the main board. Fashion work in the petite category is far more mainstream. You could find yourself modelling petite fashion ranges for advertising campaigns, posters, packaging and catalogues but, according to Pat Swift, owner of Plus Models which also represents petites, the bulk of fashion work is very much behind the scenes. 'The problem with petite models is a visual

thing. In a photograph they look no different to a regular model, whereas with a plus-size model it's obvious she's bigger.' To advertise their petite ranges, clients often use regular models and, for catalogues, they simply write 'available in petite sizes'. 'It's because of these reasons,' continues Pat, 'that petite models mainly get booked for garment fittings where they act as a mannequin for the designer.' Many designers have petite ranges, so there's plenty of fitting work and, as Pat points out, if a model is the perfect size, she can demand a sizable fee. 'Having clothes pinned and tacked onto you may not be glamorous, but it can earn the model as much as a fashion model.' Petite models can also compete with regular models for television work and consumer-product advertising, as well as for beauty advertising and editorial where height isn't a requirement.

There are many different reasons why clients choose to hire shorter models. Car advertisers, for example, often use petite models; a tall girl could look out of proportion in a small car. 'IBM uses our petite models because they make the computer look bigger,' says Pat Swift. Another reason can be because the male model is on the short side and would look ridiculous standing next to a six-footer. Certain petite models are picked regardless of height, simply because they have a particular look that fits the client's brief.

Compared to regular modelling, the petite category is still a very specialist area, but agents like Cheryl Hughes of Hughes Models are optimistic about its future. 'I believe that in the same way we've seen the plus-size field grow, petite modelling will develop into a strong market over the next few years.' In the past, clients looking for shorter models would approach glamour or promotions agencies, now they need look no further than the agencies which specialize in handling petites. Often, agencies representing plus-size models will also have petite models on their books. The market is largest in the USA, where a few top fashion agencies, including Ford, have petite divisions. At present the petite divisions only represent women, due to the lack of demand for shorter men.

If you're petite and still in your teens, you could consider joining the teenage division of a child agency. Here, girls and boys who are considerably shorter than adult fashion models get booked for a whole range of work. Teenage divisions even take on the four-foot-somethings. For more information, see the section on teenage models in the child-modelling chapter (p.46). Glamour and promotional work are other categories which don't discriminate against height.

BASIC REQUIREMENTS

You must have the physical attributes of a fashion model and a well-proportioned body.

Looks: You need to have the looks of a fashion model. See p.15.
Height: Between 5'2" and 5'6".
Measurements: Sizes 8–10 or 10–12 with a bust of 32–34 B/C.
Age: Between 16 and 30.

HELEN SLAYMAKER

'At 5'3" I don't stand a chance,' retorted Helen to anyone who suggested she should model. Helen knew the score. She had telephoned many of the fashion agencies and was fully aware that they only accepted girls who were a good few inches taller. Desperate to be in the business, she joined an extras agency. 'I thought it was probably the closest I'd ever get to becoming a model,' she says. But it was extras work that opened the doors to a career in modelling. While working on a photographic extras job, she got chatting to a fellow supporting artist whose friend ran the petite division of a model agency. Helen scribbled down the number, then dashed home to telephone Hughes Models. 'I had no idea there was such a thing as a petite model,' she says, remembering her excitement as she dialled the number.

Having barely signed up with the agency she landed her debut modelling job – a major advertising campaign for a petite clothing range. 'The client was slightly concerned that Helen lacked

experience,' explains Mandy, her booker, 'but she liked her look so much she decided to take the plunge.' According to Mandy, extras work certainly set Helen in good stead: 'As an extra she'd done photographic work and commercials, so she wasn't going into modelling completely blind.' The assignment entailed a day's shoot at a sumptuous country hotel. 'I was treated so well, and enjoyed the day so much that I wouldn't have minded had I not even been paid,' enthuses Helen, who actually raked in a huge fee for the job.

Within the space of a couple of days, Helen was booked for her second assignment, which involved modelling petite fashions on a live television show. 'I was a bag of nerves,' remembers Helen. 'I knew that if I mucked it up, the whole world would be watching – including my agent.' After hair and make-up, Helen was dressed in her first outfit: a brown cardigan, buttoned up and worn over a mere wisp of a lace dress. Because of its transparency, the stylist told Helen *not* to unbutton the cardigan. This was daytime television after all!

A 30-second countdown and she was on. As instructed, Helen gracefully sauntered over to where the television presenters were sitting. As if this wasn't nerve-racking enough, after completing a couple of pivots and turns, one of the presenters asked her to reveal what was under the cardigan. 'I panicked and my legs turned to jelly,' remembers Helen. 'The dress was completely see-through and all I had underneath was a pair of ugly, biggish knickers and no bra.' But without haste, Helen unbuttoned the cardigan, gave a speedy twirl, and walked off the set with such precision that not only could she have done it a hundred times before, but the camera didn't have a chance to focus on her modesty!

Being petite, Helen usually has her clothes taken both up and in. 'I find most of the high-street petite ranges too conservative for my liking, so I prefer to buy a regular garment and alter the size.' She's also mastered the trick of dressing in such a way that makes her appear inches taller. 'I tend to pick simple lines in one solid colour. Fussy clothes draw even more attention to your height. I also find that if I'm wearing a skirt it needs to be either maxi or mini – anything in between seems to make me look shorter. And I wouldn't dream of stepping outside without heels,' says Helen who, although she lacks height, is certainly blessed with more than her fair share of model-girl assets.

Photographed by Trevor Hurst

PARTS
MODELLING

Do you have smooth, well-manicured mitts, perfectly shaped feet or long, slender legs? If the answer is 'yes' to just one of these, you could plump for parts modelling.

'Whether it's your hands, feet or legs, your particular feature must be outstanding,' stresses Danny Korwin, president of leading New York agency Parts Models. 'You'll need to convince clients that your hands, feet, etc. knock the spots off those of any regular model.' Those whose special feature makes the grade can be hired for a wide variety of work, including advertising campaigns, packaging, television, film and editorial work.

Sarah Clive's million-dollar mitts (see profile on p.67)

The world's leading leg model, 29-year-old, American-born Laura Gens, has modelled her pins for nine years for such prestigious names as *Vogue* magazine and Liz Claiborne. Her success may have something to do with the fact that she's 5'10" with very long, shapely, but slim legs, tapering to slender ankles. And it's not just her enviably long legs that bring in the money. Laura also models her feet, hands and body. 'Her book's like a medical encyclopaedia,' laughs Danny Korwin, who represents Laura.

Don't be fooled into thinking that modelling a part of your body is a doddle. Believe it or not, parts modelling can be more gruelling than any other kind of modelling: often you're required to hold an awkward pose for hours on end, which may be extremely uncomfortable or may even cause cramp. Imagine sitting with one leg raised for over eight hours for a hosiery campaign; no doubt you'd be limping out of the studio!

HAND MODELLING

Hand modelling is the most common area of parts work. Although perfectly manicured, flawless hands are always in demand to advertise hand cream, nail polish, jewellery, etc., advertisers require a cross-section of hands to promote all kinds of products. The most popular range from the rough hands of a builder or mechanic, to the soft, pretty hands of a young mum, and from the neatly manicured hands of a businessman to well-worn, mature mitts. Nail lengths differ, too. A glamorous hand has long, painted talons, while a natural-looking, teenage hand possesses short, neat nails.

So what does it take to make a hand model? Will any old pair suffice? 'Definitely not,' says Steve Barker, MD of Hired Hands, who has around 40 male and female hand models on his books. 'Whether young or old, I look for well-shaped hands with a smooth, even skin tone and no scars or blemishes. Nails must all be of similar shape and size, and clear of any ridges or milk spots,' continues Steve. And what about age? 'We have models of all ages, but most female hand models are between 18 and 30; any older, and the lines around the knuckles and wrist start to multiply.'

Hands also need to be photogenic. What appears to be the perfect, slender hand may look too bony in a photograph. Hand models have to go to castings, especially when it's for a commercial which involves moving the hand time and time again. Supple hands are, therefore, great assets. 'One of my models was asked to pick up coins repeatedly from a table, while another had to make his fingers walk,' explains Steve. Hand modelling sounds easy, but at times it can prove to be a tricky and tiring job.

If you want to make your mitts your livelihood, you'll need to treat them like gold. This means protecting them from wear and tear by always wearing gloves for housework, or avoiding it altogether. A great excuse for not doing the washing up! In the same way that a spot can play havoc with the career of a fashion model, a cut, graze, or broken nail is catastrophic to a hand model. Until the hand heals or nail grows back, the model is out of work; that is, unless he or she is extremely lucky and the flaw happens to be on a finger or hand that's not needed in a picture. But don't think this means you can get away with anything that's less than perfect. Because most hand work involves close-up shots, clients normally scrutinize hands under a microscope before they will even consider booking you. So dry skin, flaky nails or cuts and grazes are definitely out.

Regular manicures are a must. But you should also be capable of painting your own nails and applying make-up to your hands. Most female hand models have an extensive range of nail polish, covering the whole spectrum of colour from black and glittery silvers to harlequin or natural colours. In addition to nail polish, both male and female hand models need to take a collection of varying shades of foundation to every job.

DIFFERENT PARTS

Besides hands, other features raking in the money are legs and feet. Long, slender, perfectly shaped legs are frequently needed to promote such products as depilatory creams, shavers, waxes, hosiery and shoes, as well as for magazine beauty and hosiery features. And a good pair of feet can boost the sales of shoes, nail polish, sandals, foot baths and medicinal creams. But what separates an average foot from a model foot? 'Some clients want the Roman foot,' explains Danny, 'where the second toe is longer than the big toe, but in the main they want feet where the toes form a gradual, rounded curve.' While there are requests for models with good teeth, luscious lips, perfect torsos, glossy hair and huge, sparkling eyes, there's no such a thing as an eye, hair, torso, lip or tooth model. 'In these instances,' says Danny, 'clients often hire regular models.'

Just like regular models, parts models possess a book and composite. They also need to appear in their agency's book and go on castings. A few specialist parts agencies are dotted around the world. Some represent hand models exclusively, while others handle a selection of parts. If you cannot find a parts agency in your region, approach a general model agency and enquire whether they have a parts division. It's not unheard of for hand models to earn a mint from their mitts but, in the main, parts modelling is only a full-time vocation for the lucky few.

BASIC REQUIREMENTS

Hands: Flawless skin and good, evenly shaped nails are prerequisites for hand modelling. The shape of the hands is also important. Measurements are based on the glove size 6–7.5 for women, and 6–9 for men. They should be free of broken capillaries and not overly veiny; men's hands should not be too hairy.

Legs: Shapely, smooth, long legs with an even skin tone free of veins, blemishes or scars.

Feet: Feet should be a good shape and should form a smooth curve, with evenly shaped nails. It also helps if the ankles are slender. Even-textured skin, with no broken capillaries, is also a must. Feet sizes vary. It goes without saying that feet models should not have any corns, verrucas or any other unsightly blemishes on their feet.

Eyes: Strong-coloured, often framed with thick, luscious lashes. The whites should be very white. The shapes can vary from almond-shaped to wide, round eyes.

Torso: Even-toned skin on a well-shaped body.

Teeth: Even, white teeth with no visible fillings.

Lips: Strongly defined, often full, pouty lips.

Hair: Usually thick, glossy, 'virgin' hair.

SARAH CLIVE

Minutes before Sarah Clive's very first assignment as a hand model, disaster struck. She was zipping up her vanity case when the top of her thumbnail ripped right across. 'I thought: "this may be my first job, but it's probably going to be my last",' recalls Sarah. Fortunately, not only was she able to patch the nail back on, but after all the worry her thumb wasn't even needed in the shot. Since that first, panic-stricken day five years ago, Sarah's hands have appeared in dozens of commercials and advertisements for products such as hand creams, watches and food; she's done press and radio interviews, and has been booked for many a beauty editorial. Her hands even appeared in a KY Jelly advertisement banned by magazines for being too 'in your face'.

Majoring in classical theatre, at 22 Sarah graduated with a burning ambition to perform on stage. But she knew that becoming a thespian wouldn't happen overnight – it would be a long, hard struggle. Realizing that she needed a part-time job to bring in extra cash, she was about to be employed as a waitress when she read in *The Stage* that hand artists were required. 'My mum always said that my hands were the best part of me, so I thought I'd give it a go.' Sarah approached an agency and soon became one of their top five hand models. She describes her hands as more of the 'natural-looking' and 'young-mumish' type with mid-length nails, as opposed to the more glamorous type.

According to Sarah, hand work is physically tough and requires as much – if not more stamina – than any other type of modelling. 'It can be exhausting and painfully difficult to hold a pose for ages without moving a millimetre. And it's not just your hands you have to keep still – it's your whole body.' Sarah recalls one shoot where, after holding the same position for six hours, she fainted. 'I started to feel queasy and, a few seconds later, I collapsed in a heap right onto the set.' On another occasion Sarah was suspended upside down for a whole day in order to get a shot of her hands at as vertical an angle as possible. Sarah trained as a puppeteer which, she claims, helped enormously with her movement and direction. Over the years her hands have performed many different tasks including dancing the can-can and juggling margarine tubs.

In her spare time – to the horror of her agent – Sarah enjoys messing around with glue, scissors and paint, making everything from collages and Christmas cards to glass decorations. She's also a great cook. 'When I first started modelling I was so paranoid about protecting my hands it was ridiculous; now, thank goodness, I have become much more relaxed about it.' She does, however, always wear gloves whenever she's doing something that could be potentially hazardous. 'The rubber, surgical sort are brilliant as they fit tightly and allow me to do everything from cooking and cleaning to washing my hair.' To look after her hands, she regularly massages them with warm olive or almond oil; prepares her cuticles by using a softening cream, then carefully trims them. And, a day or so before each assignment, she lets her nails stay free of any varnish.

To Sarah, hand modelling has been a godsend. 'If it wasn't for my hands, I would have found it a real struggle to support myself while I continued with the theatre. I also thoroughly enjoy the work,' enthuses Sarah, who admits that it's always satisfying when she recognizes the hands in a commercial or magazine as hers. Turn back to page 64 to see her perfect mitts.

Photographed by Rod Howe at Models 1

PART 2

THE MODEL WORLD

THE MODEL INDUSTRY

Models continue to dominate the headlines – but who are the people behind the heels, the hemlines, the hairdos and the one-dimensional faces?

THE MODEL

From Lisa Fonssagrives to Linda Evangelista, the model's role is to sell or endorse the product he or she is promoting. But who is the modern model, and where did she spring from? Starting life at the turn of the century, she was a demure, elegant mannequin, whose requisite poise and haughty stance spelled upper-class breeding.

In the forties and fifties, the model took the shape of a high-society débutante who modelled for fun between gallery visits and luncheon parties. But as hemlines rose and fashion went funky, she was cast aside for the sixties hippy chick, who cavorted around the studio to loud music, dated celebrities and lived a life of debauchery and decadence. Twiggy, Jean Shrimpton and Veruschka became some of the most famous icons on the planet; at last the model had become a household name. During the seventies, however, her new-found fame eluded her. As modelling became dominated by health and vitality, the coltish, wide-eyed waif re-emerged as the wholesome and more voluptuous all-American girl, à la Christie Brinkley. By the early eighties she had swapped her sporty look for power dressing, transforming into a glamorous all-rounder who was desired by international designers for both their catwalk shows and pan-European campaigns.

Then the model went global. And by 1988, she'd elbowed the Hollywood stars out of the limelight and given up two decades of anonymity to become a supermodel. Soon she was getting blanket exposure in the media and, by the early nineties, was an international superstar commanding exorbitant fees yet unable to do anything like the amount of work she was being offered. She went on to launch books, write for magazines, present television programmes,

open restaurants and date rock stars. Moreover, superwoman that she was, she still managed to find time to saunter down the international runways for Chanel and Versace and pose for *Vogue*.

A decade on, the supermodel is still alive and kicking, but in a more low-key way. The original supermodel label was reserved for those household names known world-wide by their first names, nowadays it is simply awarded to great models. The new species – Stella Tennant, Anna K, Esther, Guenivere, Georgina Grenville, Amber Valletta, Iris Palmer, Carolyn Murphy, Christian Kruse, Chandra North, Michelle Hicks *et al.* – have an attitude and lifestyle devoid of the traditional supermodel trappings, such as personal trainers, model merchandise and limousines.

Model, supermodel or megamodel – no matter what the label or tag – tomorrow's future models owe a great deal to that original, elitist troupe: Cindy, Linda, Kate, Naomi, Claudia, Elle, Eva, Karen, *et al.*, who proved that models were no longer mere clothes horses.

THE INDUSTRY

International fashion modelling is a multi-million-dollar industry that thrives on those fabulous faces which have the power to increase a magazine's circulation and make a mint for designers. In fact, the right model can make a big difference to the turnover figures of any company. Think how many lipsticks Cindy Crawford sold for Revlon, and the phenomenal success of the Wonderbra, thanks to Eva Herzigova. These models may earn big bucks from such campaigns, but their fees are just a drop in the ocean compared to the companies' profits.

Those who are not *au fait* with the modelling game probably find its rationale difficult to fathom.

Elite's waterbabes: contestants of the Elite Model Look final cool down in the fountains of Nice.

Courtesy of Elite

The industry can appear transient – seemingly devouring models and then spitting them out when they are no longer *à la mode*. But as Gareth Roberts, Elite Premier's head booker, explains: 'Because fashion and taste in looks are subject to constant change, it's inevitable that models who personify the current "in" look will become the flavour of a season – or two. This doesn't mean the rest disappear into oblivion, however. Far from it. They may not be hitting the headlines, but I can assure you they are still calling the shots and keeping us bookers just as busy.'

SO IS IT GLAMOROUS?

On the one hand the media portray modelling as a glamorous profession: they chart the rise of exciting new models, and feed us snippets about the supermodels, from the soirées and launches they attend to who's dating who; until that is, they decide to shift their attention to the flipside. Then we read exposés about the catfights, rivalry and backstage bitchiness. We read of tantrum-throwing models, yet the press doesn't report on the tremendous pressures that cause such outbursts: the exhaustion, the immense stress, the gruelling schedules, the strain of relentless travel. 'Yes, there are glitzy parties, shoots in exotic locations and free designer frocks,' says Gareth Roberts, 'but a model's workaday life is much more about hanging around in airports, coping with jet lag, getting up at the crack of dawn and working extremely long hours.' In what can be a skin-deep and fickle business, there's also the added stress of not knowing whether you'll still be flavour of the month next month, or where your next pay cheque is coming from.

At the end of the day, modelling is a business that consists of hard-working individuals just going about their everyday tasks. Ask any model, hair stylist, booker or make-up artist if their work is glamorous, and the answer will be a resounding 'no'. 'The world we inhabit may be glamorous, but the actual day-to-day work is not,' insists Gareth.

THE GREAT DEBATE

Too thin, too young, too rich – hungry for sensationalist headlines, the media loves to play on extremes. But any industry driven by the virulent mix of youth, beauty and money is bound to attract some controversy.

Ever since the sixties, when Twiggy triggered the debate, miles of column inches have been written about anorexia, with accusations that models look too thin, starve themselves and

Party time: Linda Evangelista, Nadja Auermann and pals.
Photographed by Niall McInerney

encourage anorexia. When the waif-like look was at its zenith, Kate Moss got all the flak. Then fear that Jodie Kidd was anorexic resulted in her being banished from the New York runways. Yet despite all the hysteria, designers continue to produce size-10 samples. It seems svelte-like models are here to stay.

Age is also an issue that sends sparks flying. A 12-year-old British model recently created a furore with critics who said that she, and other young models, should be riding ponies and playing with dolls, not working. Ironically, these models are probably the few teenagers fortunate enough to own a pony, like 15-year-old Guess? model Lonneke Engel, who bought a horse with her earnings. 'And what about education?' scream the critics. 'Agencies are very pro education,' points out Gareth Roberts, 'most teen models restrict modelling to weekends and school holidays,so it doesn't affect their schooling at all. Lots of youngsters have weekend jobs; teen models just earn more money.' Another concern is that teenage models are being exposed to drugs. 'These models are chaperoned by their parents to every single casting and job,' stresses Gareth, 'and, let's face it, they are more

likely to come across drugs in the playground.'

The supermodels have given the profession respectability. At one time, modelling was perceived as something decent girls never did; nowadays, it seems the parents are as eager as the models themselves. And besides, what other occupation offers such high rewards and opens so many doors to young people? A girl or guy from an ordinary background could be walking along the street not knowing what the future holds one minute, and the next being photographed by some of the most famous photographers, meeting interesting people, staying in five-star hotels, and travelling the globe.

WHO'S WHO
IN THE MODEL INDUSTRY

Model-industry aficionados don't just work in the business: they live and breathe it. To them it's a way of life. Perched at the top are modelling's kingpins – superagents who control the lives of their models, from brand-new faces to the major superstars. On the opposite side of the fence are the clients who hire the models: photographers, magazine editors, designers, retailers, fashion and beauty companies, advertising and PR agents.

At the industry's core are a handful of key players who hold all the trump cards and can turn unknowns into stars. The photography heavyweights include: Steven Meisel, Ellen von Unwerth, Bruce Weber, Richard Avedon, Patrick Demarchelier, Juergen Teller, Nick Knight, Mario Testino and Peter Lindbergh. The international designers such as Karl Lagerfeld, Gianni Versace, John Galliano, Donna Karan and Calvin Klein are also major power brokers, as are the bookings' and fashion editors of the most prestigious magazines including *Vogue, Elle, W, Harper's Bazaar* and *Marie Claire*.

WHO'S WHO
ON A SHOOT

Photo shoots vary considerably. Many shoots are held in studios with a paper or fabric backdrop, or a set that has been built to resemble a location, such as a living room or bedroom. Location shoots, which can be anywhere from a New York sidewalk to a white, sandy Caribbean beach, are extremely popular, but can be dependent upon good weather. By going on trips the magazines work around this. In December and January, they often shoot spring fashions somewhere hot like South Africa, Kenya or Miami. In February it's off to exotic locations, such as the Caribbean to photograph high-summer and swimwear fashion stories. Then, in April, just as it's warming up in the Med, fashion teams shoot late-summer and autumn collections. In summer the weather is good enough to shoot on location in cities such as New York, Paris and London.

Besides the photographer and model, there are a whole team of people responsible for creating an image. The photographer's assistant, make-up artist, hair stylist and fashion stylist are also an integral part of a shoot. Depending on the job, clients, art directors, PRs and other representatives may be present and, if the job is for a magazine, so, too, will members of the magazine's fashion team – either the fashion editor or director and an assistant. For a television commercial there are even more people on the shoot in addition to the usual photographic team, including a camera and sound crew, director, producer and assistants.

WHO'S WHO
AT A FASHION SHOW

Prior to D-day, the PR executive is busy getting the show on the road by sending out invitations and choosing the venue. Meanwhile, the designer or fashion company hires a show producer who is responsible for staging the whole production, from casting models and selecting music, to hiring the sound and lighting technicians. The producer is also in charge of the running order: the order in which models appear on the runway.

Backstage there's a team of hair stylists and make-up artists, along with an army of dressers who help models in and out of each outfit. At major productions a stylist is also hired to match the right outfits and accessories to each model. Finally, there's the audience. Shows presented in high-street stores or shopping malls are open to the general public, but at the international collections, unless you are part of the fashion cognoscenti, a top buyer or a major celebrity, no amount of money or bribery will get you an invitation.

MODEL FANS

For all you model maniacs who want more info about your favourite model, she or he may have a fan club you can join. For example, Marcus Schenkenberg has a fan club organized by his Paris agency, PH One. Here you'll be updated on the model's magazine and media appearances, and you may be able to purchase calendars or other model merchandise. But because fan clubs are costly to run, few models have them. However, a great way of finding out information about a model is by logging on to the Internet. If you haven't got your own computer, or are not on line, use a friend's, or go to one of the cybercafés that have recently sprung up. Click on the supermodel website, then browse through for the latest news and gossip, as well as tips, interviews and dozens of photographs. If you have a favourite, just key in his or her name.

For those who want to shower their idols with fan mail, if you know which agency represents your favourite model, send a letter (care of the agency) and it will be popped into the model's pigeonhole.

MODEL MERCHANDISE

If you're a fan, here is a list of just some of the merchandise available.

Books: Naomi Campbell, Gail Elliott, Kate Moss, Linda Evangelista, Tyra Banks, Veruschka, Jean Shrimpton. Boss Supermales, Cindy Crawford, Marcus Schenkenberg, Fashion Café cookbook.
Fitness videos: Elle Macpherson's 'The Body: Fitness & Beauty', Claudia Schiffer's 'Perfectly Fit'.
Dolls: Claudia, Naomi, Karen.
Beauty videos: Karen Mulder.
CD-ROMs: Karen Mulder.
Perfume: Frederique Van der Wal, Cameron.
Sunglasses: Lauren Hutton.
Cosmetics: Iman, products for black women.
Cards: Next model agency and the City agency have both produced a selection of their top girls on collector and playing cards, including Elle Macpherson and Yasmeen Ghauri.
Treadmill: Linda Evangelista.
Calendars: Joanne Guest, Cindy Crawford, Elle Macpherson, Rachel Hunter, Christy Turlington, Melinda Messenger, Caprice, Karen Mulder, Marcus Schenkenberg.
Fashion: Elite models' 'What we wear' – figure-hugging designs that the models wear. Elle Macpherson 'Intimates' – a lingerie and swimwear line.

Photographed by Niall McInerney

There's nothing quite like swivelling your hips down a Paris runway in an up-to-the-minute designer creation knowing that the world's press is literally at your feet.

SHOWS

The model industry wouldn't be complete without the buzz, excitement and mayhem of the shows. Each fashion season, the circus of international press, photographers and fashion buyers, together with the odd celebrity guest, descend on the fashion capitals – London, Milan, Paris and New York – to watch models parade down the runways sporting the international designers' latest collections. Here, not only can you spot the latest fashion trends, but the up-to-the-minute hair and make-up looks, too. Backstage, it's pandemonium! On the runway, it's entertainment at its best. Catwalk extravaganzas have become as spectacular as Broadway, and the invitations, not surprisingly, as elusive as the models themselves.

In an attempt to be unique, some designers either transform the venue into something of a circus, or vacate the purpose-built venues and tents in favour of warehouses, theatres or even drained swimming pools! During one season, Alexander McQueen turned the runway into a flowing stream; at a Chanel show Karl Lagerfeld sent models out on a conveyer belt; and John Galliano often has his models freely strutting their stuff around theatre stalls.

Fighting for media coverage, designers use artistic licence and shock tactics by presenting over-the-top outfits. Nevertheless, a show lacking a smattering of well-known muses is somewhat low key. You'll invariably hear the press muttering 'Great collection, shame about the lack of big girls'. Translated into normal speak, this means supermodels. To a certain extent, it's true. It's always a thrill to see a famous model who's previously only been a celluloid image or a face on a glossy magazine. Smaller, thinner, taller, more beautiful – they always seem to look completely different in the flesh.

Watching through their ubiquitous dark sunglasses from the front rows, the fashion cognoscenti appear less than titillated. They've seen it all before – last show, last city, last season. Perched at the end of the ramp is a maze of runway photographers all armed with long lenses, and all snapping away simultaneously at each model in each new outfit. After 40 minutes of sartorial indulgence and incandescent glamour, those with the passes that are even more desirable than the invitations themselves, rush backstage to voice their opinions. These usually consist of three crucial words: 'Fabulous show darling!'

BACKSTAGE

The backstage antics have become part of the whole brouhaha of the collections.

Talking, laughing, gesticulating and, occasionally, shouting – backstage at the collections is one of the rare moments when the silent stars come alive. Since the cult of the supermodel, photographers and TV crews have invaded models' privacy by flocking backstage. Their aim is to seize every precious moment on film: Helena Christensen nibbling a sandwich, Georgina Grenville with a head full of bright-coloured rollers, or Kate Moss wearing a funny hairnet with a Marlboro clenched firmly in one hand and a glass of champagne in the other.

Models are well looked after. Champagne flows freely to help them relax, and there's always a table of eats to help boost energy. While they wait for their make-up to be done, some models choose to curl up in a corner and bury their heads in a good book. But, with the frenzied activity going on around them, it's not easy. The newer girls clatter across the floor as they practise their walk in six-inch heels, while others giggle into their mobile phones or gossip with hair stylists, make-up artists or one another. Occasionally, you'll hear raised voices when a photographer exploits an embarrasing moment.

The backstage party is abruptly interrupted when the show producer calls a run-through. Everyone drops what they are doing as the models – some with their hair in rollers, others only half made-up – gather to await their cue. Tension mounts. A stuck zip, torn frock or lost shoe – such problems quickly develop into a crisis. And when models fail to turn up, or stroll in late from the previous show, it's not only the designers who are tense. Models are tired. Towards the end of a season, after four weeks of shows, fittings and parties, most are feeling a little fragile. As the countdown to the show begins, it's time for the photographers, TV crews, agents, boyfriends – and anyone else who's not one of the official backstage team – to split and leave the models to their dressers and rails of outfits. Lights are switched on and it's music, models, action …

Photographs by Niall McInerney

Top left: Caroline Park and Georgina Cooper sporting the latest in hairstyling headgear.

Centre: Backstage nibbles – Kristen McMenamy, Stella Tennant and pals try not to smudge their lipstick.

Top right: Magic make-up momemts – Kate Moss and Jerry Hall having the final touches put to their make-up.

MODEL AGENCIES

THE AGENCY

So what's it really like inside a place that represents the stars? Start by imagining hustle and bustle. Then, imagine a state-of-the-art office, where, in the thick of it – among portfolios, composites, tearsheets, charts and circular booking tables – bookers with headphones control the careers of the likes of Linda, Karen, Amber and Stella. Now you're getting the idea. The phones never stop ringing. And it's a regular occurrence to hear: '*Elle* New York on line two holding for Lucy,' and, 'Suzy from D & G press office on line four – she says it's urgent.' In this permanent state of activity, drop-dead-gorgeous models, whose countless framed covers are plastered over the walls, saunter in and, for a fleeting moment, take centre stage. Suddenly, it's all very 'dahling' and kissy-kissy! Meanwhile, photographers drop by to deliver tests, and wannabes sit patiently observing the overwhelming – but fascinating – agency antics.

AGENCY PROFILE

Yasmin Le Bon, Jerry Hall, Gail Elliot, Michelle Behenah, Cecilia Chancellor, Alek Wek – the list of models is as impressive as a page from *Who's Who*. In 1968, with little more than a telephone and three models, the famous purveyors of beauty, April Ducksbury and Jose Fonseca, started up Models 1 from Jose's attic. Based in London, it was one of the first agencies to work internationally, linking up with Paris and New York-based agencies, in particular Elite and Ford. With a 150-strong women's board, as well as new faces, men's, mature models and a management division for special bookings, Models 1 is one of the largest independent, high-fashion agencies in the world. Over the years, Jose and April have launched and handled the careers of some of the most famous models on the planet.

Twenty-nine years on, although they are ranked as one of the world's leading agencies, Models 1 still retains the warm, friendly, family atmosphere that makes it so popular with models and clients alike. Described by its models as being professional, caring and attentive, Jose Fonseca puts the secret of its success down to a relaxed atmosphere and an invaluable team of people who handle the models extremely well. 'The modelling world can be terrifying for a new model,' admits Jose. 'We make sure we get to know our models intimately; this enables us to sense when they are insecure or despondent and to guide them through it.' Jose now feels that she has a great team that gels together and makes the agency work. 'We have 16 bookers, a head booker, someone who books flights and hotels, a person who looks after the models' accommodation, a receptionist, secretaries, as well as Ellis, who's our PR and scout. Oh, and then there's myself and April, of course,' adds Jose, explaining how she is still very much hands-on, but far more relaxed than when she started 29 years ago. It's not surprising that models like Yasmin Le Bon, who has been with the agency for 15 years, never need look elsewhere.

A MODEL AGENCY'S ROLE

Nearly all modelling work is booked via agencies, so it's virtually impossible to model on a freelance basis. Agents are the experts. Once signed up, they will promote you, send you on castings, organize assignments, haggle over contracts and invoice clients on your behalf. And that's just for starters! 'There's far more to it than meets the eye,' explains Jose. 'We find models accommodation, book their flights, send flowers to their mothers – you name it, we do it. Basically, we are organizing their lives. As agents, we also act as buffers to help models deal with both rejection and success.'

Besides handling the established models, agencies like Models 1 are constantly taking on new faces to nurture and cultivate into fully fledged models. 'We are handling many girls who are still growing up and, therefore, have to deal with all the teething problems. Some new models are incredibly focused, but we find that most need guidance and nurturing. In a nutshell, you need to be a teacher and parent – firm yet understanding, and approachable yet reserved.'

Handling a stable of models is no mean feat. Undoubtedly, there's a crisis almost every day.

Imagine worrying whether a 17-year-old who's been clubbing all night will be at the studio by 8am, or attempting to encourage a model who hasn't worked for weeks. And try explaining to a client who's hired a whole photographic team that the model won't make the shoot because he's fallen ill or missed his flight. Then, there's the callous, yet necessary, task of telling a girl she must smile even though she's just been dumped by her boyfriend. It's an agent's job to meet their clients' and models' needs and, ultimately, keep both sides happy.

TYPES OF AGENCIES

Model agencies come in many different shapes and sizes. Not all agencies are quite as daunting as the big networks – the Elites, IMGs and Fords of this world. At the other end of the scale is the small, local agent or agent which specializes solely in one category of model with only a couple of bookers running the whole operation from a tiny office. Believe it or not, many of today's top agencies were conceived and initially run from a living room, and a few still successfully operate from an office located within their home. Some model agencies work internationally while others, especially agencies based outside the international modelling cities, stick mainly to their local market.

SPECIALITY DIVISIONS

The structure of an agency begins with the new faces level – a board which caters for brand new models. Next up there's the agency's largest division – the main board – which comprises the established models. In addition, some agencies have other specialist divisions. For example, Ford is one of the world's top fashion agencies, yet it also has petite, plus-size and runway divisions in addition to its women's, men's and new faces board. Child agencies normally have divisions for babies, teenage models and families, as well as their main board of kids; character agencies might also have a separate category for parts, families or extras; fashion agencies have special bookings sections for celebrity models ... and so on.

THE CELEBRITY BOARD

When the supermodels became the modern icons, Hollywood stars missed out on a large chunk of publicity. The cover of *Vanity Fair* may have traditionally been their domain, but for a while models even stole that slot. Now they have regained their glamorous image, they are competing with models for the most-coveted and prestigious media slots. And, eager to have a slice of the pie, they are turning to model agents which have set up celebrity divisions (also known as management or special-bookings boards) to cater for them.

Celebrities who are muscling in on models' ground include Tina Turner, who appeared in a Hanes advert; Juliette Lewis, who modelled for Guess?; Demi Moore and Bruce Willis, who posed for Donna Karan's ad campaign; and the face of Estée Lauder, Liz Hurley. Actor Kevin Bacon was splashed across the billboards in Romeo Gigli's campaign, and Jon Bon Jovi, Liam Gallagher, Madonna and Lisa-Marie Presley have all appeared in Versace ads.

Models who have reached celebrity status are handled in a different way to top models on the agencies' main boards. 'They are no longer casting, it's more a case of the agent pitching for work that has the right profile,' explains Jonathan Phang, who left IMG to set up Spirit Management, and now handles the likes of Jodie Kidd, Amit Mashitinger, Sophie Ward and Paula Hamilton. 'These celebrity models are looking for a more personalized service,' says Jonathan. 'It's not just about booking assignments: it goes way beyond this. We handle everything from their public and television appearances to press interviews.'

HOW AN AGENCY OPERATES

It is a model agent's job to supply models to clients. In return for this service they take a commission (between 20 and 25 per cent world-wide except in Japan, where it's 40–50 per cent) from their model's earnings. An agency finds work for its models but does not employ them. Therefore, all models are self-employed and are responsible for paying their own taxes. However, an agency does deal with all financial matters in relation to the client, from negotiating fees and issuing invoices to chasing payment when it's due. The bigger agencies have agency apartments or other accommodation for foreign models and new models who live outside the centre. The agencies usually expect to recoup this money from their models' earnings.

AN AGENCY'S CLIENTS

The type of models an agency represents will determine their clientele. A high-fashion editorial agency's clients would include fashion designers, fashion companies, fashion magazines, beauty and cosmetic clients and mail-order companies. However, the people that the bookers liase with, who are also the people casting the models, are not necessarily the client *per se*. They could be the photographer, PR officer, casting director, bookings editor, advertising agency or production company acting on behalf of the client. If, for example, Vivienne Westwood wanted to hold a casting for her spring/summer show, her show producer or PR would be in charge of casting models, while for a catalogue job it may be down to the photographer to choose the models. It differs from job to job. Clients sometimes commission casting agents whose job it is to ring around all the model agencies and hold castings to find a suitable model.

BOOKERS

Bookers (also known as booking agents) are the agency staff who handle every aspect of a model's career. Never underestimate their role. Not only do they manage models' careers, they frequently act as their best friend, mother, shrink, personal assistant … and more. You may have one booker who looks after you, or several, but remember, there will be dozens of other models for whom she or he is also accountable. Bookers show you the ropes, promote you, and aim to get you the highest fees and best working conditions possible. They will tell you when you're booked for a job and give you all the relevant details, as well as advising you on such matters as changing your image and updating your book. Your booker is neither your boss nor your employee, so respect should be mutual. Remember, a booker is the most important person to a model. Besides bookers, larger agencies often employ scouts, PRs, development managers, office managers and accountants.

SCOUTS

Fashion's insatiable hunger for new faces has led to many top fashion agencies hiring scouts to go in search of the 'Next Big Thing'. Despite being approached by thousands of would-be models each week, agencies have found that scouting is a highly successful method of finding real gems. Scouts have that 'discerning eye', and can tell from the moment they clap eyes on you if you've got 'it' or not.

Where, you may wonder, is a scout's hunting ground? To give you a clue, look at where these top models were discovered: Shalom Harlow was spotted at a Cure concert in Canada; Jan Dunning at the Glastonbury Festival; Carolyn Murphy on the streets of Manhattan; Brandi in a shopping mall in Florida; and Caroline Park in a Yorkshire chip shop! One of the most bizarre discoveries was when a scout from Models 1 nearly ran over Laura Roundel. Scouts tend to frequent places they know young people hang out. To let you a little further into the scouting secret, here are just a few of the places they might be found: model conventions, shopping malls, pop concerts, beaches in holiday locations, bars, night-clubs, restaurants, live magazine shows, exhibitions and schools.

One of the industry's top model spotters is Jessica Hallet who, after being on Storm's main board, was Kate Moss's personal booking agent for four years before becoming the agency's international scout and development manager. Jessica travels to agencies all over the world, where she holds castings, in the hope of finding potential models whom Storm can represent in the UK. On home ground she lectures at schools and holds open auditions at hotels across the country. 'You can't just leave it to chance, you have to get out there and find new faces,' insists Jessica. After many years in the business she knows exactly what she's looking for. And even when she's off duty, her talented eye is always on the alert. 'Sometimes a friend will call and say "I've seen a fabulous girl on the checkout at Sainsburys", or I might spot a girl in a shop or walking along the street,' says Jessica, who is always equipped with her Polaroid camera and a pocket full of cards. 'Some people are shocked when I approach them, saying things like, "I don't think I can model". But, nine times out of ten, they'll ring the agency within a week.'

THE MOTHER AGENCY

The original agency you sign up with automatically becomes your 'mother agency'. Kate Moss's mother agency is Storm in London, whose MD discovered her at JFK airport in New York. Naomi Campbell first signed to Elite in London, and is still with it today. Models 1 is mother agent to Yasmin Le Bon, Cecilia Chancellor, Jade Parfitt, Michelle Behenah and many other models whom it discovered and developed. Models are constantly being approached by other agents but, as Jose Fonseca explains, this is part and parcel of a competitive industry and there's precious little any agent can do about it. 'Some agencies get models to sign a contract, but we'd rather models stay with us because they're

Photographed by Rod Howe

Models 1's Ellis chooses the pick of the bunch from a model's tests.

agency. Also, models who cross into different areas may have an agency in each specific field. For example, a fashion model may also be on the books of a promotional agency.

WORKING WITH YOUR AGENCY

Agencies only make money if their models work, so it's in their interests to do their utmost to get work. Likewise, if they advise you not to do a particular job or to have your hair cut, in most cases, you should respect their judgement. As everything is organized at the eleventh hour, it is vital you keep in close contact with your agent. If you don't have anyone at home who can take messages, you must have an answerphone. Many agencies, especially fashion agencies, expect their models to telephone at least once a day, usually at the end of the day, to check if the following day's schedule has altered.

Never give out your telephone number to clients. Instead, ask them to contact you via your agency. If a client discusses fees, always refer them to your booker. You should also contact your booker, not the client, if you are late for, or unable to attend an assignment.

Whenever you attend a job, casting or go-see you are, in effect, representing your agency, so don't let them down by behaving badly. If you do, you can be sure they'll get to hear about it, and may decide to throw you off their books. 'If models mess us around by being unreliable, not turning up to castings, or being negative, there's no point in us holding on to them,' stresses Models 1's Jose. Word also gets back with lightning speed if a model complains about his or her agency to a client or other industry person. Whether it's a lack of work, unhelpful bookers, or the fact that you don't feel the agency is promoting you hard enough, tell them, rather than let them hear the complaint second hand. A great working relationship between you and your agency will help your career no end.

happy. I used to get really upset when a model left us. Now I realize that as long as you've done 150 per cent for that model, if she moves to another agency it's usually because she's unhappy with herself. In most cases, it's the unstable models that switch agencies.'

Most fashion agencies insist that a model must be exclusively on their books. However, there are exceptions, for instance, when a model belongs to a small, regional agency, then gets taken on by a top agency in one of the modelling centres. It would be pointless joining more than one agency in any particular market: you would only be competing with yourself for the same jobs and would have great difficulty juggling your time between each one. It's quite acceptable, however, for models in more specialized fields of modelling, such as character or parts, to have more than one

Photographed by Niall McInerney

TRAINING

CAN MODELLING BE TAUGHT?

Basically, you've either got 'it' or you haven't, and no amount of training will transform a no-hoper into a model. However, with a little nurturing, an unconfident, gawky teenager who's got what it takes can be cultivated and groomed into excellent model material.

HOW AGENCIES TRAIN THEIR MODELS

Most agencies prefer new recruits to be untrained rather than having attended some second-rate modelling course. 'Unless the course is of an extremely high standard, with up-to-date training, we find we have to re-educate new models to eradicate the antiquated techniques they've picked up,' says Gareth Roberts, head booker at Elite Premier. 'Coaching by the likes of Jay Alexander, who has trained some of our top girls, is very different to a school that is out of touch with the reality of the modelling world.'

Gareth explains how bookers train their new faces. 'Directly we take on a new model, we tell her what is expected, from how to act on a casting to how to use an *A to Z*. We tell her what to wear: fashionable clothes that show off her figure and make her look the part. Models should not just rely on the strength of their books. The majority of fashion and bookings editors want to be able to visualize the model in the magazine, so if she looks frumpy in the flesh, she may lose a booking. We encourage models to look neat rather than fussy and to wear shoes that will get them from one casting to another without dozens of blisters. When models are casting, make-up is kept to the bare minimum, so we show them how to apply the basics; the rest they'll pick up from make-up artists along the way. We leave hair to the professionals by sending models to a good salon. Performance in front of the camera can only be gained through experience. And poses can't be taught, either. We tell a new model to get a gist of the way models move through fashion magazines. If a model is going to do runway work, we might consider hiring a coach like Jay to teach her how to walk. However, we find most show producers are very patient with new models. Also, experienced models are usually more than willing to help put new models through their paces.'

JAY ALEXANDER'S
MODEL-COACHING METHODS

Guru model coach Jay Alexander has performed his Midas touch on some of the biggest names in the business, including Nadja Auermann, Heather Stewart-Whyte, Honor Fraser, Anna K and Claudia Mason. Wearing his trademark stilettos, his walk is legendary; this native New Yorker struts his stuff far better than any supermodel. Consequently, leading international agents such as Elite and IMG send models from all corners of the globe to his Paris studio for coaching. 'Jay's great,' says Didier Fernandez from Elite Paris, 'he's gentle and understanding towards all his models, regardless of their nationality or background.' According to Jay, himself a former model, it's not just about learning how to walk on a runway – it goes much further than this. Here, Jay explains a little bit about the coaching he gives his protégées.

'Models need shaping, both physically and mentally. And a brand-spanking-new girl from the depths of the countryside is always a challenge.

As she's about to be thrust into the fickle world of fashion and all that goes with it, I try to prepare her as much as possible. I tell her how to cope with rejection, and what to expect when she goes on a casting or assignment. A new model is in for a major surprise when she's booked for her first trip to somewhere like Marrakesh. It's no holiday. She'll have to deal with all sorts of things, like coping with climate, culture and conditions that are all alien to her. Unless someone has pointed out that she shouldn't drink the water, she could end up spending the entire shoot in bed.

'I give my students plenty of general advice. I tell them not to draw attention to their bad points, yet not be frightened of looking ugly. Then there's the presentation aspect. Some recruits come to me with their hair covered in gunge, hideous make-up and a dress sense that would make even a supermodel look like a bag lady. Usually, its not only me who's unhappy with the way they look: they know they're doing everything wrong but don't know how to change it. So once we've sorted out image, it's a big help. We talk personality. I'll tell them to warm up here, or be a bit firmer there. So many new models who lack confidence end up getting it all wrong. They think the way to deal with this cut-throat and competitive industry is to turn into a precocious little bitch. It's not!

'Learning how to walk on a runway is a very individual thing. I never say to a model "walk like me or Linda Evangelista" – it's all about what they feel comfortable with. The mental attitude always filters down to the walk: so if a girl's got confidence, she's halfway there. Some girls have great body movements, whereas others find it doesn't come quite so naturally. Unless the beat of the music happens to be synchronized with the walk, it's best to ignore it. Anyway, once models are out there on the runway, they rarely hear the music. I look at the way each individual model walks. A well-endowed girl may naturally slouch to try to hide her chest, so I'll tell her to "stick it out"!

'Different designers want different walks. For example, at the Comme des Garçons show, models walk with very little movement and show no emotion, while for Valentino they walk with elegance and sophistication. Another designer may want them to stride down the runway expressing lots of personality ... and so on. Therefore, I show models a variety of walks, such as a natural walk with less of the hand-on-hip movements, and then a more stylized method entailing added movement for an elegant saunter.

'At the end of the day, modelling is all about having confidence, being comfortable with yourself, and being aware of what lies ahead of you.'

MODEL COURSES

Because model courses are often run by cowboy set-ups which profit by teaching archaic methods to those with no potential, many agencies discourage would-be models from taking courses. However, there are still a few highly professional schools, courses and workshops – especially in the US and Canada – that are run by industry experts who offer up-to-the-minute advice. One example is the John Casablancas model centre in the US.

A course doesn't give you an instant entrée to modelling, nor does it hold any guarantees, but it can give you confidence and start you off on the right track. Before you enrol, ask lots of questions. Speak to people attending the course, or ask to watch a class. Be wary of any one-man-band set-ups: professional schools employ experts in each field, including make-up artists, hairdressers, nutritionists, etc. to teach specific skills. Find out if the course is assessed by agents or other model-industry professionals: a good school should be a regular source of recruitment for agencies. Finally, check that the course curriculum includes all aspects of grooming, information on the industry, up-to-date catwalk training, television and video experience, and photographic training. Be highly suspicious of any agency that insists that you take one of their courses before they will accept you on their books.

SUPERHINTS FOR SELF-TRAINING

As incredible as it may seem, even minutes before their debut test, assignment or runway appearance, some new models still have no idea of what is required of them. Bookers do their utmost to show new recruits the ropes, but as they are extremely busy, most are rarely able to devote as much time to this as they'd like. Understanding what is required of a model will help you appear a little less green before you set foot in an agency. And, even if you have no desire to model, you might find these tips come in handy.

Magazines: *Elle*, *Vogue*, *Marie Claire* and *Cosmopolitan* are just a handful of the myriad of fashion magazines from which you can pick up top tips on fashion, hair care, styling, make-up and beauty. Each month, invest in a couple of good fashion magazines to keep abreast of what's happening in the fashion and beauty world, and start getting to know who's who. Familiarize yourself with the names of photographers, models, make-up artists, etc. (which are printed in small text on the editorial fashion and beauty pages). Study different poses struck by models, and practise mimicking these. Editorial style involves the most unrestricted and spontaneous movement. Notice how the models not only stand, but also squat, leap, lean, sit or stride across the page. Build up a repertoire of poses and practise moving freely from one pose to another.

Mirror: Invest in a full-length mirror so you can check how you look before setting off for that all-important casting, go-see or interview. You can also practise different poses as if you were in front of the camera. Discover your most flattering angles, and practise smiling. When hired for a shoot you'll have to portray different looks and be able to express certain moods. For an evening-wear shoot you might be expected to look sultry and sexy, whereas a gregarious smile would be more suitable for a catalogue shoot. Use your mirror to try different expressions. It can also be useful for correcting your posture and perfecting your catwalk strut.

Snapshots: Whether you need a great snapshot to send to an agency, are thinking of entering a model contest, or just want to achieve better holiday snaps, fashion photographer Rod Howe has a few simple tips to help turn what could potentially be a photographic mistake into a flattering picture.

- **When** posing for a close-up/head shot, make sure your face is not concealed by unflattering dark shadows, or placed directly under a light source that might create unwanted shadows under your eyes and around your mouth.
- **Look** straight into the lens.
- **To avoid** unflattering double chins and shadows around the jawline, make sure the person taking the picture points the camera downwards, from slightly above your face, rather than angling it up from below.
- **Don't** try to mimic a very posey magazine shot; this will look unnatural in a snapshot. By all

means put a hand in a pocket or on your hip, but avoid making it appear too contrived.

- **To make** your legs look long and slender, wear high heels.
- **Dark** clothes will make you look slimmer, whereas light colours have the reverse effect.
- **Rather** than standing straight on to the camera, for a more flattering angle, rotate your body very slightly – still looking into the lens.

On film: When a photographer yells 'move', it can be the most unnerving moment of a new model's career. Regardless of how stunning you are, if you're wooden or self-conscious in front of the camera, it's unlikely you'll succeed as a model. So forget your inhibitions. You'll probably be in an uninspiring studio with a team of onlookers, but you'll need to spring into action at the first click of the camera's shutter. For some photo sessions, models are asked to sit or stand in one static position, while for others, particularly fashion shoots, they'll be expected to move naturally and fluidly, all the while striking different poses. Loud music usually blasts from speakers to help get you in the mood.

It depends on the photographer as to how much direction you'll get. One photographer works in a different way to another. The key is to concentrate on moving well, rather than posing. And if the photographer asks you to lean back further or stand in a way that is awkward, don't complain – just do it. Each time you step in front of the camera you'll be expected to reinvent yourself in a different guise: it could be anything from a fresh-faced country girl to a cool biker. The photographer may also ask you to portray different looks. Depending on the job, this could be aloof, angelic, vampish or childlike.

Winner of the Elite Model Look contest, Diana Kovalchuk, being photographed by Patrick Demarchelier in her very first photo session,

Photographed by Niall McInerney

Designer Katherine Hamnett shows Emma Blocksage how to master the supermodel strut.

Always try to get involved. Before the shoot commences find out what photographer wants from the session.

Catwalk strut: Stiffness, compared to the effortless movements of an experienced model, is the tell-tale sign of a novice. This, however, is usually due to nerves. But relax! Many models are unleashed onto the international runways without any former catwalk training at all. Walking out onto a runway with broiling lights, cameras flashing and the press scrutinizing you may sound like a daunting experience for a newcomer; but unlike an actor – who could ruin a performance by forgetting lines – the worst thing that can happen to a model is to fall over. And think of all the attention Naomi got when she tumbled over in those 12-inch platforms!

So how do you master that supermodel strut? Start by slipping on a pair of heels, although eventually you will need to be able to walk in all types of shoes, from flat pumps to platforms and even bare feet. Your job is to take on the character of the clothes and become the man or woman the designer wants you to be. Walk to everything from classical music to ballads, as well as jazz, funk and the grooviest sounds. As Jay Alexander pointed out, do not walk to the beat of the music. If you do, you will come unstuck when, halfway down the runway you find the music changes tempo. Forget about trying to master all the fancy footwork, pivots and turns. These will come later. For the moment just walk, taking confident strides. Try to relax and be as natural as possible. Before you go any further, check your posture is correct. The current look on some designers' runways may be 'the slouch, shuffle and scowl' – round shoulders, pigeon toes and a facial expression that exudes attitude – but unless you're modelling for a contemporary designer, it's unlikely you'll get away with it.

Watch as many fashion shows as you can (either live or on television) to see how the models walk. Alternatively, there are videos you can buy that give you catwalk instruction. Consider dance classes, they will help you loosen up and will improve your co-ordination. But dance fanatics watch out, as Jay Alexander often finds, professional dancers can be the most difficult to train. Sense of timing is something that will come with experience. And as for choreography, in the eighties, shows comprised complicated routines. Today, however, they are far more spontaneous and the routines straightforward. It's more likely to be shows for the public that involve complex choreography rather than the designer shows.

Informal modelling: This involves modelling clothes without a ramp in a boutique, department store, showroom or on a stand at a trade exhibition. The work entails changing into outfits the buyer or customer wishes to see – then presenting them. It's simple. You walk out from the changing room as if you were on a runway but at a slightly slower more graceful pace. Stop in front of the buyer or customer then, slowly, turn to show the back of each outfit. You may want to put one hand on your hip or in a pocket. If you're wearing a jacket or waistcoat over another item of clothing, be prepared to take it off. Remove it in a graceful manner – not the way you'd normally fling off your jacket at home. Quite often, the customer wants to feel the fabric or look closely at details, so expect to stand in one spot for a while. The secret is to stand in an elegant pose so that the clothes look as good as possible. After all, you are trying to sell the clothes.

Poise: It may sound like an old-fashioned word that evokes an image of forties débutantes swanning around with books on their heads, but the way you hold yourself can make or break your overall image. Poise is second nature to some people. However, with a little effort, you can learn to correct your posture and have model poise; although it's not *quite* as easy as shoulders back and head up. A simple technique you can do at home is as follows.
1. Start by stretching and lengthening your back – keeping your spine straight. It helps if you watch yourself in a mirror. **2.** Take a look at where your chin is positioned. It should be parallel to the floor, not drooped towards your chest. **3.** Make sure your shoulders are level and relaxed, but not unnaturally forced back into too rigid a position. **4.** Check your bottom is tucked under and your stomach is pulled

in. **5.** Now imagine that you have an invisible cord attached to your chest. Envisage this cord pulling you up. Your body should now be completely aligned. Put this into practice and, before long, good poise should come as naturally as walking.

Drama classes: These days, we are expected to be able to communicate in an articulate and coherent manner without feeling ill at ease, be it at a party, casting or interview. Confidence is the key to this. Drama classes are not only a great confidence booster, but they help you learn to speak with a clarity that will, in turn, help you to sell yourself to prospective clients, agents or employers. If you are keen to model in commercials, especially in speaking parts, the benefits of acting experience cannot be over-emphasized.

Speech therapy: How you project your voice and the tone you use can be perceived by others in many different ways. For example, if you talk in a dead-pan drone, this could be misinterpreted as lack of enthusiasm or boredom. If your voice is excessively loud, others may perceive you as being over-confident or bolshie, so stop and think about the tone of your voice. For greater clarity, tongue-twisters are also good speech aids. You can practise these at home or in the car. Start off at a normal rate and then speed up – but without a *single* slip of the tongue.

Breathing: Deep breathing is of paramount importance to your well-being. Furthermore, if you become nervous and have mastered the correct breathing techniques, each breath you take will calm you down and prevent you from hyperventilating, shaking or becoming tongue-tied. Whether you're about to attend an important interview, or take part in a speaking audition for a commercial or your first catwalk show, repeat the following breathing technique two or three times, just before the event. If you practise this exercise three times a day, you'll soon find that you naturally breathe more deeply from your stomach, not from your chest.

Breathe in deeply through your nose from your stomach – not your chest – trying to keep your chest still. Note that your stomach should expand as you breathe in and retract as you breathe out. Hold the breath for 12 counts, then exhale slowly through your mouth, making a hissing sound.

MODEL
CONTESTS
AND CONVENTIONS

In search of fresh talent and, ultimately, the 'Next Big Thing', every year, model agents from around the globe host model contests.

MODEL CONTESTS

In the world of international fashion modelling contests mean big business. And, finding that one-in-a-million face, who will make a million, is the motive. To attract contestants, model-agency competitions are either publicized throughout the media, or held in association with, or sponsored by, one particular publication. 'Entering a contest is a great way of breaking into the modelling profession and kick-starting your career,' says Storm's Sarah Doukas, who has found many great models through contests. But contests are not exclusively for fashion models: potential child, character, plus-size, petite and glamour models also get a chance to compete.

One of the biggest contests of its kind is the Elite Model Look, a competition which boasts a glittering array of winners, including Cindy Crawford,

Tatjana Patitz, Emma Blocksage and Karen Mulder. Every year, events are held in as many as 79 countries, culminating in a major international final. A week prior to the final, winners of the individual heats are flown out to some fancy destination where the gala event is to take place. During their stay, they spend time rehearsing their catwalk strut with the help of guru coach Jay Alexander, and posing in front of the camera for such photographic luminaries as Patrick Demarchelier. Broadcast on television screens across the globe, the contest is judged by a star-studded jury of supermodels, designers, photographers, celebrities and Elite's president, John Casablancas. The prize is a two-year contract worth $150,000, followed by $100,000 and $70,000 for the runners-up. And even the top 15 finalists receive a respectable $50,000 each.

Ford's Supermodel of the World, a contest offering a $250,000 contract, scours the world from Iceland to Argentina in search of potential supermodels. Ford also has its fair share of superleague winners, including British model Michelle Behenah and the Hungarian Anna Marie Cseh. Besides Elite and Ford, other agencies that host contests include The Metropolitan agency, which recently held a contest in conjunction with Max Factor and *Elle* magazine; World Top Model,

Congratulations! Supermodel Amber Valletta presents flowers to the first runner-up of the Elite Model Look contest.

a contest organized by Italy Models in Milan; and a European contest held by Berlin Models. Storm model agency is another independent agency that holds a yearly competition sponsored by Highland Spring. But it's not only the agencies who run model contests: model competitions are also organized by magazines, newspapers and television shows. One such event is the yearly MTV/*Elle* model competition.

The winner of a major international agency competition secures a contract worth a great deal of money. However, rewards on this scale are by no means typical of all contests. For most, a photo session for the sponsoring publication, or representation by an agency, is far more likely than a major cash prize or the guarantee of a lucrative modelling contract.

If you enter a contest but are not lucky enough to win, do not be disheartened. Even if you take second or third place, you could still have a modelling career ahead of you. Quite often agencies will take on runners-up and, if they've got what it takes, some of the finalists, too. Dutch supermodel

Karen Mulder came second in Elite's Model Look international final; nonetheless, she was taken on by Elite. And Linda Evangelista didn't even make it into the international final. Yet this disappointment didn't prevent her modelling career from being anything less than phenomenal.

HOW TO ENTER A CONTEST

The best way to find out about a model contest is via the media: magazines, newspapers and fashion or magazine-style television shows. Here, the publication or programme will specify the type of models they are looking for, along with the competition rules: details of the requisite age, height and measurements. Don't bother entering unless you fulfil the stated requirements. And don't think you can get away with fibbing by adding that extra inch you've always longed for, or making out that you're younger than you really are. If you're 5'6", yet you've put 5'7" on the form, you will be disqualified the moment you arrive – no matter how stunning you are!

The normal procedure for entering a contest

Courtesy of Elite

The 79 contestants take the stage at the Elite Model Look International final.

is for participants to complete an application form, filling in all the necessary details. If you are under 16, it may be necessary to include a letter of consent from a parent or guardian. You'll need to send the form, together with the specified number of recent photographs (between two and six), including a close-up and full-length shot. Professional photographs won't necessarily get you any further than a snapshot. And, in the eyes of the judges, a sharp snapshot bodes better than an average, semi-professional photograph. The pictures must be clear. Holiday snaps are usually favoured: they are often more natural looking, and a swimsuit or bikini enables the judges to see your body. If you haven't got any recent holiday photos, ask a friend to take pictures of you out of doors. Run off a whole film of you striking various poses (see p.84 for Rod Howe's tips on snapshots). This

way, you are bound to find a couple you are happy with. Don't expect your pictures to be returned: the office of every competition organizer is piled high with photographs.

If you're lucky enough to have been selected as a finalist, you will be informed by post and invited to take part in a live contest. The rules will specify whether the applicant can have undertaken any professional or paid modelling work before the date of the contest. With the major agency contests such as Elite's and Ford's, new faces models are permitted to enter the contest as long as they haven't worked over and above the number of assignments specified in the rules. Don't be disappointed if you're not selected for the final. This doesn't mean you should immediately give up on the idea of modelling. For every contest there are thousands of entries, out of which the judges

are limited to picking only a dozen or so finalists – even if 50 are outstanding.

MODELLING CONVENTIONS

The International Model and Talent Association (IMTA) organizes the biggest and most accredited model and talent convention in the world, with supermodels Beverly Peele and Joel West among their prime discoveries. Held annually in New York and Los Angeles, the convention attracts top international model agents who, as Sheli Jeffry, director of Ford's new faces division, found out, discover fabulous new faces: 'We are excited to be working with really great new faces discovered at IMTA.'

The purpose of a model convention is to unite many different industry professionals, such as agents, school owners and casting directors, with would-be models and their parents. Workshops, seminars and model contests are held, making modelling accessible to the masses. Here, would-be models can discover their potential without having to travel to cities to do the gruelling and often disheartening agency rounds.

It must be pointed out that, to cover the phenomenal cost of putting on such an event, a flat entrance fee, as well as additional fees for seminars and workshops, are normally charged. A well-run convention can offer a greater understanding of the modelling industry and, if you're lucky, you could win a contest or be signed up by a leading model agency. For model Mindy Schnoebelen, the IMTA is the best thing that ever happened to her. 'I got over 70 call-backs, signed with Ford in New York, and I am now on the editorial pages of international magazines,' enthuses Mindy.

Although conventions are regular events in both the USA and Canada, unfortunately as yet there are no conventions in Europe. Some of the US and Canadian conventions include the International Model and Talent Association, Runway to Success, World-wide Model & Talent Convention, International Model Search Invitational, MB Model & Talent Expo and Canadian Model & Talent Convention.

Before you travel miles to attend a convention, a word of warning. Unless the convention is recognized, check it out thoroughly before applying.

THE EVENT

Most model contests take the shape of a beauty-pageant-meets-runway show – a live event that is judged by a select panel of industry professionals such as model agents, supermodels, magazine editors, photographers, designers, make-up artists, hair stylists and celebrities. After the initial selection process of the contestants' photographs has taken place, finalists are notified by post and are invited to take part in a live event and, in some cases, a photo session. For a small-scale contest where there is no live show or photo session, judges usually assess finalists in person.

I was a judge at one of *Cosmopolitan* magazine's model contests. This particular competition took place at The Cosmo Show and was held in conjunction with Storm. The rules: girls had to be aged between 16 and 22 years and be at least 5'8" tall. The prize: a contract with Storm – a top international fashion agency which flaunts such big-name models as Kate Moss, Elle Macpherson, Eva Herzigova and Rachel Hunter.

The finalists of the Cosmopolitan Model Competition pose for Tony McGee. The winner, Nina McCann (front row, second left), runners-up: Alison Gulgec (back row, left), Fem Gulgec (front row, left), Rachel Steele (front row, centre).

Photographed by Tony McGee (courtesy of Cosmopolitan)

The panel: industry professionals, including fashion photographer Tony McGee, *Cosmopolitan*'s fashion director, Elaine Deed, designer Amanda Wakeley, hair stylist Anthony Mascola and Storm model agency's founder, Sarah Doukas.

Both Sarah Doukas and Elaine Deed had met the contestants prior to the final, and had a good idea of the girls they liked. But for the rest of us, the first time we clapped eyes on the girls – except for a glimpse backstage – was not until the contest had begun. As we took our seats on a podium situated to the side of the runway, we were handed details of each girl, together with a Polaroid from a shoot for *Cosmopolitan* with Tony McGee. A girl may look fabulous in the flesh, but if she doesn't photograph well she won't make a good model. Credentials such as height, measurements and age all had to be considered. Then there was the question of modernity. If the winner has the makings of a star, she must have that utterly modern look.

Ten pretty girls, who had been chosen from 5,000 entrants, paraded down the runway in clingy white hipsters and cute cropped tops, while we judges scrutinized and scribbled. I felt for them: this was a truly nerve-racking experience. Some oozed confidence, while others walked with the awkwardness expected of a novice. All were unquestionably lovely. However, four stood out as having real model potential. When the last contestant disappeared behind the backdrop we were sent backstage to confer. Incredibly, almost every judge had put a tick beside the names of the same four girls. We voted unanimously on the winner, but had great difficulty trying to choose who should take second, third and fourth place. Eventually, we decided that, as they were equally good, we'd present all three as runners-up, rather than in pecking order. The winner was announced, then the runners-up. As the audience clapped and cheered, all four girls were handed an enormous bouquet of flowers. When the contest was over, Sarah Doukas went backstage to hand her card to the runners-up. Meanwhile, the television companies and press photographers were swamping Sarah's biggest hope, 19-year-old Nina McCann.

PROFILE OF THE WINNER

Described by her booker as a dead-ringer for supermodel Stephanie Seymour and as having one of the hottest bodies she's seen in a long time, Nina McCann has already made the fashion world sit up and take notice. 'She has a quirky look which is very now,' says Marie Soulier, 'as well as a great personality.' Having just completed a foundation course in fashion design, Nina was enjoying her freedom when, browsing one lazy afternoon through a copy of *Cosmopolitan,* she stumbled across details of a model contest. 'I thought I'd enter for the sheer fun of it,' says Nina, 'and after sending off the application, I didn't give it any more thought.'

A few months later, a letter arrived informing Nina that she'd reached the semi-final and inviting her to Storm's offices to meet Sarah Doukas and her team of bookers. This elimination process catapulted Nina straight through to the final. 'I was so surprised,' remembers Nina. 'I never imagined I'd get this far.' For the finals, Nina was invited to stay in a top London hotel for three days. 'It was great fun. I met lots of girls and we were looked after really well.' Day one was a photo shoot for *Cosmopolitan* with Tony McGee, followed by a day of runway coaching by a top choreographer. On the third day it was the final itself, which was held at The Cosmo Show. When Nina was announced the winner, the look on her face was a picture of complete surprise. Many winners are so bowled over they burst into tears, but Nina just smiled. 'I just couldn't believe I'd won.' After being hounded by the press, the following day her photograph was plastered all over the national newspapers.

From that day on her life changed dramatically. 'Having finished college I was spending time just hanging out with friends until university, then suddenly it was all systems go.' After testing with a few photographers, Nina started to get bookings for magazines, shows and television. 'It's amazing how soon you get in the swing of things and lose all your inhibitions,' explains Nina. 'Winning the contest gave me a head start. I was able to gain experience in front of the camera and on the runway before I'd even gone on my first casting. It also gave me a talking point on go-sees.' After four months on the new faces board, Nina had progressed to the agency's main division and had already been placed with the prestigious Riccardo Gay agency in Milan. When I spoke to Nina she was preparing to go to Italy for a couple of months, hopefully to get inundated with magazine and show bookings. Check out the runways and magazines – Nina's is a face you won't fail to miss.

HOW TO AVOID THE
PITFALLS

Behind the glamour and gloss is an underworld rife with rip-off merchants exploiting and cashing in on the dreams of hopefuls.

COWBOY AGENCIES

Thousands of would-be models fall prey to bogus agencies who claim to be reputable. With the lure of fame and fortune, these cowboys build up the hopes of desperate wannabes and then shatter them – handing out false promises in exchange for large sums of money. Profiting by charging exorbitant fees for registration, amateur photographs, composite cards or entry into their agency book, these fraudulent agencies often insist that all recruits go on an expensive modelling course before they are prepared to represent them.

Bona fide agencies are highly selective about whom they take on, and only make money if their models work. Disreputable agencies take on everyone who walks through their door – regardless of age, height or build – and *never* have any real work available. Other scams include unscrupulous organizations which claim they will introduce would-be models to model agencies for a steep fee, and agencies, who, although they get their models work, never actually pay them.

SCOUTING HORRORS

If you were approached in the street by a so-called scout, photographer or model agent who said you had the looks to rival Cindy Crawford, you would undoubtedly be flattered. Scouting is an accepted way of finding new faces, and most top agencies now employ scouts who search the streets, clubs, bars, restaurants and shops for potential models. But beware! The cowboys have jumped onto the bandwagon and are using a scout's disguise to lure people into their agency, studio or home.

No matter how professional these sharks appear to be, it could be a cunning plot to make money out of you, chat you up or, what's worse, to get you to pose topless or nude. If someone does approach you, ask for their card. But before making an appointment, be sure to contact a reputable model agency or photographers' association to check that they've heard of them.

PHOTOGRAPHY SHARKS

Carried away with the prospect of becoming a model, some wannabes are conned into paying hundreds of pounds for a 'portfolio' of photographs. This is a complete rip-off, as no portfolio should contain pictures taken by just one photographer; professional models' books have no more than two to four prints by the same photographer. Generally, the photographs taken by these sharks are so amateurish they are completely useless. As most agents are happy to assess potential models from snapshots, a portfolio of shots is a waste of money. Once an agent takes you on, they should recommend a few good photographers for you to test with. Many of these photographers will only charge a nominal amount to cover film and processing expenses – if anything at all.

MODELLING COURSES

Model training is another prevalent scam and money spinner for the cowboys. Here, model schools and

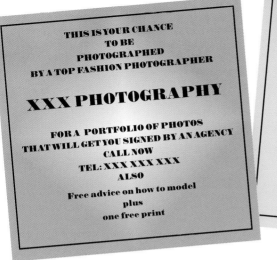

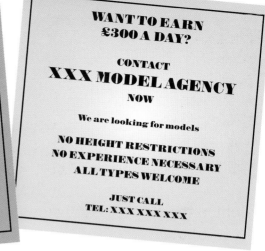

agencies which run courses make their money by insisting would-be models will only get work, or be accepted by an agency, if they have undertaken training. This is by no means true. The majority of these schools charge a high price, yet they offer participants little more than a few antiquated catwalk techniques and amateur make-up lessons. Held in tiny rooms crammed with as many people as possible (in order to make a greater profit), most organizers don't even provide a runway for students to practise on. All said, a good course run by industry experts can sometimes be beneficial – see the training chapter on p.82 for the professionals' comments.

THE MODELLING UNDERWORLD

Cindy Crawford claimed in an interview that, throughout her entire modelling career, she had never been accosted by a photographer. Like Cindy, most models haven't experienced this either. However, just as there's always the playboy casting director in the film business, it's quite likely that there are the odd one or two photographers notorious for surrounding themselves with beautiful women. As for taking this further, it's extremely rare these days. No photographer wants to risk putting his or her career in jeopardy. Prospective models would be very wrong to think that sleeping with someone would give them the edge on their rivals. It certainly won't. The only way a model gets to the top is by hard work and perseverance.

Another risky area of the underworld is where

sleazy set-ups – calling themselves model agencies – lead girls to believe they are being sent abroad to model, only to find when they get to their destination that they are employed as hostesses. This happened to one victim, who was told by an agency she was being sent to Japan to model for magazines and catalogues. When she arrived, she discovered she would be employed as a hostess in a night-club, not as a model.

CHECKLIST

- **Don't** spend money on professional photographs before you approach an agency. All agents are happy to assess you from snapshots alone.
- **Be wary** of agencies who advertise. Most reputable agencies are inundated with letters and calls from would-be models and do not need to use this method of recruitment unless they are just starting up. However, some of the big agencies occasionally advertise to promote a specific scouting event held either at their agency or a hotel.
- **Never** pay organizations claiming they will introduce you to agencies. They won't!
- **Avoid** any agency operating from a hotel: they are usually fly-by-night set-ups who'll take your money and run.
- **If** a scout, agent or photographer approaches you in the street, club, restaurant, etc. check them out before making an appointment. If

you're still unsure, take someone – preferably a parent – along with you.

- **Unlike** adult model agencies, child model agencies *do* charge an interview fee (in the UK this is approximately £20 per child). This is perfectly normal.
- **If** an agency is sending you overseas, and you are uncomfortable about it, contact the client or foreign agent and check it out. If you are not entirely satisfied, do not go.
- **Never** answer ads for extras work asking you to send a fee. Instead, approach a reputable extras or talent agency.
- **If** a model agent insists you take (and pay for) a course before they'll represent you, be highly suspicious.

If you've been accepted by an agency but are still in doubt as to whether they are bona fide, follow the golden rules:

- **Do not** part with any money up front. Remember, reputable agencies do *not* charge registration fees. Also, many agencies will advance new models expenses for composites, entry into the agency book, etc., so you may not have to pay a penny until you've worked.
- **Ask** to speak to other models who are on the agency's books. Find out if they are getting plenty of work, being sent on castings and, most importantly, getting paid.
- **Contact** magazines, large department stores or major catalogue companies and ask if they have heard of the agency. Alternatively, ask the agency who its clients are, and contact them.
- **Don't** be forced into signing anything. If you are asked to sign a contract, read it carefully; if you are still unsure, get professional advice. Many reputable agencies, however, will expect you to sign a perfectly legitimate contract that outlines their terms and conditions. This usually includes details of the percentage of their commission, as well as a clause to prevent you from working with another agency while you're on their books.

TRUE LIFE STORIES

Here are true stories of two would-be models and a professional working model who were conned. Names have been changed.

RIPPED-OFF

Nineteen-year-old Helen Keen had always dreamt of becoming a model. After being rejected by all the top London agencies she became so desperate she replied to an ad in a local paper. To her surprise, this agency actually invited her in for an interview. For a high price they promised her a glittering career as a fashion model. But at 5'2" she didn't stand a chance!

'The agent said I had the type of face that clients were crying out for,' remembers Helen. 'He told me that I would be able to work for fashion magazines, catalogues and advertising clients.' By telling Helen that out of every 1,000 models who approached him he only picked three, he led her to believe she was one of the chosen three. 'I couldn't believe it ... I thought my dream had come true.' Any reservations Helen had about her height were quickly dismissed when the agent explained that fashion models are much shorter these days – and gave Kate Moss as an example.

Helen was accepted onto the agency's books provided she pay £1,400 for a joining fee, modelling course and five photographic sessions. 'The agent assured me that I would recoup this initial cost from my first assignment. I was so excited at the thought of earning so much money, I signed up there and then,' says Helen who, looking back, cannot believe she was naïve and foolish enough to hand over such a large amount of money without checking the agency out first.

At her first training session – which took place in a disused recreation centre – Helen discovered that things weren't quite what they were cracked up to be. 'There was no catwalk, and the room was full of people with no model potential whatsoever – one person even had teeth missing. The whole course entailed nothing more than a few walks and turns, and not the extensive list of things the agent and brochure had promised.'

During the course, the agency had put Helen in touch with a couple of so-called 'professional' photographers. Two photo shoots were arranged. 'The actual sessions seemed to go okay, but the results were appalling,' explains Helen, 'I couldn't even find one decent photograph. They were nearly all out of focus and very amateurish.' By this stage Helen was somewhat reluctant to pay £600 for three more photo shoots, but desperate to start modelling, she arranged the third session. 'I was in my bedroom preparing my clothes for the shoot when mum called out to tell me there was something on television about modelling.' The programme was a documentary featuring cowboy model agencies, focusing on the very agency she had joined. 'I was gutted,' says Helen, who lost £800, had her hopes dashed and her confidence destroyed.

HOTEL SCAM

Keen to get her kids into modelling, Karen Fisher approached a model agency which turned out to be a fly-by-night organization operating from a hotel.

Karen spotted an advertisement in her local paper stating that a model agency was recruiting babies and children up to the age of 16. 'I had two children, James, eight months, and Emma, two, so I decided to telephone for an appointment,' explains Karen. The agent gave her an appointment time and the details of a local hotel where the interview was to take place. 'I assumed the agency had regular offices and was just using a hotel room for interviewing purposes.'

At the hotel, Karen was confronted by dozens of mums and dads with their offspring. After a long wait, it was her turn to see the agent. 'When my children didn't reach the agency's specified requirements I presumed they'd been rejected,' explains Karen, 'but they had both been accepted.' The agent then demanded she pay £200 per child to cover the cost of photographs and a joining fee. When Karen asked if she could have time to mull it over, the agent explained that they were only taking on a couple more children before closing their books. In a final attempt to persuade Karen to join, the agent dangled a discount. It worked! 'She said that because Emma had great potential, she was prepared to charge me less money,' pointed out Karen who, unaware she was being ripped off, handed over a cheque for £165.

Karen was then ushered to the other end of the room to the so-called 'set', where Emma was to have her photograph taken. The set consisted of an old, white sheet taped to the wall. 'The agent claimed she was a professional photographer and went on to explain that she would be taking the pictures herself. Emma didn't even have a chance to settle before the session was over,' says Karen, remembering counting only six clicks of the camera. Before Karen had a chance to gather her thoughts,

she was told that the pictures would be ready for collection the following Sunday and was abruptly shown the door.

This hurried experience left her feeling rather sceptical so, back home, she decided to check the agency out. 'I telephoned everyone from the local Citizens Advice Bureau to a major catalogue company – no one had heard of it. Eventually, I called the Association of Model Agents in London and was advised to cancel my cheque.' The following Sunday, Karen telephoned the hotel only to find what she had suspected – the agency had packed up and left town.

WORK BUT NO PAY

Former fashion model Peter Wild is now a booker for a top London model agency. But when he first started modelling, he was exploited by an agency perceived by most to be perfectly reputable. He worked for months, unaware that he would never see a penny of his hard-earned cash. This experience cost him £8,000.

Located in central London, with plush offices and pictures of models plastered all over the walls, to those unaware of its notorious reputation, this agency appeared to be bona fide. 'I was sent on several castings and was lucky enough to get most of the jobs I auditioned for, including editorial and advertising work, as well as several foreign trips,' explains Peter. Everything seemed to be going well until he raised the subject of money. 'I had been working for months without receiving any payment, but whenever I tried to discuss money, they just fobbed me off with a string of excuses,' remembers Peter. While working with another model who had been promised a long-overdue pay cheque, he became highly suspicious.

At the time, Peter was only 18 years old and didn't have the cash or the know-how to put the matter into legal hands. Fortunately, he was accepted by a top agency, which enabled him to put the bad experience behind him and start earning money. 'The thought of losing so much money makes me furious, but having worked for reputable agencies, both as a model and a booker, I am now able to see where I went wrong. I should never have continued to work for this agency without getting paid and, had I initially talked to other models on the books, I might have learnt of its bad reputation before it was too late.'

ALTERNATIVE CAREERS
WITHIN THE MODEL INDUSTRY

What does a model do when she hangs up her Manolos?

If you've had enough of standing in front of the lens, or are not exactly tailor-made for modelling, there are a number of interesting alternatives for you to consider:

BOOKER

Does the idea of handling the careers of some of the world's most gorgeous men and women appeal to you? If so, then the job of model-agency booker could be for you. A booker (or booking agent) is the person accountable for promoting models, liaising with clients, negotiating fees, booking work and developing models' careers. Essentially, you'll need to be a good salesperson; it's a booker's job to pitch to photographers and editors and convince them that a model who has never worked before is the hottest new thing. Bookers usually look after the schedules of not one, but a dozen or so models and, as the job can be stressful and pressurized, a highly strung person just would not cope. An ability to be able to tell at an instance whether a prospective model has got what it takes is also important.

Besides working for model agencies, bookers are also employed by make-up and hair agents, or agents who represent photographers. Then there are the bookings editors who work for high-fashion magazines – *Vogue*, *Elle*, *Marie Claire* and *Harper's Bazaar* – booking models, photographers, make-up artists and hair stylists for each fashion and beauty shoot. The fundamental difference between the two roles is that the bookings editor is, in effect, the client hiring models, whereas the agency booker is supplying them.

ELITE PREMIER'S GARETH ROBERTS
Gareth Roberts, head booker at Elite Premier, handles some of the world's most famous supermodels, including Naomi Campbell and Linda Evangelista. But Gareth – who has a degree in engineering – admits that before he worked in the industry he'd never even heard of Naomi Campbell, let alone the job of booker. 'I was so naïve when I first started,' recalls Gareth. 'I remember being at a model-biz bash when this woman said :"That's a nice shirt you're wearing, who's

is it?". Expecting me to reel off some designer label, she was dumbfounded when I replied: "It's mine"!'

Naïve to lipstick and lenses – maybe. But unworldly – certainly not! When Gareth chats to a booker overseas or books models on a trip to some exotic location, chances are he's been there. After graduating he spent five years globetrotting combined with a few months' stop in Sydney, where he worked for a production company booking models and organizing promos. A taste of this glitzy world and there was no turning back. On his return to London, he quickly found work assisting a fashion photographer, before being offered the job as booker at a new agency in town. 'I learnt fast,' says Gareth, 'and was booking commercials after only six months. Had I started off with a big agency, I would have still been making the tea!' With one-and-a-half years' booking experience under his belt, the big boys beckoned. Joining Elite as junior booker he soon progressed to the main board, and after only 18 months is now head booker and spokesperson for the agency.

Gareth's advice to anyone wanting to take this career path is: 'Be prepared to give up a big part of your life. You'll be living, breathing and dreaming models.' He also points out that you need to be organized and able to cope during a crisis. 'When a model hasn't turned up at a shoot and the photographer is screaming down the phone, you need to stay cool,' says Gareth. 'You've got to keep the client happy and handle the models, who constantly look to you as mother, shrink, image consultant, secretary ... If you can cope with this, it's an incredibly rewarding career. As there are no specific qualifications to become a booker, my advice is to apply to a model agency for work experience. Good luck!'

MAKE-UP ARTIST

If the thought of blending and chiselling appeals, you might want to consider a career as a make-up artist. Make-up artistry is an art form, so you'll have to be able to transform bare faces into a work of art. You could be painting Egyptian eyes for a runway show one minute, and nude lips for a magazine beauty shoot the next. Sounds glamorous huh? But, as you're often working under pressure, it can be stressful. On a trip, you'll be the one who has to get up at the crack of dawn to make up the model and, at a fashion show, you could be working on as many as ten models in a very short space of time. Therefore, tenacity, patience and an easy-going temperament are essential.

Make-up artistry is akin to modelling – an unpredictable career, but it can also be very rewarding. You travel to the world's hotspots and meet many interesting people. It can also pay well. Like models, you have a day rate which is determined by how experienced and how in demand you are. Make-up artists mostly work on a freelance basis, unless they work full time for television or theatre. Some clients are only prepared to hire one person to do both make-up and hair, so it's advisable to be able to turn your hand to styling hair. And once established, there is always the option of giving private lessons or teaching.

MARY GREENWELL

When you see Kate, Naomi, Linda, *et al.* on the runways, you can be sure that Mary Greenwell is backstage with a brush in one hand and palette in the other. Confidante, friend, 'mother' and entertainer to the supermodels, she is one of the world's most famous make-up artists. Known for her unique style and ability to find innocence in a woman's face, her first brush with the world of make-up was in LA, where she ran the make-up counter in the ultra-hip Fiorruci store. A month later this 23-year-old hippy – who never wore a scrap of make-up – moved to New York, where she was given her first – and only – make-up lesson by Ilana Harkavi in the basement of her Il Makiage salon. 'I thought, "I can do this",' says Mary, who discovered she had quite a talent. Ilana then challenged Mary to make up her first client – Brooke Shields.

After a year in the Big Apple, Mary left the USA and headed home to London. But, almost the moment she hit British ground, she became disillusioned and indecisive about her career path. 'It was that kind of British thing where you lose all your self-esteem,' muses Mary, but this didn't last long. 'I woke up on the morning of my 28th birthday and just knew that I was going to do make-up and do it extremely well.' At the time a new London model agency, Take 2, had been set up and was looking for make-up artists to test with their models. With the beginnings of a book, Mary signed up with one of the top hair and make-up agencies and was subsequently booked for her debut job – a shoot for *Harpers & Queen* with Tony McGee and Vanessa De Lisle. In 1983, Mary moved to Paris, where she was booked to do the make-up for her first magazine cover for *Madame Figaro*. From then on, Mary was on a roll. She worked for American *Vogue* with Grace Coddington and Patrick Demarchelier. She went on to perform her creations on top models for all the prestigious glossies, all the best cosmetic campaigns and all the high-profile designer shows, often teaming with Sam McKnight to make the world's most famous hair and make-up team.

'Its a fantastic job. You get to travel, meet amazing people and broaden your horizons. But the flipside is that it can be tiring, and you need unlimited amounts of stamina and patience. I realize I've been lucky. It's far more competitive today than it was when I started. Then again, there's more work around these days.' Mary suggests that those interested in a career in make-up should start off by taking a make-up course. 'This way, as well as learning the basics, you'll get to find out if you really want to spend every day of your life touching faces and nurturing models. Then, like other media careers, it's about contacts, so you can start testing to build up a good book.' If someone really doesn't have any contacts, having taken a course, Mary suggests working in one of the make-up shops like MAC or Space NK Apothecary. Here, you should meet professionals, get a chance to test and, who knows, perhaps become the next Mary Greenwell!

SESSION STYLIST

Sam McKnight, Orlando Pita, Oribe, Nicky Clarke and other stylists have become as famous as the models themselves. Many have launched their own signature product ranges, and some, like Oribe and Nicky Clarke, boast prestigious salons where clients from all over the world come to have the maestros perform their Midas touch. It is their job to tousle, twist and tease a model's tresses, and turn each head of hair into an artistic creation. To become a session stylist, apart from having the prerequisite artistic flair and a strong desire to specialize in the creative aspect of dressing hair, it is essential to be a skilled, all-round hairdresser.

If you want to take this exciting career path, you could find yourself styling models' hair for magazine shoots, ad campaigns and shows and, if you're lucky, the odd famous head or two. Like make-up artists, hair stylists are also represented by agents. Similarly, they need to test in order to gain shots for their book. But before you can work on the session circuit, unless you are very lucky, you will probably need to work your way up in a good salon, so be prepared for a long, hard haul. When you've reached the ranks of a session stylist it's vital that you're one step ahead of the fashion trends. Drawing inspiration from many different sources – books, films, clubs, past fashions – you'll need to capture the essence of each trend, translate it into a hairstyle, often exaggerating it to the limits.

COLIN GOLD

Top session stylist Colin Gold's love affair with hair began in his teens. After leaving school, he decided to take a hairdressing course. 'The course taught me the basics about hair and was an excellent grounding.' Directly after the course, Colin was offered an apprenticeship with Vidal Sassoon, but after qualifying as a stylist, he realized his style was too individual to carry on doing hair the Sassoon way, so he moved to another salon. Here, his creativity was allowed to flourish, and he soon developed an individual trademark.

It was the early eighties and the era of Boy George, Marilyn, Steve Strange and the London club scene, which Colin Gold was a big part of, hanging out and styling hair for Boy George and other famous fellow clubbers. 'Clubbing gave me a great source of inspiration,' says Colin. 'And being on the circuit meant that I was constantly styling models' hair for fashion shows. When I was asked to style hair for the Vivienne Westwood show I knew it was time to get a book together and find an agent.'

Colin's session career kicked off when he assisted at the international fashion shows in Milan. This was followed by a stint in Paris, before jetsetting around the world working for shows, magazines and ad campaigns. More notably, Colin has been the inspiration behind hair creations at some of the most prestigious shows, including Prada, Gucci and Alexander McQueen, as well as shoots for *Elle*, *Marie Claire* and *Harper's Bazaar*. 'It's been really exciting,' enthuses Colin. 'You get a chance to be incredibly innovative, especially for shows.' During the planning of a show Colin meets with the designer, studies the collection, then comes up with ideas for hairstyles that will complement the clothes. 'It's so satisfying when the season's trends stem from the styles you have created.'

Colin advises would-be session stylists to learn the basics first. 'It may be a drag, but you'll need to start in a salon or attend a course in order to have a good understanding of every aspect of hair. Once qualified, you'll need to work as a hairdresser and then assist, before eventually becoming a session stylist. Remember to develop your own look rather than be dictated to by the look of another hair stylist or salon,' says the man who broke away from bobs and bangs to create today's individual looks.

PHOTOGRAPHER

Richard Avedon, Ellen von Unwerth, Nick Knight and Steven Meisel are just a handful of the world's leading photographers. Top of the list in the glamour stakes, this profession is top of the list in competition stakes, too. This is a highly sought-after vocation, where only the determined succeed. For starters, you'll need to possess talent and creative flair combined with technical aptitude. Most successful photographers began their careers as assistants. This apprenticeship is a vital way of not only learning the ropes, but also making those essential contacts in a career where who you know is as important as what you know. As an assistant you'll get the chance to set up your own test shoots, but you'll also have to do all the menial jobs like loading the camera and making the tea. And working for a busy photographer can mean long hours. Some assistants work for just one photographer, while others assist several different photographers. There are also a number of recognized photographic courses you could take before assisting. But, before you set your heart on photography, bear in mind that places on recognized courses are oversubscribed and, assisting positions are few and far between.

Nearly all fashion photographers work on a freelance basis, and many have agents to represent them. However, you'll need to be quite well established before an agent will be prepared to represent you. The majority of fashion work includes editorial for magazines, advertisements, brochures and point of sale as well as mail-order catalogues. Most top photographers specialize. For example, a high-fashion editorial photographer would not usually shoot a mail-order catalogue as it could prejudice their future editorial work. Another area of photography is runway work, which is more akin to reportage or paparazzi-style photography.

NICK KNIGHT

Voted 'Most influential fashion photographer in the world' in 1995 by *The Face* magazine, Nick Knight is one of photography's biggest names. After taking a three-year photography course at Bournemouth College, his thesis – a project on skinheads – was not only published but became an award-winning book. Having left college in 1982, Nick started photographing fashion for *i-D* magazine. Since then, he has worked for a roster of magazines such as British, American and Italian *Vogue*, and has photographed fashion and beauty campaigns for Yohji Yamamoto, Jil Sander, Alexander McQueen, Levi's, Lancôme and Shiseido.

'Nick is not your archetypal fashion photographer,' says Charlotte Wheeler, who has been Nick's agent for 11 years and, incidentally, is also his wife. 'He was never desperate to be a fashion photographer, he just wanted to take great photographs.' Besides fashion editorial and ad campaigns, Nick has shot campaigns for non-fashion clients including Mercedes, Diners Club and the Royal Opera House. Another non-fashion project was an exhibition for the Natural History Museum. 'Nick loves a challenge,' says Charlotte, recalling how this project took a whole year. "We were commissioned to produce a permanent exhibition entitled 'Plant Power'. It wasn't just taking the photographs, we also had to do all the research.' Not surprisingly, Nick's portfolio of work is incredibly diverse. On one page you have a wild image of Alexander McQueen's blown-up head, and on another, a sophisticated campaign for Jil Sander. In 1994, *NICKNIGHT,* a retrospective, was published, which helped people understand the diversity of his work.

Nick's advice to aspiring photographers is: 'Don't try to recreate what you see in the fashion magazines. Your photographs should show people in the way you find them interesting or beautiful,' he says. Although Nick studied photography, he doesn't necessarily believe that this is the only route. 'It depends on the individual,' says Charlotte. 'Assisting is the way to learn the ropes and develop an aptitude, but you also need to start taking photographs.' Occasionally, there are assistants who have no aspirations to become photographers. But, as Charlotte explains, Nick prefers his assistants to be the type who actually want to be photographers. One of Nick's former assistants is Craig McDean, who recently shot a Calvin Klein campaign. 'Assisting is hard work and not well paid, so it seems pointless unless you're going to get something out of it in the end.' If Nick thinks someone has got to the stage where they no longer need to assist, he'll tell them. When Juergen Teller approached Nick for an assisting job, Nick took one look at his book and told him to get out there and start working.

FASHION STYLIST

If you have a sartorial passion for throwing various items of clothing together to create a stylish look, you may find that fashion styling is right up your street. A love of fashion is *de rigueur*. You'll also need a constant flow of inspiration and, if you want to follow in the footsteps of the legendary Diana Vreeland, you'll need to be something of a trendsetter. Under the fashion umbrella you could be a freelance fashion stylist – working in a similar way to make-up artists or hair stylists, having to test first, then find an agent, before bookings for magazines, catalogues, advertising shoots and shows hopefully flood in. Stylists have usually worked for a magazine or newspaper to get established before becoming freelance. Alternatively, you could be employed by a magazine as a stylist, assistant, fashion writer, fashion editor or director.

The actual role depends on the individual magazine but, in general, a fashion editor or director oversees the fashion team, covers each season's shows, plans the pages and, each month, styles a fashion story or two. If the magazine doesn't have a bookings editor, it might also be up to the fashion editor/director to choose models and photographers. It's also the stylist's/fashion editor's job to pick the clothes and then collate them along with props, shoes and accessories. The organization of each shoot will probably be left to an assistant or junior stylist.

On a shoot you will be one of the key members of the team alongside the model, photographer, make-up artist and hair stylist. Utilizing your creativity and imagination, you would arrange the garments on the model in the most suitable and stylish way. Often you need to pin the clothes to get a good shape. If you are a stylist or assistant fashion editor, be prepared to do mundane jobs, such as ironing and altering clothes to fit the model. If you work for a glossy magazine, you may have unlimited designer gear, but for a run-of-the-mill mail-order catalogue you'll have to make a cheap and nastly dress look a million dollars.

MARIE CLAIRE'S FASHION DIRECTOR, SARAH WALTERS

Marie Claire's fashion director, Sarah Walters, was studying fashion at St Martin's when she was seconded to British *Vogue* on a six-week placement. Sarah never returned to St Martin's. She was, in fact, offered the job of an assistant fashion editor. 'I was extremely lucky to have assisted some of the greats, including Anna Harvey and Vanessa De Lisle,' says Sarah, who went on to become *Vogue*'s accessories editor. Having gone straight from studying, Sarah decided to take a sabbatical, which developed into a four-year stay in Africa, resulting in the production of a film. In a no-visa situation, Sarah had to return to England. 'I still had contacts in the business and managed to freelance for a while until I was offered the job of fashion editor on *Harpers & Queen*.' After a year and a half she moved to *Marie Claire*. Today, she's one of fashion's gurus responsible for dressing the rest of us.

'Its tough to break into styling, as it's almost a closed shop,' says Sarah, who was one of the lucky ones. 'The best way to get into the business is to apply for work experience in the fashion department of a magazine. But be prepared to work incredibly hard for no money.' Sarah stresses that an artistic background is a distinct advantage and that it's also important to understand fashion culture. 'Styling is all about knowing exactly who you are addressing. A good stylist should be able to turn their hand to anything from off-the-wall stuff to incredibly straight stories.'

Photographed by John Swannell courtesy of © Condé Nast PL Tatler

PART 3

IMAGE

HOW

TO ACHIEVE THAT SUPERMODEL LOOK

You can't pick up a glossy magazine without coming face to face with perfection. Free from the usual baggage of sags, creases, bulges or (the dreaded) cellulite – models appear to have it all! So what's their secret? And how can you look and feel like a million dollars, too?

Don't be fooled by the aphorism 'the camera never lies'. It does! Not only are minor imperfections airbrushed out, but a model could be wearing any number of beauty aids, from coloured contact lenses and hair extensions, to that clever little invention – the Wonderbra. Models know all the tricks of the trade. They've mastered the art of maximizing their positive points, and de-emphasizing the negative ones. And to maintain their looks, they pay zealous attention to every inch of their bodies: no blocked pore or split end is overlooked.

You can spot a model a mile off. With a slim, black portfolio clenched firmly in her hand, she's the one who walks in such a way that, without looking too haughty, she tells the world she's proud of who she is. Her fashion trademark is individuality rather than the trendiest designs. Slick, sassy and utterly modern, she dresses to flatter her assets, cleverly teaming high-street fashion with classic pieces or vintage designer wear. On closer examination, you'll notice she's groomed from top to toe: nails are manicured and polished in some delicious shade, make-up is 'barely-there', and her mane, which is in superb condition, is tousled in an effortless, yet chic, way.

We all have the potential to look this great, but if supermodels need assistance that leaves us ordinary mortals crying out for help. You may be comforted to know that when a new model joins an agency a sort of Cinderella-turned-princess transformation takes place. Take a gawky individual who shuffles and slouches into the agency with blotchy skin and a half-grown-out, frizzy perm that has never been let loose from a scrunchie. She hasn't a clue how to dress and, as for make-up, she doesn't know what eyelash curlers look like, let alone how to use them. Start by cutting out the perm and adding style, condition and colour to her hair, pluck a few eyebrows, put her in a body-skimming outfit and show her how to accentuate her features with a little basic make-up. Mix this with a touch of poise, a change of diet and a spruced-up skin-care routine and – hey presto – you have the recipe for a ravishing beauty to rival any supermodel. The good news is that there's more help at hand than ever before. So, just like every new model, free the beauty within you and become the person you had only ever dreamed of being.

NEW-AGE BEAUTY

Consider the word 'beauty'. Is it an unquantifiable entity or is there such thing as the beauty blueprint? Just like fashion, tastes in looks are constantly changing. What was considered beautiful in the twenties was viewed as positively unattractive by the thirties. And Cecil Beaton was quite right when, in an issue of *Vogue,* he wrote: 'How imperceptibly, but quickly, our views on beauty fluctuate.'

You may be pleased to know that beauty is no longer about that single vision of a perfectly symmetrical face, pouty lips and doe eyes. This is just one reflection of beauty. And, as Naomi Campbell said in an interview with *The Face*: 'I think beauty is inside everybody. I see beautiful people every day, it doesn't mean they're physically beautiful.' Refreshingly, over the last couple of years, a far more realistic and less stereotyped look has been creeping in to the oh-so-perfect world of modelling. Along with the new breed of quirky models – who have proved beauty is about individual, interesting faces, not a blueprint – photographers like Juergen Teller, Rankin, Corrine Day and David Sims have been photographing beautiful models devoid of camouflage and clever lighting. Cutting-edge fashion photographer Rankin, who has photographed all types of models, from big girls to groovy granddads, is all for photographers documenting reality rather than fabrication. 'It's great that top models are being shown in their raw state. This is something that the public can actually relate to, rather than that unreal illusion of perfection.' Models have even been photographed with greasy hair and a face full of zits. However, in reality, if models went around looking quite so unkempt it's unlikely they'd get any other bookings, let alone boyfriends. This sort of hip-to-be-hideous trend may be taking the notion of unconventional beauty a little too far, but it has clearly helped those with more extreme looks, quirky or irregular features, to be also classified as beautiful.

The essence of modern beauty is about individuality, combined with an inner sparkle, vitality, charisma, confidence and being comfortable with your looks regardless of your size or age. And, what were once considered faults, e.g. a big nose, or widely spaced eyes, are now regarded as assets. You can't always have the texture of hair, face shape, frame or height you want, therefore, the most important lesson is to learn to love what you have. So rather than striving for perfection, follow in the footsteps of the modern models by making the most of your individual assets. Besides, a conventionally ugly girl can be far more striking, and definitely more 'now' than the archetypal blue-eyed, button-nosed blonde.

THE BEAUTY CULTURE

Models epitomize the beauty culture: a culture that places a great emphasis on appearance and worships youth. But let's face it, any one of us who has purchased a product that promises to hold back the years or make you more beautiful is, to a certain extent, a victim of this culture. You may call yourself a 'beautyphobe', but you can bet your bottom dollar you've indulged in something to better yourself, be it

VOGUE'S WHAT'S IN A MODEL'S RUCKSACK
BY CARMEL ALLEN

British *Vogue*'s assistant beauty editor, Carmel Allen, is privy to what a model carries in her bag. Here, she lets us in on the secrets:

- Books – *The Celestine Prophecy* by Michael Redfern, and mind, body, and spirit books such as those by Deepak Chopra
- Evian water
- Mints – Tic-Tacs
- Filofax
- *A to Z* of London
- Mobile phone
- Waterproof Walkman and tapes (good for playing on shoots and on the hoof)
- Favourite tapes or CDs to liven up the atmosphere in the studio
- Throw-away camera
- Marlboro cigarettes (soft packs from duty free), match books from all the bars and hotels
- Telephone cards for Italy, France and the UK
- Plasters (shoot shoes can sometimes be too small)
- Virgin upper-class blackout eye covers
- Calvin Klein sunglasses (Raybans and Persol have had their day)
- Donna Karan travel-size scented candles
- Cashmere scarf – Shatoosh
- Kiehl's lipgloss, MAC lipgloss or Carmex
- Zovirax cream
- MAC lipliner
- Eucerin cream for dry skin
- Maybelline 'Great Lash' mascara
- Eyelash curlers and gold-plated tweezers by Tweezerman
- Any bits of make-up from a make-up artist's own range (especially if they've named a piece after you); 'Jamaica' foundation from Nars for Naomi, 'Kate' lipstick by Stila
- Prescriptives flight cream
- Elizabeth Arden eight-hour cream
- Estée Lauder day wear
- Decleor neroli face oil
- Hair jewels/slides/scrunchies from Johnny loves Rosie and Tarina Lauren Tarantino
- Di Cesare paddle hairbrush for long hair, wooden comb for short hair
- Essential oils – lavender (uplifting), neroli (anti-depressant)
- Dr R Harris crystal eye drops
- Melatonin for jet lag
- Solgar 'Daily Gold' pack of vitamins

a sun tan, a bikini wax or a slick of lipstick.

There is an enormous pressure on everyone to look attractive. We have become an aesthetically literate generation. Suffice to say, the image you present to the world *does* matter. It's not about measuring how beautiful you are, nor is it about a total preoccupation with your looks: it's about the importance of paying attention to your overall appearance. With your clothes, body shape, make-up and hair you are making a statement. If you care about yourself, this will invariably be reflected in the way you look. You will have confidence which will give you the self-esteem to be successful in all areas of your life. And, as most of the supermodels have proved, beauty and brains *can* go hand in hand.

Light years ahead of the days of cold cream and

Photographed by Nick Knight courtesy of © Condé Nast PL – British *Vogue*

New-age beauties: *from left, Esther, Iris Palmer (in the tree), Laura Ponte and Kim Iginsky (on bed).*

INNER BEAUTY

Don't fret about such minor discrepancies as spots, brittle nails and dry, lifeless hair. For the moment, let's concentrate on the inside. The emphasis has shifted from what's on the outside to addressing inner beauty first. This attitude is reflected in the freer hairstyles, individual clothes and natural-looking complexions we see today. So forget disguising bad skin and lacklustre hair with coiffed hairstyles and inch-thick make-up, and start changing your lifestyle. Are you exercising regularly, eating a healthy, balanced diet, getting plenty of sleep, avoiding stress and eliminating those stimulants – caffeine and nicotine? If you really do want your spots to clear, your brittle nails to strengthen and your hair to shine, before you reach for any product change your ways.

WORK AT IT

Take action! It's easy to slip into the couch-potato mode, but if you fail to look after yourself, you might as well sit back and start counting the wrinkles. We're not talking about the no-pain, no-gain attitude, nor are we looking at endless hours of regimes, routines or rituals. Time is precious in the nineties, so the last thing you want is a high-maintenance routine. However, you'd be surprised at how getting up just five minutes earlier in the morning goes a long, long way. Models often have to be at a studio by 8am but this doesn't mean they skip their morning's ablutions.

To metamorphose into a vibrant beauty, start by thoroughly examining your pluses and minuses. Think of your overall image. Could you do with a new haircut? Do your clothes flatter your shape? Should you be working out to flatten that tummy? Draw up a mental strategy of the parts that need improving – then put it into action. Start by adopting a simple, yet effective, skin-care programme that involves cleansing morning and night, a weekly deep cleanse and mask, and a monthly facial. Skin-brushing, exfoliating and moisturizing your body will only add minutes to your shower or bath time, yet it will dramatically improve the texture of your skin. Add to that a weekly hair mask and manicure, and you're getting there. Don't forget to treat your grooming time as a form of relaxation.

Probably the most time-consuming aspect of making the best of yourself is exercising, yet keeping fit is tantamount to feeling and looking good. Think ahead by exercising now and zapping problem areas before they get out of control; it will be worth the effort

dusting powder, looking good has never been so easy. With the help of fashion and beauty magazines, sophisticated products, developments in cosmetology and accessible fashion, women and men now have no excuse but to make themselves as attractive as possible. With a little make-up even the plainest face can look striking. And a new haircut or change of colour can turn a mousy type into someone who gets noticed.

in the long run. There's nothing more frustrating or depressing than having to spend time and money battling against cellulite, bulges or saggy parts because you've left it too late.

If you're really stuck for time, streamline your regime. Opt for make-up that lasts all day, nail polish that dries in seconds, and clothes that are crease resistant or don't need hours of laborious laundering. Have your hair regularly shaped at the salon; it will be much easier to style at home and should only take a matter of minutes to look great. And if you're strapped for cash, don't worry. With minimum investment you can still look good on a shoestring by working out at home, using home-made beauty preparations and buying clothes from charity shops, thrift stores and flea markets. So there's no excuse!

TRICKS OF THE TRADE

A tuck here, a collagen injection there, a new nose, breast enlargements ... you can have practically any part of your body altered or improved. But thanks to the increasing number of modern fashion and beauty solutions, you don't have to opt for the scalpel. Always wanted blue eyes? Then simply emulate Naomi Campbell and wear blue-coloured contact lenses. If your hair is too short or lacks fullness, you could, like Naomi, Elle Macpherson and many other models, consider hair extensions. False nails or nail extensions will hide bitten-down or broken nails, and a fake tan or bronzers will give you an evenly toned skin and a natural glow.

Next, on to your body. Cultivate all your feminine curves. You can uplift and sculpt those less-than-perfect bits with exercise and body treatments, but you may need a little extra help. If so, there are the bottom-raising knickers for an uplifted and more shapely bottom; knickers that flatten your tummy and give you that nipped-in waist; tights with control tops for slimmer thighs, cellulite reduction and a slender stomach; and, for that cleavage to die for, there is, of course, the push-up bra. But if you've got nothing to lift, don't worry. For a more voluptuous bosom, slip a pair of silicon-gel pads into your bra. If you want to go bra-less, tape is a great trick for pert breasts.

Now for the face. Plump up wrinkle-prone zones with the latest wrinkle miracle pads. In the long term, facial exercises or the non-surgical face-lift (Caci) will tone muscles, improve fine lines and give you chiselled cheekbones. If you really want to cheat, do what cover girls do, and use tape to lift your face. But ensure you conceal the tape with your hair. Luscious lashes can be yours with the help of eyelash tints and false or individual lashes. And having your eyebrows reshaped will make all the difference to your face. For bee-stung lips, dab on lip-plump balm. Trick nature by giving your lips a natural, cherry-coloured hue, adding definition to your lash line or filling in missing brows with semi-permanent make-up. So now you know the trade secrets, don't let others put you in the shade.

SIMPLE STEPS TOWARDS SUPERMODEL LOOKS

The next few chapters are devoted to the quest for that supermodel look. So if you're one of the millions who aspires to look like Helena, Naomi, Amber, *et al.* – aspire no longer. Even if you're the most self-confessed 'beautyphobe', this section of the book will hopefully convert you into a beauty buff. Starting today, you can do something positive towards achieving that model look. Below is a taster to help you kick-start your regime. If you can only manage one or two of the steps, it will still be a step in the right direction.

BRILLIANT BROWS: Give your face an instant lift by reshaping your eyebrows. Dab clove oil on to numb the area then, using tweezers, pluck from underneath the arch. If you haven't had your eyebrows shaped before, it's advisable to go to a salon to get the initial shape. Darken brows by tinting with an eyelash dye; condition by applying Vaseline; and keep in place by brushing with clear mascara. Define brows with eyebrow powder or a brown eyeshadow that matches your brows. Check out the make-up chapter (p.116) for more details.

LUSCIOUS LASHES: For naturally dark eyelashes, darken with an eyelash tint. To open up your eyes, curl lashes before applying mascara. If you don't want to wear mascara, to hold the curl in place, coat eyelashes with Vaseline or clear mascara. For thicker lashes, dust powder over eyelashes before applying mascara. For super-thick lashes try lash thickeners, which use fibres to build up thickness and length, before applying mascara. Alternatively, plump for falsies. To give the illusion of thicker lashes, dot eyeliner (preferably liquid) by the root of each lash. Keep lashes conditioned with Vaseline. Check out the make-up chapter (p.116) for more details.

PERFECT POUT: Prime and plump up lips by exfoliating. Ruby Hammer has the trick: 'Before showering, cover your lips in balm. Then, take a child's toothbrush into the shower and scrub.' Another trick to make your lips look fuller is to hold an ice cube onto your lips or use a lip-plump balm which fills in lines with wax. If you want your lip colour to stay, apply fixative before the colour or choose one of the long-lasting lipsticks. For a natural-looking hue, fill in lips with a lipliner as close to your own lip colour as possible, then cover with gloss. Naturally glossy lips can be achieved by applying Vaseline, gloss or balm. Check out the make-up chapter (p.116) for more details.

CHISELLED CHEEKBONES: For those who aren't blessed with the razor-sharp cheekbones of Kate Moss, Jodie Kidd and the majority of models, top make-up artist Maggie Hunt has a great tip for contouring the face. 'Suck in your cheeks, and apply semi-matt bronzing powder or brown eyeshadow with a brush to the hollows, blending back towards the ears.' Consider facial exercises or the non-surgical face-lift; in the long term they really do give you more prominent cheekbones. Check out the make-up chapter (p.116) and skin-care chapter (p.128) for more details.

GLOSSY TRESSES: For a head of shiny hair, spritz hair with an instant-shine solution or apply a serum. Brighten dull-coloured hair by using colour shampoo. Have hair cut into an easy style so you can have that just-stepped-out-of-the-salon look every day. If you've been asked out for a date, but haven't got time to wash your hair, Colin Gold has a tip for hair that looks great in a matter of seconds: 'Spritz hair with styling lotion, turn your head upside down, then blast with the hair dryer.' Check out the hair chapter (p.122) for more details.

STUBBORN SPOTS: If you have a stubborn spot the morning before an important night out, whatever you do don't squeeze it. Apply a soothing spot lotion that will calm it down, reduce the redness but not over-dry it. When it comes to make-up, use a fine layer of colour corrector followed by concealer, applied with a brush. If it's in a sensual place – e.g. above the lip – you could turn it into Cindy Crawford beauty spot by colouring it with an eyebrow pencil. Check out the skin-care chapter (p.128) for more details.

GLOWING SKIN: Skin-brushing from head to toe will help to increase the circulation and give you that all-over glow. After skin-brushing, exfoliate in the shower. For a quick exfoliator, Champneys' Kathryn Paling advises you to grab a handful of salt from the kitchen, then rub it all over your body (not your face). Having slathered on your favourite body lotion, spray on or apply fake tan. Next apply a body sheen to shoulders, arms, décolleté and legs. For a radiant face, apply fake tan, sheer foundation and a little bronzing powder or blusher. Check out the beauty chapter (p.134) for more details.

EVENLY TONED SKIN COLOUR: Beauty expert Alison Young, claims that the secret for an even skin tone all over the body is to use fake tan, preferably the spray-on kind that dries almost immediately and means you can get dressed within five minutes. Use just a little for a glowing, even skin tone, and a bit more for a golden tan.

EAT FOR BEAUTY: Eat plenty of fresh fruit, vegetables, fibre and wholegrains and avoid toxic foods. Cut down on tea, coffee, sugar, refined and processed foods. The basic message for eating to look and feel good is, as dietician Priscilla Marmot points out: 'Eat less fat, especially saturated fat and eat more fibre in the form of vegetables, fruit, cereals and grains, with moderate use of salt and added sugars.' Drink as much water as possible. And to detox, eat nothing but fresh fruit until lunchtime. Check out the nutrition chapter (p.152) for more details.

HEAVENLY HANDS: When exfoliating your body, don't forget your hands. Always wear gloves for washing up and when it's cold. Apply hand cream whenever you wash your hands, and massage in cream before you go to bed at night. For a special treatment, take a tip from hand model Sarah Clive and cover hands in warm olive or almond oil, then put your mitts into warmed cotton gloves and leave to nourish overnight. Check out the beauty chapter (p.134) for more details.

NEAT NAILS: Care for your nails by lavishing rich cream onto hands and nails. Give yourself a weekly manicure. And, to protect nails from breaking, paint on a strengthener. Keep nails varnished, as it helps to protect them. If you don't like coloured varnish, select a French polish or a clear or nude varnish instead. Check out the beauty chapter (p.134) for more details.

INSTANT PICK-ME-UPS: Put a couple of drops of your favourite aromatherapy oil on a tissue and inhale. To freshen up your face, spritz with toner, drying the face with tissue straight afterwards. To freshen up tired eyes cover with cold, used tea bags or cucumber slices. To get the blood flowing, shake your head upside down. For a general pick-me-up, Champneys' Kathryn Paling suggests rubbing aromatherapy oil (blended not neat) onto the soles of your feet. Check out the chapters on beauty (p.134), skin care (p.128) and natural beauty (p.140) for more details.

INDIVIDUALLY YOU: Wear something individual, be it unusual-coloured or metallic nail varnish, a bright-coloured jacket or coat, feather boa, vintage dress, beaded handbag, and hair accessories such as jewels, feathers, roses, etc. This way you'll stand out from the crowd. Check out the fashion & style chapter (p.110) for more details.

INNER GLOW: Don't just focus on external beauty, address your inner beauty. A warm, happy person with charm and charisma, whose eyes sparkle and face lights up when they talk is far more attractive than any static beauty. Smiling and laughing bestows the feel-good factor and is one of the best beauty tonics. The old cliché – if you feel good you will look good – is certainly true.

FASHION & STYLE

Whether you dress to impress, are a fervent follower of fashion, or fling on any old thing – what you wear and the way that you wear it is your trademark.

Fashion is eclectic: sharp tailoring contrasting with pretty chiffon dresses, and bohemian prints with minimalist neutrals. But with such a bewildering choice, where do you begin? Most women want modern clothes that are wearable yet have a hint of glamour and, ultimately, make them look and feel good. They want to be sexy without looking obvious, and comfortable without looking boring. Guys want to stand out in a crowd in an effortless way. Whatever your personal style – super-sophisticated, subtle and safe, classic-chic, casual-chic or young 'n' funky – the key to modern dressing is to maximize your potential and achieve individual style without losing sight of your shape or lifestyle. Fashion allows you the freedom of choice to reflect your personality and character, but doesn't stop you taking on as many different roles as you wish: flaunt your femininity in a scrap of lace one minute, and get serious in a slick suit the next. After reading this chapter, hopefully reinventing your image should be fun, challenging and not quite so daunting.

MODEL STYLE

Send a model down the runway with a black plastic bin-liner or curtain wrapped around her and she'll still look great. With legs that go on forever and curves in all the right places, models have a great advantage over the rest of us – almost anything looks good. And,

like top model Tina Harlow, they have the confidence and know-how to dress to their best advantage. 'I choose clothes that make my legs look longer, accentuate my waist and give me a good bosom,' says Tina. 'There are some brilliant skinny shirts and tight-fit tops with darts which I find great for flattering your curves.' Tina has developed a look she is happy with. 'In summer I wear simple dresses or short skirts with little tops, teamed with a pair of chunky-heeled, strappy sandals. And in cold weather, I stick to slimline pants, with fitted tops, shirts or cardigans and ankle boots.'

When they're not barely clad in those to-die-for, sexy party numbers and Manolo Blahnik mules, models tend to go in for no-nonsense, simple basics. They choose pieces in body-hugging fabrics that show the lines of their physique, yet are wearable enough to get them from casting to airport without looking completely dishevelled. Storm's new faces booker, Marie Soulier, tells her new models to keep it simple. 'If they can't afford new clothes, I'll tell them to wear jeans with a white, fitted T-shirt. By the time they start earning, they already have good fashion sense and know which clothes suit them.'

Models understand fashion – they have to, its their job. They have fashion sense, but are not slaves to fashion, preferring to mix rather than be sold a complete fashion statement. And they're not

Photographed by Miles Aldridge courtesy of © Condé Nast P.L.

111

necessarily dressed from head to toe in designer gear either. Most have got a fashion stylist's knack of teaming high-street clothes with vintage pieces or designer labels. Above all, they strive to be individual. At castings, however, there is a kind of model uniform: black is always popular, as are short skirts, slimline pants, minuscule tops, slip dresses, fitted cardis, tight shirts, sweaters and brightly coloured tops for guys. The models' main consideration is to wear modern clothes that accentuate their bodies and look good on video or Polaroid. Elaine Deed, fashion director of *Cosmopolitan,* feels it's important for models to show off their assets on castings and go-sees. 'We need to see their bodies, so short skirts are always popular. For colder weather I advise models to invest in a good, long coat; this way they keep warm, look good, and can still wear a mini underneath.'

For a long time male models have got away with the scruffy-jeans-and-leather-jacket look but Boss Models' Karen Long explains, this is changing. 'Clients expect guys to look the part these days. So we suggest they invest in a good blazer, which they can wear with a turtleneck or V-neck top and smart/casual trousers.'

TRENDS

Designers are continuously drawing inspiration from various sources, including different cultures and past decades. They then reinterpret these looks and add a modern twist. The first place to spot the latest trends is on the runway but, before you can even say 'couture', the key looks are dotted all over the high street. Fashion certainly has its moments. What looks great on the runway often looks out of place for work or play, which is why many of these fashions are diffused into more wearable versions. Lets face it, few of us are going to venture out in bumster trousers, or schoolgirl knickers under the scrap-of-chiffon look that littered the runways.

To give your clothes a modern edge you don't have to go the whole hog. You can simply inject a touch of the latest catwalk-inspired trends into your wardrobe by investing in a couple of key fashion items in the hottest colour or most up-to-the-minute style. Even the odd accessory can update your look. Hemlines continuously go up and down, but the most popular lengths with staying power seem to be the mini, knee-length or maxi skirt.

Don't become a fashion victim; choose clothes primarily because they suit you. It's preferable to defy fashion rather than wear a style that is unflattering to your shape. Besides, unless you can carry it off, a trendy item could inadvertently make you look terribly dated or downright ridiculous. And this won't win you any prizes in the book of style.

SENSE OF STYLE

It's not what you wear but the way that you wear it. Give two women the same, basic shirt and you can bet that the results will be different. One woman might wear it open over a T-shirt or camisole and jeans, while another may add a silk neck scarf and slip a tailored jacket over the top. By wearing the shirt in a different way, each one is adding their own individual identity to it, which is what style is all about. You may have a wardrobe full of designer clothes, but they are utterly useless if you don't have that essential commodity – fashion sense.

Impeccable style doesn't come easy. And as Sarah Walters, *Marie Claire*'s fashion director points out – it's indefinable. 'Style is an instinctive thing. You can't buy it, nor can you steal it from someone else. It's about the whole image, not just the clothes, hairstyle or earrings.' Susie Faux, image consultant and author of *Wardrobe,* also sums up style as a total look: 'A good haircut, the right make-up and well-cut clothes that fit you in good-quality fabrics with the least amount of trimmings,' says Susie. 'Less is definitely more when it comes to stylish dressing.'

Here are a few tips to help you acquire the knack of stylish dressing:

- **Style** is a very individual thing. It's easy to buy an entire outfit from the same designer or shop, but intelligent dressing requires mixing and matching to create a look that not only suits you, but is unique to you and reflects your personality.
- **Look** through fashion magazines for inspiration. Notice how the stylists team certain clothes together, how they mix and match (or mismatch) colours and prints, and which accessories and shoes they add to an outfit to complete the look. Keep pages of the looks that you would like to achieve, then adapt them to suit your own image and shape. If, for example, you love the style of a particular top shown with a mini, but don't have the legs to wear it, think of suitable alternatives such as slimline pants or a longer skirt.
- **Don't** be lured by designer clothes for the sake of a label. Invest in the quality of fabric and cut.
- **Team** your latest fashion purchase either with a classic piece you've had for years, or with one-off, vintage numbers. Wearing something like a vintage three-quarter-length bouclé coat, either bought from a second-hand designer store or borrowed from your mother, is guaranteed to get attention; just think – no one will be wearing the same.
- **What's** in the shops, magazines and on the runways is not the only barometer of fashion. You can be highly fashionable without having to succumb to current fashion.

- **Try** to add a personal touch to your outfit. Choose something unusual that gives you personal identity: perhaps a faux-fur hat, printed coat, boa, vintage wrap, hair accessories, unusual shoes, wacky handbag or a special piece of jewellery.
- **Keep** accessories simple. Susie Faux points out: 'The older you get, the less jewellery you should wear. However, I don't feel women are properly dressed without earrings.'
- **If** – and only if – you've got the confidence to carry it off, have a daring sense of style and unashamedly show a leg, expose a midriff or flaunt a cleavage. A glimpse is all you need.
- **Experiment** with combinations of separates that you would not normally wear together.
- **Consider** using an image consultant or personal shopper. Many department stores now have consultants on site who help put outfits together for customers. As long as you make a purchase there is usually no charge. But as Susie Faux, the pioneer of image consultants, points out, make sure *they* have a good sense of style.
- **Add texture** to your wardrobe rather than sticking with boring and bland fabrics.
- **When** dressing, take your age into consideration. 'We call it the decade dump,' says Susie Faux. 'As you get older, not only should you change your hair and make-up, but also the style and colour of clothes you wear and, equally importantly, what you wear them with. A 20-year-old can wear the same suit as a 40-year-old, but with different shoes and accessories.'

CHEAP CHIC

During lean times, look for items of clothing that transcend the seasons. Choose versatile garments that can be worn with several different pieces from both your autumn/winter and spring/summer wardrobe: winter trousers can be teamed with a summer top and strappy sandals; a light summer shirt can be worn under a winter jacket. Also, look for all-occasion wear. Take a tailored jacket, for example. You can wear it over jeans for a casual look, with leather trousers for a smarter image, and over a black dress for evening.

Pared down for day or jazzed up with accessories and snazzy shoes for evening, many clothes double up as day and evening wear. For instance, wear your simple summer shift dress in the day with pumps or sandals. Then, when dusk falls, swap your pumps for a high pair of strappy slingbacks, add your favourite earrings, a smart jacket or wrap, throw an evening bag over your shoulder, and hit the town.

If it's the latest designer labels you crave, but you can't afford to pay the prices, did you know that many top designers are creating collections for high-street chains and department stores at a fraction of the cost of their own label? Look for the 'designed by' signs.

If you want to trade your old clothes for new, if they are in good condition take them to a nearly new shop or second-hand designer boutique which should be happy to take them on a sale-or-return basis.

SECRET PLACES

Now for those unconventional shopping haunts. Models often raid children's clothing departments for fitted shirts, jumpers and tiny tops. Another well-kept model secret is the underwear store. Here you'll find everything from that perfect little party frock, floaty summer slip dresses, sheer camisoles, fitted bodies and bustiers, to simple silk or cotton vest tops. During my days working at *Elle*, the fashion team was amazed when I told them that my silk Jasper Conran lookalike was actually a £10 satin slip from the underwear section of a department store!

Next stop: cut-price designer wear and high-street fashions. Look out for designer sample sales or factory shops that sell nearly perfect seconds. Often items will be sold at a fraction of the normal retail cost simply because the colour didn't match the rest of the batch. Then there's the army surplus store: a great place for casual wear, men's wear or military-style garments.

VINTAGE CLOTHES

The model's favourite has to be the second-hand designer shop. This is not about cheap chic, but individual style. Vintage clothes may conjure up an image of the grunge look – but grunge they're not. Grunge was a deranged look: scruffy clothes worn with DMs and messy hairstyles. Besides, models and fashion pundits were scouring second-hand shops long before grunge was in. These shops enable us to buy clothes from different periods and mix them together with up-to-date garments to create a timeless look. Search for good-quality clothes in mint condition, and check the labels for fabric content. If it's an original twenties Chanel jacket you're after, you might spend your whole life searching. But if you go with an open mind you may be surprised at what you find.

In addition to vintage shops there are flea markets, jumble sales, thrift stores and charity shops. You may find yourself rummaging through a load of old jumble but occasionally there are real gems to be found. Warning – it can become quite addictive!

COLOUR PALETTE

Fashion is more colourful than it has been for decades. To instantly brighten your wardrobe, add a splash of vibrant colour. The not so brave can either use colour to accent (a coloured top under a neutral suit, for example), or can opt for coloured accessories or shoes. Be careful not to put hard-to-wear colours too close to your face: they can leave you looking pasty and can accentuate a less-than-perfect skin. Ideally, key colours are the ones that suit you, not necessarily the ones dominating the magazines and shop rails. And forget colour-coding, this is far too restricting.

Choose from tempting palettes of screaming bright, citrus or candy colours; new pastels in such cooling shades as mint green, lilac, pale pink or ice blue ... and so on. Muted shades of beige, tawny, camel and taupe are always popular, as are the rich winter colours of deep plums and purples, vivid reds, greens, navy and chocolate browns. Then there's the monochrome look of black and white that, no matter what colour is in fashion, always looks chic. Black has been the colour worn by the fashion pack for years, even when they declared brown the new black. Black is stylish, slimming and simple, but worn alone it can look unadventurous and dull. Black does, however, look great punctuated with colour.

Basics of black, brown, charcoal grey, olive green, white and navy all make great building blocks to team with other colours. For example, you could wear chocolate brown with mustard, purple, blue, camel or orange. Different shades of the same colour can also work. An electric-blue top could look great teamed with pants in the right shade of light blue. But make sure the shades contrast not clash – unless that's what you intend! Take care with red. For example, an orangey shade of red wouldn't look good worn with a burgundy-toned red. The final word on colour: to avoid colour overload, only mix a maximum of three colours or shades of colour at once.

CUT AND SILHOUETTE

There are many different permutations of one item of clothing. Take pants. From tapered, flared and bootleg, to palazzo, waisted, hipster or flat-fronted, there are at least a dozen variations. You probably don't possess all these styles simply because they wouldn't all suit you. This is wise. The biggest fashion mistakes are unflattering fashion items were Lycra leggings. At the height of the leggings trend, regardless of their size or shape, women were seen revealing every lump and bump in skin-tight leggings. Another diabolical shape was the puffball skirt, which is now regarded as one of fashion's more embarrassing moments.

When shopping, don't get depressed if you try on what you thought was your normal size, only to find it is two sizes too small. Many clothes, especially the high-fashion stuff, are sized too small. These days, there is no such thing as a standard size – annoyingly, what is a size 10 in one shop is a size 14 in another.

HOW TO FLATTER YOUR SHAPE

Think of the lines of your body as a sculpture, and always aim to keep a narrow silhouette. Whether the shapes are structured or unstructured, fashion expert June Marsh, who also writes for *Encore,* the magazine for large sizes, explains that the trick is to find clothes that help balance your proportions, disguise your bad points and maximize your potential. 'Study your shape in a full-length mirror and work out your best and worst parts. Emphasize your plus points, such as good legs or a slim neckline, and camouflage the bad,' says June, who suggests that anyone not in possession of a full-length mirror should immediately go out and buy one. 'When it comes to buying clothes, the most important thing is the fit,' she stresses. 'Clothes shouldn't be too small, otherwise you'll feel awkward and uncomfortable. What you wear underneath is also important. The right underwear will produce a smooth line on the outside.' Here are some of the typical shape problems and tricks on how to disguise those less-than-perfect parts.

FULLER FIGURES: Keep your silhouette in slimline proportion by avoiding bulky or chunky clothes that may be comfy and cosy but do little to flatter your shape. Instead, opt for figure-skimming clothes. 'The worst mistake a larger person can make is to hide under big baggy clothes,' says June Marsh. 'Instead, they should wear tailored clothes to streamline their figure.' Avoid the sack-of-potatoes effect by not wearing baggy tops together with baggy bottoms, as these will swamp you and make you appear bigger. Dark colours will make you look more streamlined but, as June points out, this doesn't mean you should avoid wearing colour: 'Bright colours and prints can act as a camouflage and draw attention away from your size. When it comes to fabrics, choose clothes in fluid, natural fabrics rather than bulky synthetics. If you're on the larger side, you tend to perspire more easily, therefore, it's wise to avoid synthetic fabrics.'

PEAR-SHAPED: If you're large around the bottom or hips, June Marsh suggests avoiding clothes such as cropped jackets and waisted dresses that draw attention to this area. 'You need to balance your shape by building up your top half,' she explains. 'Choose jackets that have a strong shoulder line rather than a soft one. And if you're wearing trousers, cover your bottom with a jacket, long-length top or loose shirt.'

BIG-BOSOMED: Those with big bosoms should avoid tight, clingy tops, but this doesn't mean hiding your cleavage. June Marsh recommends wearing V-necks or a lower neckline as opposed to a round neckline or high neck, which can make you look bustier. 'Opt for fitted rather than loose jackets, or you will look too matronly. Avoid double-breasted jackets or fussy tops with pockets or frills that draw attention to your bust.'

SMALL-BOSOMED: Lucky you! You can wear all those chiffons, strappy dresses and vest tops without a bra that bigger busted girls can't get away with. To give yourself a cleavage, go for the Wonderbra or silicon-gel pads.

LEGS: Bootleg trousers that flare out at the hem can slim and lengthen the appearance of your legs. If you've got slender legs, you can wear short skirts and dresses, but leave out the micro mini unless you are very young. 'If you've got heavy thighs,' warns June, 'beware of skirt lengths that end at the largest part of your thighs; this will only accentuate their size further.'

PETITE: If you're petite, avoid clothes that swamp you and make you look even smaller. Steer clear of very high heels that will only draw attention to your height. 'Petites have much more choice than those with fuller figures,' says June Marsh. 'They can wear petite, teenage or children's ranges as well as many of today's fashions which are sized so small.'

LARGE HIPS: The secret is to de-emphasize and balance your hips to your proportions. For example, if you wear clothes that give you a nipped-in waist, your hips will look even larger. June Marsh advises wearing A-line styles, shift dresses and clothes that skim the waist rather than accentuate it. 'Avoid clothes that stop on, or flare out from the hip,' advises June. 'Cropped jackets and tops that stop at the waist will also over-emphasize a less-than-slim hip, or a big bottom.'

PODGY STOMACH: According to June Marsh, the trick is to make your stomach as inconspicuous as possible: 'Don't wear tight-fitting tops or belts that will draw attention to it. Wear clothes that cover your stomach, such as waistless shifts, tunics and longer-length jackets, and avoid tight-fitted, bias-cut or pencil skirts.'

FABRICS

Take advantage of the endless choice of exquisite, eye-catching fabrics – velvets, lace, PVC, sparkly Lurex, faux fur – and add richness to your wardrobe. Wear it alone or use one of these fabrics to punctuate an otherwise plain outfit. Interesting textures such as bouclé, chenille, mohair, chiffon and suede will add detail and style to an outfit. A sheer shirt will transform a bland, wool-mix suit into something exotic. Stick a plain, cotton shirt underneath, and it reverts into an ordinary, workaday outfit. In summer, choose from light-textured fabrics such as flyaway chiffons, crochets, slinky, fluid jerseys, crisp linens and opulent-coloured shantung silks. For body-hugging clothes that flatter your figure, look for garments containing Lycra or other fibres that add stretch to even the heaviest fabric.

From geometric patterns to checks, stripes, animal prints, paisley or florals, there is an abundance of prints, from small to big and bold. If you want to wear prints together, juxtapose one printed garment with another by using a colour connection. You'll need a skilled eye, however. To avoid a hotchpotch look, only wear one printed item.

ACCESSORIZE

Accessories dress up an item and give an outfit your stamp of individuality. The trend has gone from the cluttered look to the bare minimum, and back to the more decorative but selective look. Overuse of accessories can make you look like an overdecorated Christmas tree, which can cheapen even the most expensive designer outfit. Then again, an accessory like a low-slung chain belt or brilliantly coloured scarf can add a touch of style; and jewellery can transform day wear into evening wear. Expensive designer accessories – a Gucci belt or Prada bag – are a clever way of instantly upgrading cheaper clothes. Shoes also make a big difference to your appearance. Often it's the shoes that date an outfit quicker than the actual clothes. Tights can make a difference to an outfit. You may want to stick to neutrals and shades that match your clothes but, if you're wearing a plain skirt, textured, patterned or coloured tights can add that decorative touch.

CAPSULE WARDROBE

Invest in a couple of good-quality pieces, such as a classic jacket, that will last season after season. Build up a base of versatile, interchangeable separates. Trousers are an integral part of a modern wardrobe, as are fitted/skinny shirts, and both work well together or with other separates. You'll also need a few simple basics – a little black dress, crisp-white shirt, T-shirt, cardigan, etc. Constantly reassess and reinvent your wardrobe. Take the classic trouser suit you bought two seasons ago. Mix it with the latest-style shirt or top, together with modern boots or shoes, and you've instantly updated a classic item. If you find colour-co-ordinating difficult, your staple wardrobe can be based around neutrals, adding a dash of colour here and there. Whenever you are about to buy an item of clothing, use your fashion intelligence and think what other items in your wardrobe it will work with. It's no good buying a red jacket if you have nothing else to team it with.

MAKE-UP

Do you boldly define your features or only dare tease them with the brush? Regardless of how little or how much make-up you wear, take advantage of cosmetics technology and reinvent yourself.

Make-up should flatter your features, enhance your appearance, camouflage your imperfections and, ultimately, give you the confidence you'd lack if you ventured out with the bare-faced alternative. The last few years have witnessed a mini make-up revolution, with new make-up ranges designed by make-up artists including Françoise Nars and Bobbie Brown, and the opening of make-up boutiques such as MAC and Space NK Apothecary, where every shelf and counter is piled high with rows of lipsticks, powder and blushers. There's also help at hand from the pros: you can purchase videos, CD-ROMs and books that give you a step-by-step guide or, alternatively, attend one of the make-up workshops now on offer from several of the major cosmetic houses, including Estée Lauder, Clinique, Clarins, Prescriptives and The Body Shop. And don't forget the fashion and beauty magazines: they are the cardinal way to keep up with the latest trends and product launches. Once you have read this chapter and gleaned the experts' advice, prepare yourself for a total make-up rethink.

A MODEL MAKE-OVER

Top make-up artist Maggie Hunt, who has made up such famous names as Cindy Crawford, Naomi Campbell, Niki Taylor, Lisa B and Yasmin Le Bon has devised a step-by-step guide to model make-up. Maggie believes in using brushes for almost every stage and has, therefore, created her own set of 11 brushes shaped from the finest pony, kolinsky and sable hair, which are a favourite with models and make-up artists alike. If you want to apply make-up like a model and look like a model, follow Maggie's guide, which includes many of her insider's secrets and tips.

BASE

Choose a cream foundation that is the same tone as your face. Apply evenly with a sponge so that it appears like skin, not a mask.

CONCEALER

Using a brush that is of a similar shape to a lip brush but softly pointed, disguise blemishes with concealer or foundation until they've softened or disappeared. To eliminate shadows, look straight in the mirror and paint on a light-coloured concealer or a lighter foundation than the one you use on the rest of your face. Start from the corner under the eye, along the dark shadow. Blend with the same brush and, if necessary, pat lightly with your little finger. Lower eyelids and brush an even coat of light base all over the eye zone, especially those hollows on the side of the nose. Blend.

POWDER

Before foundation has had a chance to set, powder lightly using a translucent powder applied with a powder sponge or Velcro powder puff.

FACE SHAPING

Using semi-matt bronzing powder or brown eyeshadow (mid brown for

white skin and dark brown for skin) with a brush that is slightly smaller than a blusher brush, you can contour your face. If your face is too round, suck in your cheeks, and apply in the hollows, blending backwards towards the ears. Soften a high forehead with a sweep of powder around the hairline. To narrow a wide nose, brush down either side, and to shorten the length, brush a touch on the tip of the nose.

EYES

STEP 1 – Using a spade-shaped brush (the largest of all eyeshadow brushes), and an ivory eyeshadow, sweep all over the eye area, from lashes to eyebrows, including hollows.

STEP 2 – Using a contour brush (slightly smaller than your first eyeshadow brush) give eyes shape and depth when using a semi-matt brown eye-shadow. Create

definition in the eye socket with light, steady, back-and-forth movements (avoid the ivory brow-bone area and an oval-shaped area on the inner eyelid). Gradually work upwards towards the brows. Apply the brown eyeshadow under the lower lashes and to the outer corner of eyelids only, sweeping upwards and outwards towards the temples (but no further than where your eyebrow ends) until the shadow blends imperceptibly into the skin tone.

STEP 3 – Now for a hint – just a hint – of colour on the eyelid. Pick an eyeshadow in the colour and texture of your choice, and with a pointed, spade-like brush apply to the inner half of the eyelid, below

the crease. This lid colour should not extend more than two-thirds of the way towards the outer edge of the eyelid.

STEP 4 – Using a tiny, spade-shaped brush, define the outer third of the eyelid with a dark brown matt eyeshadow in a half-diamond shape (>) below the socket. Smudge gently into the shadows applied.

STEP 5 – With a pencil, start at the inner corner with a very thin line, getting thicker at the centre of the eye and lifting up towards the outer corner. Then, starting where the lashes begin naturally, draw underneath lower lashes. Soften with a brush. If you prefer to, use cake or liquid liner, using a small pointed brush.

STEP 6 – Apply mascara to both sides of the upper lashes. Mascara on the lower lashes smudges easily, so it's best to avoid it. After applying, use an eyelash brush to avoid clogged lashes.

BROWS

Using the same brush as in Step 5, define brows by applying eyebrow powder or eyeshadow as close to your natural eyebrow colour as possible. Comb eyebrows into shape.

BLUSH

Now smile. Then, using a blusher brush, blush the upper part of the cheekbone which will be clearly defined by that smile. Begin your sweep of blush no further in than the centre of the eye, stroking along the cheek towards the ear and hairline.

LIPS

Enhance the shape of your lips with a lip pencil. Then coat your lip brush with your chosen lipstick, gloss or both, and apply smoothly to lips.

UPDATE YOUR MAKE-UP

With catwalk-inspired make-up trends – purple eyebrows, citrus-orange lips or bruised eyes that look as if you've been in the ring with Mike Tyson – it's no wonder most of us stick to the same old shade year in, year out. But as top make-up artist Mary Greenwell points out: 'You need to update your make-up not just for the colour, but for the texture, too.' Take Mary's advice by trying out new textures, brushing up on techniques, and flirting with different shades. You'll be delighted when you find that eyeliner you'd only ever contemplated buying, gives you those cat-like, Evangelista eyes.

Don't get caught in the make-up time warp by using those same old three, six or eight products you've had for donkey's years. 'Every few months re-evaluate your make-up,' says leading make-up artist Ruby Hammer. 'Then update it by adding a couple of new items. If you want to give your make-up that modern edge, but don't have the type of skin to be able to get away with the latest sheer bases, add a touch of shimmer to your lips or eyes.'

COLOUR CRAZY

Fashion's infatuation with colour extends to make-up. There is now a kaleidoscope of colours ranging from candy shades and acid brights to pale pastels. 'Colour make-up is a refreshing alternative to neutrals, but if you don't apply it correctly, you can end up looking like a clown,' points out top make-up artist Arianne Poole. 'Diffuse colour eyeshadow by using beige or taupe as a base. Then, add just a light wash of a shade such as lilac, lavender, powder blue, rose, soft gold, or apricot to the lid. To avoid overkill and to counter-balance, keep lips pared down by wearing sheer-textured, rather than opaque colour. Chocolate-browns and plum colours work well as long as they are kept sheer.'

FROM DAY TO EVENING MAKE-UP

Ruby Hammer points out why it is a myth that you need different palettes for day and evening. 'You can still use the same colour, just more of it. If you're going out straight from work, the idea is to repair and polish up your make-up rather than start from scratch. Add a touch more eye colour and blusher. If you've been wearing mascara, brush eyelashes to de-clog, then reapply. This way you won't have the hassle of removing all your eye make-up. A couple of eye drops will help tired eyes

look brighter. For lips, add more colour and a slick of gloss or a touch of shimmer.'

CHEAP OR COSTLY

You don't need to spend a fortune on items of make-up to look good. Make-up guru Stephen Glass is an authority on make-up and uses 20–25 brands ranging from the cheapest to the most expensive. 'If it works for you, then use it regardless of price,' says Stephen. However, most make-up artists agree that it's worth investing in a good base. When going for more daring colours, experiment with the cheaper brands to make sure the colour suits you before diving straight in at the pricier end.

WATERPROOF MAKE-UP

Waterproof make-up has come on in leaps and bounds since the very first waterproof mascara. When purchasing waterproof make-up, bear in mind that there is a difference between waterproof and water-resistant. While the latter performs well in humid conditions it cannot, unlike the former, withstand a good cry or a deep-sea dive. After use, it's important to remove waterproof make-up thoroughly with specially formulated products.

SEMI-PERMANENT MAKE-UP

A method that tattoos the skin by using a coloured pigment. If you're fed up with having to keep drawing that same old under-eye line day in, day out, then semi-permanent make-up may be for you. If you are interested in having semi-permanent make-up, go to a qualified practitioner *not* a beauty therapist.

CASTING MAKE-UP

Mary Greenwell's advice to high-fashion models is to go to castings bare-faced: 'Models can still look great with clean, shiny hair and fashionable clothes.' If you have to, add a touch of mascara, a tiny amount of blusher and lip gloss, but wear nothing on your skin. For other models and models going on castings which involve a screen test, Ruby Hammer suggests wearing a sheer base, concealer, blusher, lipstick and basic eye make-up. 'Define eyes with mascara and keep lips in a neutral colour so you look natural, but not entirely washed out.'

NEUTRALS/BARELY-THERE

Neutrals flatter almost anyone and give a fresh, healthy look without appearing as if you've tried too hard. For the barely-there look, which is so subtle few people will realize you're wearing any make-up, opt for the paler end of the spectrum. For more definition, choose deeper tones. Arianne Poole explains how to wear neutrals. 'For eye colours, choose from the nude shades of champagnes, beiges and taupes to the deeper tones of russets and chocolate browns. Good neutral colours for lips are beigey-rose and terracotta. You can use stronger shades such as chocolate browns or plummy tones as long as they are sheer. Older women, in particular grey-haired, should use a coral, soft-red or a pinkier lipstick to prevent them looking drained. Bronzing powder makes a great blusher for the natural look; otherwise go for pinky-brown, apricot-brown or red-brown. Keep your base sheer, add a little clear or brown mascara and eyeliner if you wish, but no harsh lines.'

MAKE-UP FOR MEN

Believe it or not, men are dipping into women's make-up bags, not just for spot cream, but for foundation, concealer, bronzing powder and even mascara! For all you guys who want to enhance your features – go for it. But a word of warning. The aim is for no one to know you are actually wearing the stuff. This means carefully matching your base and concealer to your skin tone, and very clever application indeed.

MAKE-UP
PERFECT BASE

A thickly applied base that makes you want to reach for the chisel is passé. These days less is more. Aim for minimal coverage that evens out the skin tone but still looks natural and allows your skin to show through; hence the popularity of the barely-there look and the sheer, dewy complexions both on and off the catwalks. This means wearing a light base, ideally a sheer formulation, light-reflective foundation or tinted moisturizer, with little or no powder. For an ultra-natural look, do away with base, applying concealer to blemishes or under eyes.

Colour correctives are colour tints in shades of green, purple, yellow and white which will tone down and even out your skin tone if you have particularly high colour or are battling with blushing. Colour correctives do, however, need to be worn under a foundation or tinted moisturizer, which can make for a rather thick base.

Foundation comes in liquid, powder, mousse, cake, stick or cream form. Choose a formulation that suits your skin type and lifestyle, and pick a shade that matches your skin tone, not one that is darker or lighter. However, you may want a lighter shade if you are using foundation as an under-eye concealer. If you want a sun-kissed effect, use self-tanning cream as opposed to a darker shade of foundation. Test foundation on your face rather than your hand, and always check it in natural daylight before purchasing it. Apply sparingly with a damp sponge, patting on and blending in circular movements for a smooth, even finish. To hide any tell-tale signs, blend it under your jaw line.

Concealer is used to cover spots, blemishes and thread veins, or to disguise dark shadows around the eyes and on the sides of the nose. You may want to use a slightly lighter shade than your own skin tone. For concealing scars, Arianne Poole suggests using a waterproof concealer. When using concealer under your eyes, apply with a sponge or brush before foundation. To cover spots, thread veins or to fill in lines, apply with a brush and set with powder. But as Stephen Glass explains: 'Avoid filling in lines in the mobile areas of your face, otherwise, when you start talking or smiling, the concealer will start collecting, and the lines will look even more noticeable.'

Powder comes in different forms: loose, compact and gel based. Nowadays, many powders are made without talc and are, therefore, less drying. Go easy. A light dusting to areas such as forehead, nose and chin is often all you need. Remember, the more powder you apply, the more matt your face will appear. Translucent powders are good as they don't add colour to your face. If it's a healthy glow you desire, use a bronzing powder sparingly.

BLUSH BABY

Blusher can lift the whole face, but it should be applied sparingly, otherwise you could end up looking like a painted doll. For a healthy bloom, Arianne Poole suggests applying a small amount of blusher to the apple of your cheeks. To give your face that sculptured look, she advises sweeping the blusher slightly under your cheekbones out towards your hairline, blending well. If you over-apply, Arianne recommends toning down with translucent powder rather than rubbing or having to remove your make-up. Bronzing powder makes a good alternative to blusher. To find your natural colour do the natural blusher test and pinch your cheeks. Now choose a blusher that is closest to this colour.

BRIGHT EYES

The purpose of eye make-up is to emphasize and draw attention to your eyes, not the make-up. For longer-lasting eye colour, apply foundation or concealer before eyeshadow. When applying eye make-up remember to use brushes and blend, blend, blend. See Maggie Hunt's model make-up for advice on which brush to use where.

Eyeshadow now comes in all the colours of the rainbow and in different textures: shimmering, pearlized, semi-matt and matt. Pick the right texture for the type of make-up; matt is probably more suited to daytime, while shimmering or pearlized looks great for evening and party time. Pale shades, such as ivory, can be used to highlight the brow bone. When using strong eye colours, your lip and cheek colours should be pared down.

Eyeliners come in different forms: pencil, liquid, powder or cake. Pencil gives a softer effect, whereas liquid pens and liners result in a bolder effect. You can wear eyeliner either on your upper or lower lashlines, or both. To soften a hard line use a brush, pointed cotton bud or eyeshadow over the line. For a more natural look, smudge brown eyeshadow close to the lashline. To give the appearance of thicker lashes, without having to draw an obvious line, the trick is to apply small dots of eyeliner (preferably liquid pen liner) along the lash line as close to your lashes as possible.

Eyebrows frame the eyes, so it's important to shape them carefully. Only pluck eyebrows from beneath. To add definition, use a brow pencil or, for a softer effect, brown eyeshadow or eyebrow powder. For darker, bolder brows, consider having them tinted. To keep eyebrows in place, brush with clear mascara, eyebrow mousse or Vaseline.

LUSCIOUS LASHES

Models would never be without their Tweezerman eyelash curlers. For sensuous lashes that draw attention to your eyes and open them up, curl top lashes. Squeeze for a couple of seconds, but do take care or you could end up with no lashes! Never curl lashes once you have applied your mascara; they will stick to the rubber and could be pulled out. If you don't want to wear any mascara, hold the curl fixed with a coat of Vaseline or clear mascara.

Mascara comes in black, brown, navy, bright-coloured or clear forms. Unless you have very dark hair and eyebrows, opt for brown, dark brown or nearly black, as black can look too hard. Save crazy colours for parties. Apply to top lashes and only sparingly, if at all, to bottom lashes. Always brush lashes with an eyelash separator before the mascara dries. For thick, long lashes use lash builders before you apply mascara.

False eyelashes can transform even the dullest eyes into a seductive gaze. You can now buy very fine lashes that don't look false at all. If you don't like the idea of complete falsies, there are individual lashes that, applied to the outer corner of your eyes, can look incredibly sexy.

PERFECT POUT

A slick of lip colour brightens up even the plainest face. Plum, cappuccino, aubergine, damson: there are an infinite number of shades available that sound good enough to eat. Choose shades that complement your skin tone: berry-browns, beigey-neutrals, plummy-reds, pinky-browns and terracotta look good, regardless of skin tone. Lipsticks come in different finishes. For shiny lips, pick a glossy formulation, for dense colour without shine, a matt lipstick, and for a more subtle look, a sheer finish. The beauty of lip colour is that you can easily mix lipsticks to create your very own shade. When buying a new lipstick, always test it on your lips – not your hand. With the new, longer-lasting lipsticks that stain the lips, colour is locked in for hours. However, as they can be quite drying and dense in colour, Arianne Poole suggests using a fixative.

Before applying any form of lip colour, prime lips first. Ruby Hammer suggests applying balm then using a child's toothbrush to scrape away dry skin; this will also help plump up lips. Now add lip balm. Lip pencils make a good base and help prevent lipstick from bleeding. If you use a lipliner, avoid ending up with that unsightly, dark, obvious line by finding a shade that matches your lipstick. Apply lipstick with a brush. For that barely-there look, colour lips with a lipliner then apply gloss. Alternatively, add a little lipstick to your gloss to dilute the colour. With the emphasis on full, sensuous mouths, Arianne Poole has the trick for making your lips look fuller: 'Apply a fixative all over lips. Then, with a pinky-brown lip pencil, draw slightly outside the line. After filling in lips with lip colour, add slick of gloss to the centre of your lips.'

HAIR

Today's hair philosophy is about wash 'n' go – easy to care for, effortless hair that looks fabulous yet only takes minutes to style. Bad hair days are now a thing of the past!

A daring new haircut or dramatic change of colour is by far the most spectacular way to reinvent yourself. Models know that if they want to continue to grab the limelight, they must succumb to the stylists' scissors and the colourists' palettes. Nineties hair is about healthy-looking tresses that are cut well and styled with minimum fuss. It's also about finding a modern, individual look that suits your face shape as well as your lifestyle. 'Choose a style that makes you look and feel great,' says Sam McKnight, who is one of the world's leading session stylists. 'Take care of your hair and make it look as though you take care of it. But this doesn't mean you need to spend hours styling it – 20 minutes is ample.' The good news is that today's hairstyles are freer and easier to achieve. With colour, cut, styling aids and a pinch of creativity, you have a whole range of looks at your fingertips.

MODELS' HAIR-CARE KIT

Models' hair is covered in gunge every day, and, during showtime, often several times a day. Therefore, when they are away from the runway models need the right products to care for their hair. Sam McKnight suggests that the following items should be in every model's hair kit: a light-weight, non-detergent shampoo for frequent washing; a detangler rather than a normal conditioner; a deep-conditioning mask; a soft, natural-bristle hairbrush; a wide-toothed comb.

HAIR CARE

Beautiful hair is thick, glossy hair that has body and bounce – but how do you achieve it? A great hairstyle begins with healthy, well-cared-for hair. Dry, damaged, lacklustre hair will not only spoil your hairstyle, it will let down your whole appearance. Hair is constantly subjected to a hammering from chemical processes, as well as styling aids, heated appliances, sun, poor diet and ill health, so you'll need to counteract this by protecting your hair as much as possible from these offenders and restoring its condition.

Models often have their hair restyled several times a day. But because they care for their hair, it remains glossy and luxuriant. If you want the sort of hair that shines, has natural bounce and attracts attention, have your hair trimmed regularly, protect it from the sun and heated appliances, and always use a conditioner. According to Anthony

Mascola, the man behind the famous Tony & Guy salons, cut is a priority. 'A short hairstyle usually starts to go out of shape after four to six weeks. I suggest people have it cut as soon as it starts to play up. Long hair can last a couple of months, but in order to keep it healthy I recommend having it cut every four to six weeks.'

One of the best hair nourishers is to eat a good, balanced diet. Supplements that can be beneficial to the condition of your hair include cod-liver oil, as well as vitamins C, E and B complex.

Ignore the myth that brushing you hair 100 times a day will improve its condition. It won't. Over-brushing can damage the hair shaft. 'You wouldn't brush a wool jumper every day – it would wear it out,' stresses Philip Kingsley, leading trichologist and author of *Hair: an owners handbook*.

WASH 'N' GO

Philip Kingsley believes that for a healthy head of hair you should wash your hair daily, but only shampoo once. 'You wouldn't go days without washing your body now would you?' quips Philip. Over-washing with harsh, detergent shampoos can strip out more lustre from your locks than any intensive conditioner can ever attempt to replace, so use a gentle, non-detergent shampoo that is right for your hair type. If you have oily roots but dry ends, a product for oily hair types will only dry out the ends further. Instead, shampoo using a rebalancing or gentle product, then condition the ends separately.

If your hair is fine or you want extra body, you may want to take advantage of the volumizing shampoos. When it comes to the two-in-one combined shampoos and conditioners, listen to Philip Kingsley and avoid them at all costs. You should not be conditioning your roots, nor shampooing the ends of the hair. If you're in a hurry, opt for a leave-in conditioner instead. Avoid using harsh, anti-dandruff shampoos too often. Instead, choose products with natural anti-dandruff ingredients such as tea tree oil. If you have a continual scalp problem, consult a trichologist.

When shampooing, spend time massaging it into your scalp, which will step up blood flow and, in turn, nourish the roots. Always rinse thoroughly to ensure you remove all traces of shampoo and conditioner. Give hair a final rinse with cold water for extra shine, or mineral water to soften hair.

CONDITION

It's a well-documented fact that the moment hair emerges from the scalp it is dead. However, the condition and the moisture level of hair can be improved by using products containing ingredients which penetrate the hair, so as Philip Kingsley points out: 'Conditioner is vital.' If you have split ends, the only solution is to have your hair trimmed: no product can actually mend them, only temporarily seal the ends by binding them together. Apply conditioner every time you wash your hair. Spend time massaging it into the ends, then gently ease a wide-toothed comb, not a brush, through your hair, working from the ends upwards and taking care not to tug or pull. Treat coloured and permed hair once a week with an intensive conditioner or hair mask. Virgin (untreated) hair, only needs a treatment once a month.

DRY AND STYLE

Before blow-drying or using other heated appliances, protect your hair with a spray-on solution. When blow-drying, switch your hairdryer to the coolest setting and hold it at least 12 inches away from hair. Keep the hairdryer moving, directing the air down to avoid frizziness. Be careful not to over-dry or hair will become brittle. Before you style your hair, rough dry by either finger-drying, dabbing with a towel or blow-drying until hair is about three-quarters dry. Only at this stage should you reach for the styling brush. Rather than weakening your hair with lethal weapons such as heated rollers, tongs, hot-brushes and straightening irons, opt for Velcro rollers or a rounded brush to straighten, add volume or curl. Teasing and backcombing can cause damage. Use a brush, which is gentler than a comb.

STYLING PRODUCTS

The days when styling products turned hair as stiff as cardboard are long gone. 'Hair-product technology has changed dramatically,' says Sam McKnight. 'Nowadays we have easy-to-use components which, while still holding the style in place, also care for your hair by protecting and conditioning.' When testing his signature range of nine styling products, Sam McKnight had the best possible guinea pigs – the supermodels. Today you'll find most supermodels have at least one of his products in their tote bags. When styling hair, Sam often mixes products to get the right texture. 'You can mix gel and mousse to get the exact effect

you want,' explains Sam. When applying a styling product, only use a little at a time; if you overdo it, you'll end up having to wash it out. Instant-shine sprays and serums coat the hair shaft so it lies flat, therefore reflecting light and leaving your hair with a natural-looking sheen. But, as Colin Gold advises, go easy on these: overuse can make hair look lank. His tip is to rub a little bit of serum in the palm of your hand, then coat the hair.

QUICK FIX

If you only have a matter of minutes to transform unwashed hair into a crowning glory, Colin Gold has the answer: 'Spritz hair with styling lotion, turn you hair upside down and blast with the hairdryer. If you have short hair you can always slick it back, or scrape it back into a pony tail if it's long.'

HOLIDAY HAIR CARE

Sun, sand, sea salt and chlorine all contribute to dry, brittle hair that leaves it even more vulnerable to everyday wear and tear. And if your hair is coloured, this combination could be disastrous: you could arrive home with green- or purple-tinged hair to complement your tan. To avoid this risk, protect hair with a gel or cream containing a sunscreen. Alternatively, keep it under a hat. Avoid using lemon juice to lighten your hair in the sun, as the acid can damage your hair.

COLOUR

Colour is your hair's most important cosmetic. Unless you're lucky enough to be a brilliant blonde, have velvet-like, raven hair or are a natural redhead, hair without colour is like a face without make-up. Colour also adds body to fine or limp hair and depth to dull hair. Ultimately, changing your hair colour is a great way of revamping your look without having to alter the length or style of your hair.

'The supermodels have helped turn hair colour into a fashion accessory,' says leading colourist, Jo Hansford, who has coloured many a supermodel's head of hair. But before Jo colours hair she takes each client's skin tone, eye colour and lifestyle into consideration. 'You must be aware of the upkeep and cost involved in colouring hair,' stresses Jo. For those who want to take the plunge for the first time, but don't want too drastic a result, Jo has the answer. 'Going one or two shades lighter or darker than your natural hair colour will give the most natural-looking results. You'll also find the regrowth is less obvious. And rather than a solid tint, plump for highlights or a tone.' For the best results, to avoid the risk of damage, always have your hair coloured by a professional and, if possible, a colourist rather than a general stylist.

Colour maintenance: Maintain colour by using colour-enhancing or colour-maintenance shampoos. Between salon visits, to make roots less noticeable, Jo advises using vegetable colours. Unfortunately, there is no such solution for those who lighten their hair. But don't fret, Jo has a great tip. 'In-between salon visits, put a little bit of dry-shampoo powder along your parting and dust off any excess. This will defuse the darkness of the roots.'

Blonde: With shades ranging from shimmering platinum to pale mink, blondes have more fun. If you want to go lighter you can opt for fine highlights, bold streaks or chunks of colour rather than solid tints where, unless you are already quite fair, root growth quickly becomes noticeable. Blonde hair suits most skin tones, although if you have olive or dark skin, avoid the lighter shades. If you want your hair still to look shiny, remember: the deeper the shade of blonde, the glossier the hair will appear.

Brunette: Rich shades of brown, such as deep mahogany, plum, chestnut or hints of hazelnut can enliven even the dullest head of brown hair.

Raven: Daringly striking and guaranteed to make an entrance, raven hair is suitable for the palest to the darkest skin tones. Raven-coloured hair looks fantastic on sleek, glossy hair and is particularly devastating with blue eyes. But before rushing to your salon, be aware that not only can it look very hard, but it has a habit of highlighting any imperfections on your skin. You'll also find you may look washed out without make-up.

Redhead: Whether you want to look like a flame haired temptress, crave a carrot-coloured mop or auburn tones, shades of red will make heads turn. Russet, auburn, plum, carrot, copper, ginger – there are many different shades to choose from.

DIFFERENT TYPES OF DYE
Colour mousses are perfect for an instant change.
Colour-enhancing shampoos enrich your own natural hair colour by coating the hair cuticle.
Wash-in wash-outs add subtle tones and shades that last a couple of washes. Great for adding warm tones to brown hair.

Tone-on-tones contain low levels of peroxide and are suitable if you want to enhance your own colour or add a richer shade.
Vegetable dyes are a gentle way of dyeing the hair and can also deepen or enrich the colour.
Semi-permanent is colour that lasts up to six washes. Won't lighten hair.
Permanent colours contain peroxide and do not wash out.
Highlights use permanent tint to lighten hair. Highlights are either woven through ultra-fine sections of the hair for a subtle effect, or applied in chunky slices for more noticeable results.
Lowlights use the same method as highlights but use darker colours, such as golden-browns and reds rather than blonde.

YOUR HAIRDRESSER
Good communication with your hairdresser is the key to getting a great hairstyle and avoiding those all-too-often salon disasters. Utilize your hairdresser's expertise. He or she will be more than happy to advise you on various styles that would suit you, and different ways to wear you hair. Hairdressers agree that a picture is the best way to give a clear idea of the style you want. But as Anthony Mascola points out, 'If you arrive clutching a photo of your favourite model or celebrity, don't expect your hair to turn out exactly the same. If you have a strong idea, a photograph is very helpful. But you must bear in mind that even the top stylists cannot alter the fact that your hair is probably a different texture to the hair in the picture.'

CHOOSING THE RIGHT HAIRSTYLE
A new hairstyle can be a fantastic boost to your confidence – even if it's only a simple change. 'Today's cuts are more individual rather than just carbon copies of one or two styles,' says Anthony Mascola. Take a good look at your hair – how does the style affect your overall look? Your hair should balance your proportions. If you are short with a large head, a bouffant hairstyle will do little but emphasize your lack of height and shape of head even more. Face shape and texture of hair are also important when choosing a hairstyle. Use your hair to conceal imperfections such as sticking-out ears or a large forehead. And if you want to maintain that just-stepped-out-of-the-salon look, choose a style that requires minimal upkeep which you can easily recreate at home. Once you have found a

style you like, Sam McKnight suggests wearing it in different ways. 'You can wear it up, use styling products to give it a different texture, add an accessory like a rose, or simply change the parting.'

HAIRDOS

LONG TRESSES

Long hair undoubtedly has the most mileage. Wear it long and sleek, sweep it up in a topknot, curl or crimp it or, for that just-got-out-of-bed look, tease and tousle it. Unless it's waist-length or poker straight, hair that is all one length can often drag a face down. Layering and chopping around the front is softer and, therefore, flattering to most face shapes. It also adds individual style and versatility to your hair. Get your hairdresser to start at the level most flattering to your face shape – fringe length, eye-level or chin level, for example. Hair worn up has never been so popular or so stylish as today – wear it tousled and dishevelled or neat and tidy. If you want what Colin Gold calls a naturally sexy hairstyle, do the following: 'Sexy hair is the type of peep-through hair that falls onto the face or over the eyes. Make sure your hair is in beautiful condition, then wear it slightly undone.'

THE CROP

If you have never worn your hair short, you are probably worried that without a mass of hair to hide behind you are exposing your face to the world. But short hair is the easiest style to handle, and can look the most striking of all. Choose from a variety of styles and shapes: short and sharp, geometrical, soft and layered. For a change, wear short hair slicked back with gel or pomade, smoothing it back off your face.

MODERN BOB

The nineties version of the bob is a longish bob with a modern twist that is more about shape and softness than hard-to-wear geometric cuts. The bob comes in varying lengths: jaw-length, shoulder-length or somewhere in between. Think of Helena Christensen's hair before she had the chop, and Liz Hurley's soft and loose style. This graduated bob is easy to wear and flattering to all ages. You can wear it layered or you may want to keep it all one length in a blunt cut. For a change, curl your hair or use a hotbrush to flick out the ends.

THE BANG

There's the long fringe that falls into your eyes, the short fringe cut halfway up your forehead, the heavy or the feathered fringe. Growing out a fringe can be a real nuisance, so before you take the plunge be sure it will suit you. If you are just toying with the idea, you could always try a fringe hairpiece.

PERMING

You may want to do away with the hassle of curling your hair and go for the permanent solution. Charles Worthington suggests that, before committing yourself, you try experimenting with curling tongs or bendy sticks to see if curly hair suits your face shape. 'Thanks to modern technology, today's perms are much more gentle and will not compromise the condition of the hair, even if it's fine and relatively fragile,' says Charles.

WIGS/HAIRPIECES/EXTENSIONS

Always fancied long, flowing tresses or wished you could be blonde for the day? For a total change, without affecting you own head of hair, try a wig or add streaks of colour by just pinning in hairpieces. To give the impression of long hair, add a false bun or pony tail to short hair. Hair extensions, which are bonded or woven into the hair, look completely natural and are suitable for adding length or fullness to most types of hair. If you don't want permanent extensions, there are now clip-on extensions, which means you can wear them for a party, then remove them before you go to bed.

STRAIGHTENING

There are different methods of temporarily or permanently straightening hair. For sleek hair, rough-dry hair until it is 80 per cent dry, then spritz with styling lotion. With a circular brush, blow-dry sections of hair straight. If you want poker-straight hair, you can always use straightening irons after blow-drying. Do not use these too often, however, as they will damage the hair. The more permanent solution is to have your hair chemically straightened at a salon. Just like perming, hair-straightening rearranges the hair's structure so it lies straight. Relaxing is a form of straightening used for Afro hair.

CURLS AND WAVES

Cherub curls, soft waves, unruly curls, corkscrew or ringlets – curls and waves are making a comeback. For a head of waves, kink with waving irons or plait hair before you go to bed. Another interesting way to wear your hair is to crimp it with crimping irons. If you already have slightly wavy or curly hair, you can create a tighter wave or curl by applying mousse or styling lotion then, using a diffuser attachment on your hairdryer, scrunch hair with your hand while drying it.

CHARLES WORTHINGTON'S GUIDE TO CURL

The type of curl you want to achieve will determine the tools you use. Here, leading hairdresser Charles Worthington, recently voted British hairdresser of the year, has a simple guide.

Using rollers: Rollers can create soft curls for a really glamorous look. Generally, the smaller the roller, the more defined the curl. Roll each section under. Only remove the rollers once hair is completely dry. If you have too much curl, gently comb your fingers through your hair, then spritz with hairspray.
Using pin curls: Divide hair into one-inch sections. Place two fingers against the scalp, then wind each section around them, beginning at the root and tucking in ends. Slide fingers out and secure with a clip. When dry, remove the clips and shake out.
Using bendy sticks: Divide hair into one-inch sections, then take a bendy stick, place it next to the scalp and wind hair around it. Fold ends to secure. When hair is completely dry, unravel and separate hair with fingers.

General tips on curling hair:
*   **Insert** rollers into blow-dried hair while it is still warm, that way you get maximum root lift.
*   **Before** putting rollers in, spritz each section with styling spray.
*   **Ensure** hair is completely dry before taking rollers out, supporting the curl at the root to prevent tugging.
*   **Curly** hair shouldn't be handled excessively. Avoid using a hairbrush; simply rake fingers through the hair to style it instead.

ORLANDO PITA'S 'UPDO'

He invented the 'Updo', he's Madonna's favourite hair stylist, he hasn't shampooed his hair for a decade and he's artistic director for John Frieda – you've guessed it, it's Orlando Pita. The man behind today's catwalk hair has devised a step-by-step guide so you, too, can sport the look.

'One of the most versatile looks to emerge from the catwalks and transcend the seasons is the relaxed and informal topknot – it not only looks great but is actually quite easy to do yourself.
• The aim is to create a look of spontaneity. Start by gently combing the hair through with a wide-toothed comb, then pull it all back off the face and make a sleek pony tail near the top of the head. Secure this lightly with a covered band. Give the pony tail a perfect smooth, shiny finish and eliminate any stray hairs by smoothing over a light coat of hair serum.
• Next pull roughly three-quarters of the pony tail back up through the band, creating a loop at the back, and secure this with an extra twist of the band. Wrap the remaining part of the pony tail once around the band to cover it, and pin in place.
• Then take the last remaining ends of the original pony tail and dress with a wax to create a separated, spiky, almost feathered effect. These short spikes can then be pinned randomly around the wrapped section, so that they stick up to create a sort of crown. Finish off with some modelling spray to hold in place and add a final gloss.'

NICKY CLARKE'S VOLUME

Whether big hair is in or out, unless the hairstyle means wearing hair close to the head, most of us want body at the roots. Here, hair maestro Nicky Clarke gives his tips for creating volume.

'To create height when blow-drying, tip your head upside down or sweep hair in the opposite direction from where it lies naturally, directing heat at the roots and shaping with a large, round, bristle brush. For amazing volume, wait until your hair is about 80 per cent dry, wind a few large Velcro rollers onto the crown, spray with volumizing lotion (which coats the hair with a fine film of polymers to make it thicker) and dry on a medium heat. Leave for ten minutes, remove rollers and tease into place. Remember always to make sure that your hair is 100 per cent dry before going outside; hair will drop if it's the slightest bit damp. The actual haircut is also important – layering can give your hair instant volume if done well.'

SKIN CARE

We are all searching for the perfect beauty elixir. With the help of a little hocus-pocus from leading skin-care specialists, this chapter aims to help you achieve perfect skin.

SKIN CARE

Faced with a plethora of skin-care products, it's difficult to know which way to turn. Alpha-hydroxy acids (AHAs), ceramides, enzymes and other state-of-the-art ingredients claim to repair, rejuvenate and replenish. But there's no point slathering on copious amounts of potions, lotions and age-defying creams if you neglect your skin, eat junk food and puff on cigarettes all day. Susan Harmsworth, MD of aromatherapy- based company E'SPA, which runs clinics throughout the world, is concerned about the amount of people mistreating their skin: 'Its amazing how many people, including models, are still ignorant of basic skin care, or are just doing far too much to their skin.' So before you rush out and buy new products, educate yourself on skin care and understand your skin's needs, and you will be over halfway to achieving beautiful skin.

SKIN TYPES

Your skin is affected by factors such as climate, pollution, sun, stress, emotions and hormones and is, therefore, constantly changing 'type'. Even if your skin is normal for most of the year, you may find it becomes dryer during the cold winter months. Leading skin-care consultant, Eve Lom, believes that skin rarely falls into one type and, because of this she stresses that we should constantly review our skin: 'Be your own physician and assess your skin. If you need help, go to a qualified beautician rather than taking advice from cosmetic-counter staff, who are sales people, not skin-care specialists.'

As children, most of us have normal skin – smooth, clear, often porcelain-like with tiny pores. But once we hit puberty all hell breaks loose: our skin loses its natural balance and becomes dry, oily, spotty, congested or sensitive – or a combination of the lot. If you are one of the small minority who've been blessed with normal skin, don't be tempted to neglect it: it can quickly turn dry, sensitive or congested if it's depleted of moisture or not cleansed thoroughly.

If your skin isn't quite as smooth or as flawless as a baby's bottom, here are the most common skin types, together with advice on how to care for each type's particular needs.

DRY SKIN

Susceptible to the signs of ageing, if your skin is dry, it needs constant nourishing and protecting to prevent premature lines. Dry skin may feel tight and rough to touch or, in more extreme cases, the skin may actually flake or peel. As water can dehydrate skin, thick, wipe-off cleansing creams, rich lotions or milks are preferable to facial washes or cleansing bars. Soap is a definite no-no. Use a rich moisturizer to replace natural oils and, for a smoother appearance, slough away dead surface cells with a gentle exfoliant. Special treatment oils, vitamin E oil and hydrating masks can also help dry skin retain moisture. When skin is dry you should replenish from the inside by having plenty of olive oil on salads, eating oily fish regularly, drinking lots of water and, if necessary, taking supplements that are rich in gamma linolenic acid (GLA), such as evening primrose oil or starflower oil.

OILY SKIN

You've probably been told that your skin won't age as fast as those with normal or dry skin. It's true. When skin is oily, the oil acts as a natural moisturizer. But this is no consolation when you've a face as greasy as a chip pan. Due to fluctuating hormone levels that occur during teenage years, oily skin is often one of the downfalls of adolescence. Because the sebaceous glands are over-active, the excess sebum blocks the pores, making the skin more prone to spots and blackheads. Avoid the temptation to use harsh, medicated, detergent or strong, alcohol-based products, as they strip the skin's acid mantle and can, when overused, make the sebaceous glands work even harder, thus producing more oil. Instead, choose gentle products that aim to normalize oil production through balance, not dehydration. Many medicated products now come in gentler formulations for sensitive skin and are less likely to over-dry your skin.

Cleanse with a gel, facial wash or a light cleansing lotion rather than a rich, oil-based cleanser. Oily skin should not need moisturizing. However, if you feel certain areas need it, apply a light, oil-free, non-comedogenic moisturizer, avoiding the oily T-zone (forehead, nose and chin) completely. Any cosmetics you use, such as foundation, should also be oil-free and non-comedogenic. Control oil and prevent shine by dabbing on an oil-absorbing lotion. Those with oily skin should steer clear of fatty or sugary foods, drink plenty of water, and eat a diet rich in vitamin B. (See also acne section on p.132).

COMBINATION SKIN

Many people have combination skin, with an oily chin, nose and forehead, together with normal skin or dry patches on the cheeks and around the eye area. The aim is to restore the pH balance (the skin's acid mantle) by using gentle balancing products. Where skin is oily, avoid using moisturizer.

SENSITIVE SKIN

Sensitive skin is not a skin type, it is a skin that has become sensitive: red, itchy, inflamed or, as Susan Harmsworth puts it – sick. 'Sensitive skin needs to be calmed down and allowed to normalize,' says Susan. Aggravated by harsh or fragranced products, pollution, stress or extreme weather conditions, more and more people are complaining of sensitive skin. Skin can also flare up due to a reaction to certain medicines, foods, caffeine, alcohol, or because of illness or drastic climate changes.

To minimize sensitivity, treat sensitive areas of the skin with natural-based products such as aromatherapy-based preparations, aloe vera, calamine, or other gentle products that have a calming and soothing effect. Cleanse and moisturize with fragrance-free, anti-irritant products. Products containing AHAs are known to cause sensitivity and should not be used by those prone to sensitive skin. Baby products in the form of lotions, talc and bath oils are suitable for those with sensitive skin. If you have a sensitive reaction to any product, natural or otherwise, stop using it.

CLEANSING

According to Eve Lom, who produces what *Vogue* describes as 'probably the best cleanser in the world', cleansing is the most crucial part of your skin-care regime. 'I cannot over-emphasize the importance of cleansing,' says Eve emphatically. 'If it's done properly with the right product, your cleanser should be a cleanser, toner, decongester and exfoliant all rolled into one.' Eve also believes in spending time massaging the cleanser into your skin: 'It's amazing how many people have congested skin. Massage helps eliminate the build-up of toxins in the muscles.'

There are several different types of cleansers to choose from. Wipe-off cleansing lotions, milks and creams effectively cleanse and remove make-up, but, as some leave a residue, you may feel you want to splash your face afterwards. Facial washes, gels and cleansing bars are more suitable for morning use or for make-up free skin. If your cleansing routine involves washing, splash several times to ensure you have removed all traces of residue, make-up and grime. If you're still using soap – which not only strips your skin of precious oils but leaves a residue – fling it out!

TONING

Some skin specialists, including Eve Lom, believe that if you are cleansing your face thoroughly there's no need for a toner – be it an astringent, clarifier, toner or skin freshener. 'It's just as beneficial to splash your face with water and, besides, if you are using water when cleansing, you will have already toned your skin,' says Eve, who can't understand how skin-care companies can charge exorbitant amounts for water and a bit of witch hazel. 'If you want to use a toner, do not leave it to dry,' she advises. 'Tissue it off, or it will dehydrate your skin.' No toner can close enlarged pores, but it can leave your skin feeling refreshed. Avoid alcohol-based astringents that strip the skin of its natural oils. Instead, choose toners with natural plant extracts that will not dehydrate the skin.

MOISTURIZING

Over the last few years there's been a major

breakthrough in anti-ageing ingredients, which can make choosing a moisturizer a perplexing task. However, it should be remembered that moisturizers with anti-ageing properties only contain a small amount of the active ingredient which can merely treat the *stratum corneum*, the skin's outer layer. If these products contained any more than the specified amount, they would need to be classified as a drug and not allowed to be sold as a cosmetic.

A good moisturizer should maintain, preserve and enhance the skin. And, because it also acts as a protective barrier, most skins need some form of moisturizer. There are rich creams to replenish dry skins, oil-free lotions for oily and combination skins, day creams, night creams, special treatment creams and serums. One vital ingredient most day creams contain is a UV sunscreen.

Many people question the benefits of a night cream, and the skin specialists are sceptical, too. 'There are certainly times when you need a richer cream, but I don't believe the skin knows the difference between day and night,' says Susan Harmsworth, whose E'SPA range has one moisturizer that can be used at both morning and night.

Choose the correct moisturizer to suit your skin's needs. Too much moisturizer can clog the pores, leading to spots, blemishes and open pores. At certain times, during warmer weather, for example, you may feel you need to swap to a lighter moisturizer. Eve Lom has the answer: 'Wet your hands with cold or warm water before applying your cream, this will dilute even the richest cream.'

EXFOLIATION

Skin renews itself every 21 days. This cycle can be boosted and dead cells sloughed away, by regular exfoliation. Unlike the body, where skin is thicker and more tolerant, you should only exfoliate your face once or twice a week at most, or you'll risk stripping away live cells as well as dead ones. Sloughing dead cells stimulates blood circulation, leaving behind a fresher-looking complexion that is easier for moisturizers to penetrate. But choose the wrong one, and you could find the harsh grains actually scratch the skin's surface. Thin, transparent or sensitive skin requires a gentle exfoliant such as the rub-off peel type, or simply a rub with a face cloth.

AHAs (Alpha-hydroxy acids), also known as fruit acids, have become extremely popular in speeding up the skin's renewal cycle. However, according to skin-care specialists, using cleansers, moisturizers and exfoliants all containing AHAs is overdoing it. Therefore, if you want to use AHAs, only use one product, not an entire skin-care range. But, as Eve Lom warns: 'Unless you have a genetically thick skin you should not use AHAs, or you could be stripping away protective layers of skin.' 'If you do use them, always wear a sunscreen.'

EYE CARE

The skin around the eyes is thinner, with fewer sebaceous glands than the rest of the face and, therefore, needs special attention. Because it is so delicate, the eye area is one of the first places to show signs of ill health, ageing, or a life of debauchery. Always use a separate eye cream or gel morning and night, which will protect, moisturize and minimize puffiness, thus preventing fine lines and crepiness. Eye products are designed to be much lighter than regular moisturizer, so take advantage of them. Avoiding your eyelids, apply sparingly, or the eye area will become puffy. Eye make-up should be wiped away gently with eye make-up remover – not your regular cleanser – on dampened cotton wool.

Dark rings can be caused by tiredness, illness, sinus congestion or where the skin has become thinner and more transparent due to age, thus making veins more visible. You can temporarily conceal dark rings with make-up but, with the exception of veins, for a permanent cure you need to address the cause. Another common problem is puffiness, which can be caused by too much eye cream, water retention or excess fluids that accumulate while we sleep. Reduce puffy eyes by using eye gel and by placing cucumber, cold tea bags or witch-hazel pads over your eyes for a few minutes each day. Avoid salt, processed foods, alcohol and coffee. To instantly brighten eyes, use whitening eye drops, but only occasionally. Used too often, they can have an adverse effect.

FACIALS

There are different methods and techniques used in facials, with deep-cleansing and massage-based facials being the most popular. Deep-cleansing facials rid the skin of impurities and leave a smoother, clearer, more radiant complexion. Some salons use machinery such as the galvanic current in Catheodermie or skin vacuuming, whereas others prefer the traditional, hands-on approach. Steam, while still used in some facials, is now believed to be damaging to the skin, causing broken capillaries, and should only be used on the thickest and most tolerant skins.

Massage is playing a far more important role in facials. Susan Harmsworth believes that for maximum benefits, facials should stimulate the systems rather than the skin: 'Our concept is to use massage to release toxins by stimulating pressure points, then eliminate the waste via lymphatic drainage.' The philosophy behind E'SPA is the holistic approach, which has led it to devise a facial that includes a neck, back and scalp massage. Some salons are offering acid-peel facials that claim to reduce wrinkles and acne scars. However, due to the risk of side effects, if you want a skin peel, take Susan Harmsworth's advice: 'I believe these peels should only be administered by a dermatologist or skin specialist, not by a beautician.'

FACIAL WORKOUT

Growing old isn't just about wrinkles and lines: ageing causes saggy skin, drooping eyelids, jowling around the mouth and a distorted jaw line. Sounds depressing, huh? But don't fret – help is at hand. Exercising your facial muscles promotes a firmer, smoother skin, gives you more prominent cheekbones, and improves and prevents the appearance of fine lines. Pioneered by Eva Fraser, there are now dozens of books and videos on exercises for the face. You don't have to stick to one particular expert's routine. Pick and choose exercises that suit your needs. When exercising your face, ensure you wear a moisturizer or, even better, a barrier cream such as Vaseline. To relax muscles after your workout, lightly tap your face with the tips of your fingers. Practise your facial workout for a couple of minutes each day and witness the difference!

ELECTRICAL TONERS – 'NON-SURGICAL FACE-LIFT'

Many beauty salons now offer electrotherapy facial treatments such as Caci – the highly acclaimed, original, non-surgical face-lift, which uses a gentle, low-frequency, electrical micro-current delivered by tiny impulse pads and prongs, to stimulate and tone muscles. The lazy alternative to facial exercises, the benefits of electrotherapy can be as effective. Caci recommends a course of ten followed by six boosters a year. You can purchase electrotherapy facial machines to use at home, but they are not as effective as salon treatments.

MALE MATTERS

Except for make-up removal and shaving, these days there is very little difference between a man or woman's beauty regime. Some men still reach for the soap, yet others spend as much time and effort looking after their skin as their wives or girlfriends. Men are lucky: their skin is generally tougher and more tolerant than women's. But this doesn't mean they can get away with not cleansing, moisturizing or exfoliating. To pave the way for a smoother, closer shave, men should exfoliate regularly. When shaving, men with acne should take extra care and use a razor with a blade instead of electric or battery-operated razors.

ACNE, SPOTS AND BLEMISHES

Spots take different forms and levels of severity from blackheads, or the occasional pimple, to full-blown acne. Nowadays, most skin problems can be effectively treated. And, as doctors begin to realize the long-term psychological effects acne has on a person, they are more willing to prescribe treatment or refer the patient to a dermatologist. Some conditions can be treated with lotions and creams or herbal and homeopathic remedies, but more severe and persistent acne usually only responds to stronger medication.

SPOTS vary from a tiny red lump to a bubble of pus or an angry, red boil. Basically, they are pores blocked with sebum and dead skin cells that have become infected with bacteria.

BLACKHEADS take the form of little plugs of sebum trapped in the pores. The black top is not dirt, it is caused by oxidation on exposure to air. Blackheads can be removed with a blackhead extractor or your fingers wrapped around a tissue, but on certain areas such as the chin and nose, they only return. Before tackling, open pores by applying a hot cloth to face.

WHITEHEADS are white bumps under the skin (known as milia) that start as liquid, then eventually become hard and can lie dormant for long periods of time. Whiteheads are far more difficult to remove than blackheads. One way of getting rid of these lumps is to disperse them by gentle massage as soon as they appear. Don't try to extract a whitehead: leave it to a professional. If it gets pushed deeper into the pore, it could cause a stubborn spot.

AVOID – if you are prone to spots or acne, avoid fatty and sugary foods, citrus fruits, caffeine and alcohol. Although they won't actually cause spots, they can aggravate the condition. Leave your skin free to breathe, covering pimples and scars with concealer or flesh-coloured spot cream. If you must wear a base, use a light, powder-based or oil-free foundation or a tinted moisturizer. Avoid dehydrating the skin by sunbathing, or overuse of anti-bacterial products and spot remedies containing alcohol or hydrocortisone. If the surface of the skin becomes too dry, sebum will become trapped under the layer of dry skin and the problem could get considerably worse. Finally, avoid that temptation to squeeze spots – this can spread bacteria under the skin and lead to permanent scarring.

ACTION

Fresh air, early nights and drinking plenty of water all help acne. Also, make sure your digestive system is not sluggish by eating plenty of fibre. A glass or two of warm water with a dash of lemon juice, taken first thing, helps cleanse your system.

ORAL TREATMENTS

Skin problems due to a hormone imbalance respond well to certain types of contraceptive pill. There are particular brands that doctors prescribe for acne. Evening primrose oil and starflower oil can also aid hormone balance, therefore improving acne. For severe acne, roaccutane (available on prescription only) is a major breakthrough in treating acne and is the first permanent cure. A course of antibiotics can also clear up bad skin but, as they only suppress the problem, the spots normally return. If you are prescribed antibiotics, take *lactobacillus acidophilus* (either in yoghurt or supplement form) to replenish your body with the good bacteria.

TOPICAL TREATMENTS

Combat spots by keeping skin scrupulously clean. Wipe affected area only with a gentle or diluted anti-bacterial lotion before using your regular cleanser. Zap spots topically with a blemish-control gel, antibiotic lotion or a gentle, antiseptic lotion such as tea tree oil (apply to spots only).

Dermatologists can inject a spot or whitehead with cortisone, which will dry up a whitehead instantly, and takes a couple of days to clear up a stubborn spot.

Products containing Isolutrol, such as Ketsugo, applied to the skin can regulate the sebaceous glands by blocking the production of the male hormone, androgen, which triggers acne in both men and women. If used regularly, this can be an effective remedy.

Retin A – a vitamin-A derivative (on prescription only), can help clear up acne, but it causes initial peeling and can make the skin more sensitive to the sun.

Supplements known to help acne include echinacea, evening primrose oil, starflower oil, herbal supplements containing burdock, herbal blood-purifying tablets and propolis (a natural antibiotic). Vitamin B slows down oil production, while zinc and vitamin C help fight infection.

SCAR-HEALERS

Help reduce reddish scarring by using vitamin E oil or a calamine-based product.

Vitamin B complex taken internally helps speed up the healing process of scars.

YOUTHFUL SKIN

As we grow older, elastin, proteins and collagen fibres start to break down, lines and wrinkles appear, and the skin starts to slacken and sag. This process begins as early as 20, although visible signs don't show on most people until they reach their thirties. Moisturizers, night creams and anti-ageing creams may keep the skin's surface smooth, but they cannot reverse the ageing process. No matter how well you look after your skin, genetic factors such as an imbalance in hormones, or external factors such as stress, illness, UV rays and pollution can upset the skin's delicate balance and can cause premature ageing.

AVOID: The worst offenders of all are exposure to the sun, drug-taking and nicotine. Regarding the latter, scientists have proved that skin ages considerably faster for smokers than non-smokers as it causes the skin to lose its elasticity and thickness. If you really can't give up smoking, take large doses of vitamin C. Other vices that speed up the ageing process include weight loss and gain, which affect the skin's elasticity; stress, which exacerbates free radicals; and excessive amounts of alcohol and eating too much junk food, which both prevent your body's intake of essential vitamins and minerals.

ACTION

Eat a healthy, balanced diet, whch includes essential fatty acids, olive oil and oily fish, and drink eight glasses of water a day.

Massage your face (either with your cleanser or moisturizer) gently for at least a minute each day to help drain the lymphatic system, boost circulation, and promote skin cell renewal.

Regular facials can improve the texture of the skin and make it look younger.

Be gentle with your skin and use gentle, natural-based products that contain the highest possible natural ingredients.

Supplements, including anti-oxidants, evening primrose oil, starflower oil and echinacea all improve skin's texture. Youth pills such as Menetolin and Imedeen are thought to work, but this is still disputable.

Facial exercises or electrotherapy can tighten muscles, thus helping to prevent skin from slackening.

Exercise and fresh air help combat free radicals. Breathe deeply to help enhance oxygenation of cells.

HRT (hormone replacement therapy) can slow down the ageing process in post-menopausal women .

AHAs can help speed up skin renewal, but should not be used excessively or on sensitive skin.

Retinova gel (prescription only), which contains retin A, can help reduce fine lines when used regularly over a period of a year. When using this product you must wear a sunscreen at all times.

Anti-wrinkle miracle pads plump up skin with a high dosage of vitamin C and make wrinkles less noticeable.

Sleep lines can be prevented by sleeping on your back. If you can't sleep in this position, apply a dab of Vaseline to vulnerable areas, notably your neck and décolleté, before you retire to bed.

BEAUTY

New-age beauty demands regular body care – from your head to your fingertips right down to your toes

MODELS' BEAUTY CABINET

Beauty expert and key consultant to the cosmetic industry, Alison Young, lets you into the secrets of the type of products models keep in their beauty cabinet. 'Standing under broiling lights, working long hours, and having gunge plastered over their hair and face results in ultra-sensitive skin and hair damage. So those in the know will use natural-based products that are gentle, more caring and are least likely to cause a reaction,' says Alison.

Skin: Cleanser, toner, spray toner (not water), moisturizer, a richer moisturizer, face oil, or serum for when skin needs extra nourishment, eye cream/gel, exfoliant, hydrating mask, eye mask, deep-cleansing mask and lip balm.
Body: Mild, non-detergent shower gel, body scrub, rich body lotion, body sheen, concealer (to cover birthmarks, spots etc.), razor and shaving emollient.
Colour: Spray fake tan (which dries in minutes), fake tan remover and instant tan enhancer.
Nails: Along with nail kit (see p.138), natural-looking pale varnishes and a white varnish for a French polish.

BODY CARE

From your neck right down to your toes, your body is all too often neglected. Before revealing our bodies to the world, in a desperate attempt to get in shape, most of us pummel and preen or make a mad dash to the beauty temples: the salon, gym or health spa. But to achieve the optimum body beautiful requires all-year-round commitment and – you've heard it before – the holistic approach. Combine a body-care strategy with regular exercise and a healthy diet, and you'll achieve that to-die-for body.

WASHING

When showering, to prevent dehydration, use a mild, non-detergent shower gel rather than soap. Gels containing moisturizers will leave your skin feeling soft and smooth – especially in areas where water is hard. If you're a bathing beauty, or enjoy the occasional long soak, add a couple of drops of aromatherapy bath oil or moisturizing foam to the water. After bathing, rinse skin thoroughly with a shower attachment to avoid leaving any residue which could dehydrate your skin. Then – if you can bear it – douche yourself in a spray of cold water to stimulate circulation. Finally, rub yourself briskly with a flannel or towel.

EXFOLIATION

Exfoliating your body sheds dirt and dead skin cells, boosts blood circulation, sloughs away rough skin on elbows and bottoms of feet, encourages cell renewal and thickens the skin, leaving you with a polished-looking, silky, spot-free skin. You can exfoliate your body as often as every other day, while taking a shower or bath by using either an exfoliating scrub, loofah, body mitt or simply a handful of salt.

SKIN-BRUSHING

Elaine Williams, head of Grayshott Hall health spa's natural therapies stresses the importance of skin-brushing. 'It does far more than improve the skin's surface, it works as a great overall tonic by stimulating the organs of the body. Using a firm, natural-bristle body brush, skin-brush your body before you shower or take a bath. Starting at your feet and working upwards including your neck, take five minutes (if possible) to brush in sweeping movements working towards the heart. This will rev up your circulation, help break down fatty deposits, improve your skin's texture, and give you that all-over glow.'

MOISTURIZING

To counteract dryness and keep your skin soft and supple, apply body lotion liberally after your bath or shower. The longer you spend massaging lotion into those not-so-hot body zones, such as your upper arms,

stomach, buttocks and thighs, the firmer they'll appear. Massage also helps boost the circulation and enhance your skin tone. While skin-firming products help tighten the skin and improve its texture, the effects are superficial, and should be used in conjunction with exercise and massage. Body lotions have become as sophisticated as skin-care products, and most now contain active hydrating formulas. If you have sensitive skin, opt for fragrance-free lotions or products that are designed for babies' and children's skins. For that special occasion, to give a dewy gleam apply a body-sheen product to shoulders, décolleté, legs, or other exposed areas of the body.

BUST

Unless you are totally flat-chested you should always wear a bra to support and uplift your bust; this will prevent your breasts sagging or stretchmarks forming. Lotions that claim to make the bust firmer only tighten the skin's surface. Splashing cold water on the area is just as effective. If you can bear it, shower for two minutes. Swimming the breast stroke regularly is a great bust firmer.

NECK

Most of us neglect our necks, yet it's one of the first give-away signs of age. Even the most beautiful, youthful-looking face will be spoilt by a saggy, crepe-like neck that has deep lines. When cleansing, toning, moisturizing and exfoliating your face, include your neck; not forgetting under your jawline, which is an area prone to spots. Finally, for a firm neck and jawline – exercise. A simple exercise involves sticking your tongue out and as close towards your nose as possible.

FEET

When applying your body lotion don't forget your feet. For a special treat, massage foot cream into feet, pull on cotton socks, and leave overnight. Remove dead skin with a pumice stone or a dead skin remover. Treat the nails on your feet as you would your hands by giving them regular pedicures. Soak feet in a herb infusion, adding a couple of drops of essential oil.

CELLULITE

Cellulite is fatty tissue – found mainly on the bottom, thighs and upper arms and caused by toxic build up – that leaves a dimpled, orange-peel effect on the body. Exacerbated by poor diet and lack of exercise, there is no simple cure for this stubborn condition, which affects 90 per cent of women. Even the most effective anti-cellulite creams will not work in isolation. According to Grayshott's Elaine Williams: 'You need a healthy diet, regular exercise and some form of stimulation, such

as skin-brushing, to improve circulation. Correct breathing and good posture are also important.'

Anti-cellulite treaments

- **To** disperse these fatty deposits, unless specified, a cream needs to be combined with vigorous massage on the affected area daily.
- **Skin-brushing** every day on the cellulite zone helps break down fatty deposits.
- **Good** diet helps prevent the build-up of toxins that lead to cellulite. Cut down on tea, coffee, alcohol, sugary and spicy foods.
- **Regular** exercise is particularly beneficial in combating cellulite.
- **Bursts** of cold water, interspersed with warm on the area can be effective. Use your shower attachment; but it needs to be fairly powerful.
- **Salon** treatments such as detoxifying wraps, electrotherapy, including Caci's electro-cellulite massager, Ionithermie or Fisiotron, can help.
- **Medical** treatments including cellulolipolysis – where needles are attached to electrodes and inserted under the skin – have been known to remove cellulite. Mesotherapy – injections that burn the fat – can also help reduce cellulite.

STRETCHMARKS

Stretchmarks are permanent. No cream will magically make them vanish, though it can help them appear slightly less visible. Found on the thighs, bottom, breasts and stomach, stretchmarks are not only limited to those who are overweight, have given birth, or whose weight fluctuates. To prevent stretchmarks, eat a diet rich in vitamins A, C, E, B6 and zinc. Used in conjunction with massage, anti-stretchmark creams, cocoa butter and vitamin E oil can help prevent them forming. Retinova gel, Caci skin rejuvenator and laser treatments have been known to reduce stretchmarks visibly.

BODY TREATMENTS

There are a whole range of body treatments available either at a spa or your local beauty salon but, as Elaine Williams points out, for any treatment to be effective you must prepare your body by skin-brushing and exfoliating before your treatment, and maintain it afterwards. Here are some of the treatments available.

Body polish – exfoliating scrub followed by body lotion or massage leaves skin glowing and squeaky clean.

Body wraps – a mud, clay, seaweed or algae wrap is applied, followed by a heated blanket. For instant inch loss, some salons cover the body in mud- or seaweed-soaked bandages to help sweat out excess fluids and toxins. However, the inch loss only lasts a few days.

Electrotherapy – using electronic micro-currents, treatments like Caci can tone the muscles and resculpt the body, leaving it taut and firm.

Reiki – uses laying on of the hands to balance mind and body.

MASSAGE

'Massage can ease tension, reawaken the senses and improve the condition of the skin,' says Elaine Williams. There are various massage techniques to choose from at Grayshott. Here are some of the most popular techniques.

Aromatherapy massage: Using essential oils helps relax the body and mind, eases muscle tension, stimulates the circulation, and aids lymphatic drainage.

Lymphatic massage: Through lymphatic drainage, this massage rids the body of toxins and improves skin texture.

Shiatsu: A Japanese massage technique which uses finger pressure on the acupressure points and meridian lines to release energy flow.

Swedish massage: This is a deeply relaxing massage which eases muscle tension and increases blood flow.

Hydrotherapy: Underwater massage using jets to tone parts of the body such as thighs and buttocks.

G5 vibro-massage: Using a vibrating machine, this vigorous form of massage works into muscles to reduce tension and break down fatty deposits.

Clarin's Paris method: Using rhythmical movements, combined with essential oils for a relaxing massage.

SUN CARE

We all love a golden tan – it makes us look and feel healthy, slim and twice as sexy. However, since it was confirmed by dermatologists that 90 per cent of wrinkles are caused by the sun, it is now a well-documented fact that the sun is the greatest contributor to premature ageing, not to mention all the other hazards such as sunburn, sunstroke, allergies and skin cancer. Yet, in spite of these danger warnings, no sooner has the sun started to shine than many of us rush to soak up its rays, even though we now have excellent sun-free tanning alternatives. For those who still want to expose themselves to the sun, the only answer is to protect. SPF (sun protection factor) measures the amount of UVB protection a product gives you, and indicates how long you can stay in the sun. The higher the factor, the greater the protection. More recently, a star system has been adopted to indicate the level of UVA protection. The more stars, the more protection. Don't be fooled into thinking sunbeds are any less harmful than the sun – they're not. All said, sunshine in very small doses helps stimulate vitamin D production and lifts our spirits.

ACTION

- **Wear** a total sunblock on your face and a high protection factor on your body, which you should re-apply every hour. Once you have built up a tan

you can lower the factor. Keep your lotion out of the sun, and discard it after two years.

- **Wear** sunglasses wherever possible.
- **Always** use a day cream containing a UV filter of SPF 15, even in winter or when the sky is overcast.
- **Wear** a hat or apply a product designed to protect hair from the sun.
- **When** the sun goes down, apply an after-sun product or a rich body lotion like cocoa butter.
- **Retin-A** products such as Retinova gel (on prescription only) can be beneficial in healing sun-damaged skin.

SELF-TANNING

Thanks to great self-tanning products, we no longer need to expose ourselves to harmful UV rays to achieve that sun-kissed look. Most products on the market bestow a completely natural-looking tan and, as long as you spread the lotion evenly, will not streak. Some formulations are tan coloured, so you can see exactly where you have applied it. There are even products to correct any mistakes you might make. Self-tanning products are also good to top up a tan or fill in bikini or strap marks.

Prepare your body for self-tan by exfoliating. Then, apply to a dampened skin, preferably after a bath or shower. Unless you are using the spray-on type, which dries in minutes, it is advisable to wait at least 30 minutes before getting dressed. Within a matter of hours, you'll have an all-over golden tan. Instant tans and bronzers that wash off are good for an immediate effect. For a model, it's essential to have an evenly toned skin. Therefore, most models need to control their body colour and even out irregularities by using fake tan. 'For some assignments models are expected to turn up looking tanned, while for others, paler,' says beauty expert, Alison Young. 'So it's important they have a good fake tan, as well as a fake-tan remover. The best types are spray-on, as they give an even colour and dry quickly.'

THREAD VEINS

Tiny thread veins, also known as spider or broken veins, are caused by capillaries that have dilated due to such factors as taking the contraceptive pill, exposure to the sun, or extreme conditions of heat or cold. These veins are also common in smokers, who are depriving their skin of oxygen. If you are prone to broken capillaries, you should avoid washing your face in very hot water, taking too many saunas or steam baths, or spending too long in them.

ACTION

- **Use** a concealer such as Dermablend to cover veins. Waterproof foundations and concealers also provide long-lasting cover.

- **Retin-A** (by prescription only) products thicken skin and, therefore, make veins less noticeable.
- **Thread** veins can be effectively removed by a process known as hyfrecator, which is performed by beauticians and dermatologists.
- **Copper bromide** lasers are another up-to-date method of removing veins.

SKIN DISCOLOURATION/PIGMENTATION

Brown patches of melanin the size of freckles, or in the larger shape of age spots, can be caused by the sun or hormonal changes often triggered off by the contraceptive pill. While freckles can enhance your looks, larger patches of pigmentation are unsightly. Age spots are areas of hyper-pigmentation that increase with old age or constant exposure to the sun. If you are on the pill and have noticed a change in pigment, consider coming off it. There are fade-out creams available, but you must be aware that these products, although effective, can leave behind a white mark.

POSTURE

No matter how tall or how beautiful you are, if you're slouched over with hunched shoulders you'll go unnoticed. Poor posture is unattractive and, what's more, can cause back- and neckache, migraine, bad circulation or digestive complaints. Correct your stance and you'll immediately appear taller, more self-confident and in control. Dance improves your posture, as do body-conditioning routines such as Pilates. If your posture is particularly bad, consider osteopathy, or the Alexander technique that, over a series of sessions, teaches you the art of good posture.

NAIL AND HAND CARE

Hands, like faces, are continuously exposed to the elements. As they are nearly always on show, unless you look after them, chapped, lined hands are the biggest give-away of your age. And bitten or unmanicured nails are a sure sign of neglect. Brittleness, ridges, and other nail problems are mostly caused by poor diet. A healthy nail should be strong, with a pinkish appearance. Ridges on the nails can be caused by illness, or could be an indication that the body is lacking certain minerals. However, any vertical ridges on nails naturally become more visible with age. Other problems, such as brittle nails that split and peel, or white/milk spots, can be helped with good diet and regular nail care.

ACTION

- **Multi-vitamins** and minerals that include calcium, magnesium, zinc, iron, iodine, selenium and silica. Vitamin B complex and a protein-rich diet are also

good. Zinc is good for white/milk spots.
- **Apply** nail-strengthening creams and varnishes.
- **Always** wear gloves when washing up or using a strong detergent.
- **Change** nail varnish regularly.
- **Use** nail clippers rather than scissors.
- **Use** an emery board.
- **Massage** hand and nail cream into nails, backs of hands and palms at least twice a day.
- **For** naturally shiny nails, buff nails once a week.
- **Take** care when undoing buttons, bottles or anything that could potentially tear your nail.
- **If** you break one nail, file the others down.

MANICURE

Heading for the beauty salon every time your nail varnish starts to chip is costly and time-consuming, so learn how to do your own home manicures. Never before have there been so many wonderful shades of nail polish to choose from. Along with the pinks, reds, whites and natural shades are choices of citrus colours, pastels, metallics, as well as the darker shades of purple, plum, chocolate and red. There are even special shades for men! Nail varnish also comes in a pen, ideal for touching up tips. Long nails can now be yours with the help of false nails and tips. And you can even patch up your nail if it tears.

STEP-BY-STEP MANICURE

Tools: Emery board, orange sticks, nail buffer, cotton wool, acetone-free nail-varnish remover, cuticle clippers, cuticle cream, nail strengthener, repair kit, nail brush, base coat, nail polish of your choice.

1. Remove nail polish.
2. Using an emery board, file nails in one direction only, not from side to side.
3. Massage nails with strengthening cream.
4. Exfoliate hands, clean nails with brush, then soak hands in warm water with almond oil for a few minutes. Dry thoroughly.
5. Gently push back cuticles with an orange stick, apply cuticle remover and trim cuticles if necessary.
6. Buff nails.
7. Apply a base coat to stop the varnish staining the nails. Now apply one or two coats; this will depend on the density of shade you choose.

For a French polish, apply a pale-pink or neutral varnish to nails as above. Then, when it's dry, apply one coat of white nail varnish to the tips of your nails.

TEETH

There's nothing quite like a dazzling set of perfectly straight, pearly-white teeth. For those not lucky enough to be blessed with such teeth, there is help at hand from cosmetic dentistry. Procedures include crowns, – the existing tooth is filed down and covered with a porcelain layer; implants – individual false teeth are screwed into the bone; veneers – a layer of porcelain is bonded to the tooth; bonding – a substance is stuck onto the tooth; whitening – using a form of bleach. If your teeth are not straight, this can be corrected by orthodontics. Although the alignment of teeth can be altered in adulthood, it is a much slower progress. On a day-to-day basis, brush teeth for two to three minutes, not forgetting gums, and floss once daily.

COSMETIC SURGERY

For some people, especially Californians, a visit to the plastic surgeon is almost as simple as going to the beautician or hairdresser. But those considering cosmetic surgery must be aware that it may not fulfil all expectations. The most successful operations are performed on individuals who are having the surgery done for themselves – not to please a partner or revive a bad relationship. And even if an agent suggests it, models must remember that a new nose or bigger boobs are no guarantee they will get work.

Top London plastic surgeon Douglas Harrison has kindly helped compile details of some of the most popular cosmetic procedures. These run the gamut from the major surgical changes, such as nose reshaping, to the more simple procedures such as dermal fillers, which are used to plump out lines, wrinkles and pitted scars caused by acne or chicken pox. 'Collagen is one of the most widely used substances,' explains Douglas Harrison. 'However, it's not long lasting and needs to be redone every six months. The alternative to collagen is GoreTex, which is threaded under the skin and can be removed, and Hylaform which, according to the manufacturers, lasts longer than collagen. Hylaform is a very new substance, so we have yet to see the outcome.' Douglas Harrison warns that silicone, in liquid-injection form, should not be used for dermal fillers or lip reshaping. 'If you react to silicone, it can turn rock hard and cannot be removed. To reshape lips the substances now used include collagen, GoreTex, Hylaform or lipodermal graft. With lipodermal graft, fat and skin are taken from the patient's body and injected into lips. The downside of this procedure is that, once in the lips, it can dissolve. However, if your body picks up the graft, the results will be permanent.'

Other procedures that do not need a general anaesthetic include ear pinning for sticking-out ears and eyelid surgery. Lower-eye surgery can reduce under-eye bags by removing or redepositing the fat. 'This procedure (known as transconjunctival),' says Douglas, 'is performed either from the inside of the eye or through an incursion made along the lower lash line.' Drooping eyelids can also be dramatically improved by upper-eye surgery. Though highly effective, as they are so close to the eye, both these operations can cause discomfort, swelling and bruising.

Skin resurfacing can eliminate fine lines, acne or chicken pox pits and dramatically improve the texture of the skin. The three methods used include dermabrasion – which uses rotating wire brushes to remove top layers of skin; laser therapy – using a silk-touch laser; and chemical peel – where skin is coated in an acid-type peeling agent. 'I still prefer to use dermabrasion,' says Douglas, 'you can control it better and, therefore, get the most accurate results. Whichever method you choose, you are still burning the skin.' He also points out that added drawbacks of chemical peel are sensitivity to the sun and the risks of pigmentation. And as it is difficult to anaesthetize the face completely, for any form of resurfacing to avoid suffering pain, he recommends a general anaesthetic. After surgery a crust forms to uncover softer, smoother skin. The skin feels sore and expect to be out of action for two weeks.

One of the most popular forms of cosmetology is nose reshaping. Noses can be lengthened, shortened, made narrower, wider or retroussé. 'The resetting of the bone and cartilage removal is performed inside the nose, leaving no visible scarring; although I find the more difficult noses benefit from what is termed as "the open approach", as it makes access more easy.' Another procedure that enhances the face shape is cheek augmentation. Douglas Harrison explains: 'Pre-shaped proplast implants are inserted into cheeks via the mouth to give the patient more prominent cheekbones. There is no visible scarring, but oral hygiene is essential to prevent post-operative infection.' Breast augmentation is one of the most popular procedures. But, it seems that after the silicone scare, fewer women want to risk it. 'Silicone in this form, unlike the fluid, has still not been proved to be harmful,' says Douglas, 'there is now an alternative – trilucent soya bean, but the shape is not as good as using silicone.' Other cosmetic procedures include face-lifts, liposuction, breast reduction and chin augmentation.

Cosmetic surgery always carries risks such as infection or permanent scarring, and should not be undertaken without serious consideration. If you are contemplating cosmetic surgery, it is *essential* you find a highly reputable plastic surgeon. Approach your doctor and ask him or her to refer you to, or recommend, a good surgeon. Avoid answering advertisements. If you fall into the wrong hands, at best you could be disappointed with the results, and at worse, you could be scarred for life!

NATURAL BEAUTY

NATURE KNOWS BEST

As more high-tech things are foisted upon us, we are turning to nature for subtle and gentle solutions. Companies like E'SPA, Origins, Philosophy, Kiehl and Aveda have anticipated these demands by producing natural-based products. And, many of the cosmetic giants are now enriching their products with aromatherapy oils, herbs, plant extracts and other natural ingredients. 'The great thing about natural-based products is, because of the high content of natural ingredients, they are kinder to the skin,' says Alison Young, beauty expert and key consultant to the cosmetic industry. 'Aveda, for example, uses a natural carrying agent not mineral oils or detergents.' These companies aren't only producing cosmetics, from self-tanning products to hair care, washing-up liquid to perms, they cover the whole gamut.

PRODUCT FACTS

While the eighties witnessed cosmetic companies churning out products for every square inch of the face and body, today they are favouring the more simplistic approach and multi-purpose products. For example, you can buy creams which can be used on lips, hands, dry patches and stretch marks; cleansing gels for both face and body; and moisturizers which double up as hydrating masks.

You've probably noticed the word 'hypoallergenic' written on products, but what does it really mean? 'Very little,' replies Susan Harmsworth from ESPA. 'With products that state they are hypoallergenic, you could still be allergic to a certain ingredient in the product, even if it's natural.' And what about the contents of natural ingredients in a product? 'No product can be 100 per cent natural as, if a product is to last, it must have some form of preservative,' continues Susan, 'although we are very close to producing a natural preservative.'

Other common jargon found on pots and packaging includes 'non-comedogenic' and 'non-acnegenic', which in normal speak both mean the product should't clog the pores. An easier one to decipher is 'fragrance-free', which means that no fragrance has been added.

Fortunately, there are now many cosmetic companies against animal testing. If the product has not been tested on animals, it will say so. If this is not specified on the packaging or product, it is highly likely that it has used this method of testing. Some companies who do not test on animals have had to change their wording to 'this product has not been tested on animals', as ingredients common in most cosmetics have, in the past, been tested on animals.

AROMATHERAPY

Aromatherapy uses extracts from wild and cultivated plants, flowers and herbs. A key ingredient in many of the leading skin- and body-care ranges, essential oils have a wide variety of uses, not just for their beautifying properties, but for their aroma and therapeutic value, too. Add to a bath, place in a burner, inhale, or use for face and body massage.

Essential oils are now widely available and are sold either pure, blended or diluted with carrier oils such as almond, wheatgerm or jojoba. But Susan Harmsworth, whose E'SPA range is aromatherapy based, warns that people should take care when using essential oils. 'It's far safer to use a blended aromatherapy product as opposed to neat essential oils. When putting oils in the bath, blended oils have a dispersant to make them go milky, while pure essential oils sit on the water and can cause skin sensitivity.' When buying essential oils, Susan strongly recommends going to a reputable supplier or aromatherapist to ensure you get quality oils.

Essential oils should never be taken internally and must always be diluted before applying directly to the skin. Pregnant women and children should not use essential oils without the guidance of an aromatherapist. To dilute essential oils, use two drops of essential oil to one tablespoon of carrier oil. There are over 30 essential oils available; here is a list of some of the most widely used and their key properties.
Stimulating: Juniper, rosemary, peppermint, lavender, lemon, mandarin, pine, eucalyptus.
Antiseptic: Tea tree, lavender, eucalyptus, clove.
Relaxing: Rose, sandalwood, neroli, geranium, lavender.
Soothing: Sandalwood, rose, lavender, ylang-ylang.

HERBS

Thyme, mint, rosemary, parsley, lavender, camomile and comfrey are all common herbs found in many beauty products. Culinary herbs are widely available, easy to grow, and make good, natural ingredients for home beauty products. Highly nutritious, herbs are both tasty and decorative when sprinkled on salads and other dishes. They also make excellent teas and tisanes. Grow herbs either in your garden or indoors. If you don't want the bother of growing them, buy them from the supermarket in fresh or dried form.

To make preparations for use in beauty products it's simple.
Infusion: Place herbs (preferably fresh) in an infuser. Steep for ten minutes. The more water you add, the weaker the infusion will be. For a strong infusion, use only enough water to cover the herbs.
Poultice: Mash fresh or dried herbs into a pulp using a pestle and mortar. If you are using dried herbs; you may need to add a drop of boiling water to soften them.

MASSAGE

The effects of a facial massage are extremely beneficial. Even massaging your face with cleanser or moisturizer for a few minutes each day will help decongest skin, rejuvenate cells and promote a healthy glow.
Self-massage: Using a blended aromatherapy oil especially formulated for the face, start massaging your cheeks with small, circular movements, not forgetting to pay attention to your jawline and chin. Use index fingers to massage your nose around the outer nostrils. With your thumb and first finger, spend a few moments massaging your earlobes. Then, just beneath the delicate, under-eye skin, gently glide your index finger both clockwise and anticlockwise around your outer eye area. Now move out towards the temples, stopping to press for a few seconds on the pressure points. Finally, sweep your palms

in an upward direction over your forehead. A scalp massage will also do wonders for your complexion.

HOME FACIAL

There's nothing quite like a salon facial – not only does it give your skin a radiant glow, it leaves you feeling totally relaxed. In-between your monthly facials, beauty expert Alison Young suggests doing your own home facial once a week. Here is a simple facial you can try.
1 Cleanse your face, spending longer than usual massaging the cleanser into your skin.
2 Apply a warm face cloth to your face and leave for a minute.
3 Exfoliate either with the face cloth, using circular movements, or with an exfoliant suited to your skin.
4 Massage a blended aromatherapy oil onto face, neck, shoulders and scalp for at least ten minutes. Remove.
5 Apply a mask of your choice and relax for 15 minutes.
6 Rinse off mask, tone and moisturize.

NATURAL BEAUTY PREPARATIONS

With a little time and effort you can easily make your own beauty preparations. If the ingredients are not already in your kitchen cupboard or bathroom cabinet, you should be able to obtain them from supermarkets, pharmacies or health-food stores. Instead of buying off the shelf, ask your pharmacist to dispense ingredients like kaolin, fuller's earth, aqueous cream, witch hazel and rosewater; they are much cheaper to buy this way. And when you want a refill, just take your jar or bottle back to the pharmacy and it will cost you even less.

Avoiding too many messy and perishable foods, here is a range of preparations using natural

ingredients. With the exception of the face and hair masks, most of the preparations below will last at least a few weeks if kept in an airtight container.

NATURAL PREPARATIONS CABINET

Foods: Honey, lemon, fine oatmeal, finely ground sea salt, rock salt, cucumber, egg.
Liquids: Witch hazel, glycerine, rosewater.
Cream bases: Aqueous cream, beeswax, coconut oil.
Powder: Fuller's earth, kaolin, bicarbonate of soda, crushable vitamin C, borax.
Oils: Almond oil, wheatgerm oil.
Essential oils: Neroli, tea tree, geranium, sandalwood, mandarin.
Herbs and plants: Thyme, camomile, basil, mint, rosemary.
Tools: Jars and bottles (preferably airtight), saucepan, blender, pestle and mortar for crushing herbs and infuser – the type used for tea or tisanes is fine.

BALANCING FACIAL WASH

6 tablespoons glycerine
3 teaspoons coconut oil
1 teaspoon borax
4 drops geranium essential oil
Melt coconut in saucepan, add glycerine and essential oil, then beat in borax.

CAMOMILE CLEANSER

½ teaspoon beeswax
3 tablespoons almond oil
2½ tablespoons camomile infusion in hot water
½ teaspoon coconut oil
¼ teaspoon borax
Prepare infusion and dissolve borax in infusion. Melt beeswax and coconut oil in a saucepan over a gentle heat. Add almond and essential oil slowly. Then add infusion (a few drops at a time), stirring vigorously. Remove from heat and beat with a fork or whisk until it forms a smooth paste.

SIMPLE TONER

Rosewater

Witch hazel

Mix one part rosewater to one part witch hazel. For dry skin, mix two parts rosewater to one part witch hazel.

CUCUMBER FRESHENER

Cucumber

Witch hazel

Put cucumber in blender, blend to a pulp, extract juice. (Put pulp aside for a face mask.) Add one part cucumber juice to two parts witch hazel.

HONEY SKIN FIRMER

1 teaspoon honey (runny)

8 tablespoons witch hazel

Mix teaspoon of runny honey with witch hazel until completely dissolved.

REPLENISHING MOISTURIZING CREAM (for dry skin)

1 teaspoon beeswax

3 tablespoons wheatgerm oil

$2^1/_2$ tablespoons thyme infusion in hot water

4 drops neroli essential oil

$1/_4$ teaspoon borax

Prepare infusion and dissolve borax in infusion. Melt beeswax in a saucepan over a gentle heat. Add wheatgerm and essential oil slowly. Then add infusion (only a few drops at a time), stirring vigorously. Remove from heat and beat with a fork or whisk until it forms a smooth paste.

GENTLE EYE MAKE-UP REMOVER

3 tablespoons aqueous cream

3 tablespoons almond oil

Mix both ingredients together.

EYE TREATS

Puffiness: Slices of cucumber, pads soaked in rosemary infusion or pads soaked in witch hazel.

Dark circles: Pads soaked in mint infusion.

Eye bath: A pinch of salt in boiled water. Allow to cool before use.

SPOT ZAPPERS

Tea tree oil, lavender oil.

POST-ACNE SCAR HEALERS

Wheatgerm oil.

FACE MASKS

Choose one of the following masks to suit your needs. Apply with a brush (any old make-up brush will do). Leave on for 15 minutes. Each recipe is for one mask only.

DEEP-CLEANSING MUD MASK

1 tablespoon fuller's earth

3 teaspoons infusion of rosemary

Prepare a strong infusion of rosemary and allow to cool. Mix the ingredients into a paste and apply to your face immediately. This mask will dry hard.

REVITALIZING MASK

Pulp from 1 cucumber

1 tablespoon kaolin

Blend cucumber, strain off the juice (use for toner). Mix kaolin with cucumber pulp. Apply immediately.

MOISTURIZING ANTI-WRINKLE MASK

1 teaspoon honey (runny)

1 teaspoon wheatgerm oil

1 vitamin C tablet (crushable)

Crush vitamin C tablet in a pestle and mortar. Mix honey and oil together. Finally, add vitamin C powder and apply to face.

GENTLE FACE EXFOLIANT

3 tablespoons fine oatmeal

3 teaspoons honey (runny)

3 teaspoons wheatgerm oil

Mix all ingredients together into a paste.

INVIGORATING BODY POLISH

4 tablespoons rock salt or finely ground sea salt

1 tablespoon strong mint infusion

1 tablespoon glycerine

4 drops tea tree oil

Prepare a strong mint infusion and allow to cool. Mix in salt, glycerine and oil.

HYDRATING BODY LOTION

1 teaspoon beeswax

3 tablespoons almond oil

4 drops sandalwood essential oil

$2^1/_2$ tablespoons infusion of basil in hot water

$1/_4$ teaspoon of borax

Prepare infusion and dissolve borax in infusion. Melt beeswax in a saucepan over a gentle heat. Add almond and essential oil slowly. Then add infusion (only a few drops at a time), stirring vigorously. Remove from heat and beat with a fork or whisk until it forms a smooth paste.

ANTI-STRETCHMARK POTION

1 tablespoon coconut oil

$1/_2$ tablespoon wheatgerm oil

2 drops mandarin essential oil

Melt coconut oil, then add oils, stirring vigorously. Decant into a pot, then leave to solidify.

MOISTURIZING BATH

1 tablespoon oatmeal

Piece of muslin

Place oatmeal in a piece of muslin. Tie it up so that none of the oatmeal can escape and put it into your bath.

RESTORING HAND AND NAIL TREAT

1 tablespoon warm almond oil

Cotton gloves

Warm almond oil in a pan. Massage into hands and nails then cover with cotton gloves. Heat gloves on radiator first. Leave on for an hour or overnight if possible.

LEMON JUICE NAIL CLEANSER

1 lemon

Squeeze the juice from one lemon and wipe over nails.

NOURISHING HAIR MASK

1 tablespoon almond oil

1 egg yolk

Mix oil with egg yolk, then apply immediately. Leave for ten minutes.

FITNESS & VITALITY

Beauty is the by-product of a fit body and healthy lifestyle.

Get into peak form by exercising regularly. Whether it's a vigorous workout on a step machine, pirouetting around the floor in a dance studio, or sitting in the lotus position while practising yoga, you'll reap such benefits as a taut, toned body, together with an abundance of energy and a more positive outlook on life. And, as model fitness trainer Rob Lander advises: 'Combine this with rest, relaxation and a healthy diet, and not only will your not-so-hot body look amazing, but you will sparkle with vitality.' Take time out for yourself and try to learn how to relax, detox your mind and body and get stress under control. For that total fitness and relaxation experience, retreat to a spa. Get and stay motivated. Kick-start your fitness routine by walking rather than taking the car, and opting for the stairs instead of the lift.

EXERCISE

Exercise leaves you bursting with energy and is the key to good health and vitality; it helps you achieve a certain level of fitness and lose weight; it can also resculpt your body, improve muscle tone and boost collagen production. Nigel Sapsed, fitness trainer to the stars, suggests that to achieve a healthy level of fitness, you should work out three times a week for at least 40 minutes each session. Because exercise encourages blood flow, after several workouts you'll notice a visible difference to the texture of your skin: it will appear smoother, silkier and younger looking. Beauty benefits aside, exercise helps eliminate stress by releasing tension build-up; it heightens your ability to concentrate and, by triggering the release of feel-good brain chemicals – endorphins – gives you a zest for life.

From the most sophisticated health club to the church hall, or even a towel on your bedroom floor, it doesn't matter where you exercise, as long as you exercise. Not having the cash for membership fees, personal trainers or a treadmill is no excuse – exercise is free! There's no quick-fix method to getting fit. Joining a gym with all good intentions, then giving up after a few weeks, is pointless. To get on the road to fitness – and maintain it – you'll need heaps of self-discipline. Don't set unrealistic goals or you'll give up before you've even started exercising. And, as Nigel Sapsed points out: 'Choose an activity you enjoy, so you don't see exercise as a chore. If you have difficulty motivating yourself, work out with a friend or join a class. Pick a form of exercise that suits your body's needs. It's no good doing weight-training if you don't want to build up muscle definition.'

Some people favour the gym, while others prefer a less strenuous form of exercise such as yoga. Whichever exercise you pick, build up gradually; this way you'll acquire strength and stamina, together with a supple, firm body – without injury.

TARGET TRAINING ZONE

If you want to achieve maximum results from cardiovascular exercises such as swimming, power-walking, cycling, jogging or aerobics, before you start you need to find out your target training range, then maintain it. Nigel Sapsed explains how:

'To find out your individual maximum heart rate (MHR) take 220 beats per minute (the clinically determined maximum heart rate), then minus your age. Everyone is born with a MHR of 220 bpm then, each year of our lives, we loose a beat. Now calculate 70–85 per cent of your maximum heart rate. These figures are your personal training range. During your exercise session, take your pulse for one minute, counting the beats. (It's probably easier to time 30 seconds, then double the amount.) Your aim is to get your heart rate in-between the two ratios and maintain it throughout your workout. By doing so, you will safely increase your level of fitness by promoting the efficiency of your heart and lungs, lose weight, tone muscles and feel great!'

Example of a 20-year-old's training range: 220 bpm less 20 years = 200 bpm maximum heart rate; 70–85 per cent = 140–170 bpm. Therefore, a 20-year-old should aim to get his or her heart rate somewhere in-between 140 and 170 bpm and maintain this heart rate throughout the workout.

POPULAR FORMS OF EXERCISE

SWIMMING

There's nothing quite like swimming for leaving you feeling totally invigorated. And, according to Nigel Sapsed, it's probably the best exercise for overall fitness. 'Swimming strengthens and builds long, lean muscle. Also, as you're supported by water, there's no risk of injury. And the breast stroke really does give you a firmer, more pert bosom!' To maximize the benefits, if you can, alternate your stroke every ten lengths. To exercise the buttocks and thighs use a kick board, keeping your legs straight and kicking hard. Swim at a fast pace for at least 30 minutes. If you want to turn your swim into a training session, Nigel suggests swimming a certain amount of lengths while timing yourself. 'Each week try to swim an extra length, staying within your original time limit.'

WALKING

Probably the easiest and most civilized form of keeping fit, walking is rated by Nigel as the second-best form of overall exercise. If you are getting fresh air, i.e. in the country or by the sea, it will be doubly beneficial, as the oxygen intake will help ward off free radicals. Wear training shoes or walking boots to support your knees and lower back. Aim to walk briskly for 40 minutes. 'To improve your level of fitness,' advises Nigel, 'you need to walk at a speed of at least four miles per hour. And don't forget to move your arms to exercise your upper body. If you're power-walking on a treadmill, increase the speed rather than the gradient.'

JOGGING

A form of aerobic exercise which improves the cardiovascular system, strengthens legs and boosts stamina. However, as Nigel points out, jogging can be harsh on your body. 'If you do want to jog, stick to a treadmill or grass, not hard surfaces. Even then, a good pair of training shoes is essential to prevent any back or knee injuries.' If you have never jogged before, take it slowly to begin with. To lower the risk of stiff muscles or injury, it's important to warm up by doing a few stretching exercises first.

CYCLING

Cycling is a cardiovascular activity that works your legs and buttocks and improves stamina. If you don't have a bicycle, cycle machines are popular both for home use and in the gym. 'When using a cycle machine, combine this with upper body exercises,' explains Nigel. 'There are different cycle machines – the upright, conventional cycle and the recumbent cycle. The recumbent is fantastic for firming up those buttocks.'

ROLLERBLADING

This fun, outdoor activity is a great way to keep fit. Go to parks where rollerblading is permitted and make sure you wear all the protective clothing, including helmet, gloves, knee and elbow pads.

'I'd put this high on my list of best overall exercise,' says Nigel. 'The advantage that rollerblading has over jogging is, because it's smooth, there's no impact on your body. You're also exercising your upper body.'

WEIGHT MACHINES AND FREE WEIGHTS

Weight-training, using weight machines and free weights, gives the body a defined look, as well as building muscle strength and endurance. 'If you don't want to build muscle,' explains Nigel, 'keep the weights low.' He recommends combining weight-training with some form of cardiovascular exercise. 'If you're in a gym, use step machines, cycles or treadmills. If you don't feel motivated to work out on your own, join a circuit-training programme or hire a personal trainer.'

PERSONAL TRAINING

A tailor-made exercise programme devised by a trainer is guaranteed to get you in tip-top condition – ideal for those who cannot motivate themselves. But beware! It can be gruelling – especially if the trainer is at each session with you. A personal trainer will either come to your home or will work out at a gym with you. The attraction of personal trainers is twofold. The trainer will work on specific areas you want improving and will make sure you are exercising correctly. Also, the one-to-one aspect means you can't cheat!

AEROBICS CLASSES

Aerobics (high or low impact), such as step or aerobics classes, increase your stamina and improve the efficiency of your heart and lungs. Step mainly strengthens the legs, whereas general aerobics classes are good for the whole body. This exercise should be taken regularly for maximum benefit, or combined with other forms of exercise. 'Aerobic classes are great from a motivational point of view and for all-round exercise, but if you want to firm up certain body zones, you may not find it specific enough,' explains Nigel.

AQUA AEROBICS

Aerobics classes held in swimming pools have become extremely popular. Because you are immersed in water, it's far more gentle on the body than general aerobics. 'The water acts as an extra weight to work against, yet it supports you, thus preventing injury,' says Nigel enthusiastically.

YOGA

Improves flexibility and helps you obtain a more supple, toned body. By focusing on deep breathing and meditation, yoga cleverly combines exercise with relaxation. This ancient form of exercise is ideal for combating stress in today's hectic society.

STRETCH

Like yoga, stretch is a gentle exercise that helps you become more supple and gain greater mobility in all parts of your body. Stretch can be used either as a flexibility exercise, or can be combined with other forms of exercise. 'You should always stretch after exercising,' insists Nigel, 'it's particularly important to do at least ten minutes of stretching after a workout in the gym.'

BODY-CONDITIONING

Body-conditioning will improve body shape and muscle definition and make you more supple. Pilates is a gentle form of body conditioning which tones the whole body, improves flexibility and encourages good posture.

DANCE

One of the most pleasurable ways of keeping fit, dance offers more benefits than just a great physique. Many forms of dance improve poise and co-ordination, as well as giving you the feel-good factor. Choose from ballet, contemporary, jazz, ballroom, Latin, salsa, tap-dancing, Irish dancing, line-dancing, ciroc, belly-dancing, flamenco and limbo, among others.

SPORTS

For a competitive way of keeping fit, take part in sports such as tennis, basketball, badminton, squash, netball, football, hockey, rugby, kick-boxing, karate, volleyball, surfing, etc. 'Enjoy sporting activities at the weekend, or as a social thing,' says Nigel, 'but not as your main form of exercise.'

HOME FITNESS
THE FITNESS VIDEOS

Claudia Schiffer, Elle Macpherson and Cindy Crawford are just three of a long line of celebrity models who have launched their own fitness videos. If you find it too intimidating to work out with the perfectly proportioned supergirls, choose from a whole selection of videos made by fitness gurus, personal trainers and celebrities. The type of workout i.e. stretch and tone or aerobic, should determine your purchase. Stick with it – avoiding the temptation to switch off halfway through – and the benefits will be almost as good as a class, without the hassle of having to get there.

MINI-TRAMPOLINE
A fun and energizing way to work out that won't have any impact on your lower back.

SKIPPING
All you need is a piece of rope and a space where there is no risk of knocking down priceless objects, and you're away.

STEP
Step classes have become a popular form of aerobics. If you don't want to join a class, purchase your own step from a sports shop.

STAIR-CLIMBING
If you live in a house or apartment with stairs, simply run up and down a dozen or more times for a free aerobic and leg-strengthening exercise.

WEIGHTS
You can either buy dumb bells or make your own lightweight ones by simply using cans of food or filling plastic bags with sugar or salt.

CAT STRETCHES
Throughout the day – especially if your work involves sitting at a desk – stand up and stretch.

THE MODEL WORKOUT

From cropped tops to figure-hugging trousers, today's body-baring fashions reveal more parts of our anatomy than ever before. Rob Lander, fitness guru and personal trainer to models, has devised a special workout for the readers of this book to target all the normal areas of concern – stomach, breasts, bottom, thighs and upper arms.

Note: Exercise should only be carried out after taking illness, injuries, medication and medical conditions into consideration. Seek advice from your GP if you are exercising for the first time. If any exercise hurts too much – stop immediately. Wear loose clothing.

PERT BREASTS
FLIES
Using a couple of cans of food or light dumb bells, lie down on a bench or the floor. Place the weights in your hands and onto your chest. Now push the weights up so they are above your face. With your elbows unlocked and slightly bent, lower your arms out in an arc until you are in the crucifix position. Now bring your arms back above your face in a nice arc, keeping your arms straight but not locked. Repeat around 12 times. If you find you can do up to 16 repetitions easily, increase the weights so that 12 is quite hard.

Points to remember: Make sure your back is supported at all times as lower-back problems are common. Remember to breathe! Breathe out on exertion and in on lowering.

FIRM BUTTOCKS AND TONED THIGHS
SQUATS
Stand with your feet shoulder-width apart. Now place your hands on your thighs, bend your knees and sit back onto your heels as if you were sitting on an imaginary chair. Slide your hands, then elbows, onto your knees. You should find that your knees are at a 90-degree angle, and your back at 45 degrees. If you're not in this position, correct yourself until you are. Your feet should be flat on the floor, but your body weight should go through your heels so that you are able to lift your toes very slightly. Now stand up, head first, keeping your back at 45 degrees. Repeat approximately 12 times. If you find it too easy, hold your cans or dumb bells.

Points to remember: Do not arch your back; keep it flat and your head up. Breathe – or you will pass out.

TONED UPPER ARMS
BICEP CURLS
This exercise can be performed seated or standing. Standing is preferable, as seated will lower your heart rate and, therefore, have less effect on your fitness levels. Stand with feet shoulder-width apart, holding either dumb bells or cans in your hands, at each side of your body. Keeping your elbows fixed to each side, bring your hands up to shoulder

level, then lower back down in a slow, controlled manner. Repeat around 12 times. If you can do this easily, increase the weights in your hands.

Points to remember: Fix your elbows to the side of your body, but don't use them as a lever from which to lift the weight. Breathe steadily.

TRICEP DIPS

This exercise helps tone that flabby-prone area at the back of your arms. Sit on the edge of a chair with your hands tucked underneath your bottom. Holding onto the edge of the chair, lower your bottom down towards the floor until your elbows are at 90 degrees. Your bottom should not touch the floor. Now straighten your arms and bring your bottom back up, keeping it close to the chair. To begin with, your feet will probably be positioned quite close to the chair with your knees bent. The further away you move your feet from the chair, and the more you straighten your legs, the more difficult the exercise will be. Repeat exercise until you tire.

Points to remember: Keep your hands forward and elbows pointing backwards. Keep your back close to the chair and do not bend the elbows greater than right angles, as this could damage your joints.

FLAT, FIRM STOMACH

CRUNCHES

Lie down on your back with your knees bent and feet on the floor close to your bottom. Place your hands on your thighs. Now contract your stomach so it feels tight and hard, and push your lower back into the floor. Next, lift your chin away from your chest, and slide your hands up onto your knees. Hold this position. Your tummy should be as tight as possible; if you can't feel anything, you are not squeezing hard enough. Now lower your head and shoulders back down to the floor. Breathe out on the way up and in on lowering. Repeat 10–15 times. If you find you can do more, you are not squeezing hard enough. If you want to make this exercise harder, place your hands at the side of your head. However, do not lock them behind your head as this could damage your neck.

Points to remember: keep the tension in your tummy all the time until you cannot lift anymore. This is far more effective than lots and lots of repetitions.

FITNESS AND HEALTH

Exercise will go a long way to making you look and feel great, but if the stress of everyday living in the nineties is taking its toll, you need to look at different aspects of your lifestyle and find ways to relax, de-stress and bring your body and mind into harmony.

SLEEP

Sleep keeps mind, body and soul healthy. A good night's sleep is probably one of the best beautifiers. Although the majority of us need around seven or eight hours a night, some can survive on considerably less, while for others even eight hours is inadequate. The effect of lack of sleep through late nights or insomnia is cumulative; eventually your health and looks will suffer. After a few late nights, or some nights of disturbed sleep, you may find that your skin becomes dull and greyish, with dark circles or bags under your eyes. Lack of sleep can also make you more susceptible to spots and blemishes.

During sleep, the body is continuously renewing itself. If sleep is disturbed, or you are stressed, regardless of how many hours you are sleeping, its benefit is undermined. Sleep also becomes less effective the later you go to bed; unless this is a regular pattern due to unusual working hours. Remember – early to bed, early to rise, keeps you healthy, beautiful and wise. If you have difficulty sleeping, try herbal supplements. And a drop of lavender essential oil on your pillow (away from where you put your face) can work wonders. Before you disappear into the land of Nod, prepare to pep up your looks by applying treatments to parts of the body that need a particular boost, such as your face, lips, hands, feet and hair. If you can try to sleep on your back, this way you are less likely to get sleep-induced lines and wrinkles.

RELAXATION

Relaxation is an important part of general well-being. It calms the mind, body and nerves, enhances peaceful sleep and aids concentration. Search for that perfect place to relax, be it a candlelit bedroom, a peaceful spot out of doors, or a long soak in an aromatic bath. If you're relaxed, you are far better equipped to deal with everyday problems than if you're on edge. And your looks certainly won't tolerate a permanent state of tension. Throughout the day be aware of your standing or sitting position. Ensure that your shoulders are relaxed and that your hands and feet are not tensed up. Deep breathing is a great relaxant and cleanser. Take a deep breath through your nose, hold your breath for six counts, then exhale slowly through your mouth.

If you have trouble relaxing, from soothing voices to relaxing music or bird songs, there are a variety of relaxation tapes on the market to help you on your way

MEDITATION

Another way of cutting off from the world, eliminating tension and stress and clearing your mind from the everyday clatter is by practising meditation. There are different methods of meditation, some focus on repeating a word – your mantra – silently, while other techniques involve chanting aloud. Meditation has a positive result on both mental and physical well-being. Generally, people meditate to find their inner self, to seek spiritual or mental enlightenment, or as a form of combating stress and reviving lost energy. When meditating, it is important to sit in the correct position – the lotus position or crossed-legged, keeping the back straight. To get yourself in the mood, burn incense and play spiritual sounds.

MIND

Don't underestimate the importance of being mentally fit. To cope with life's ups and downs and to enjoy it to the full, you need a healthy mind. Without positive thoughts and an optimistic outlook, your mind can start to control you, allowing you less control over your life. Stress, anxiety, depression and negative thoughts can have devastating effects on your health: you will be more susceptible to illness, your sleep patterns will be disturbed, and your looks will be affected. The proverb 'a problem shared is a problem halved' most certainly works for most people. So, if you develop a problem, tackle it immediately by getting help.

Detox your mind daily by either relaxing, meditating or taking time out for yourself to gather your positive thoughts and re-energize your mind.

HEAT TREATMENTS

Saunas, Turkish baths (steam rooms) and steam cabinets are a great way of ridding your body of toxins and leaving you with thoroughly clean, glowing skin. If you prefer not to have your face and head submerged in heat, plump for a steam treatment. Only spend 10–15 minutes at one time. A cold shower or dip in a plunge pool afterwards will have an invigorating effect.

SPAS

Gone are the regimented attitudes of the eighties-style health farms, labelled 'fat farms', where you exercised until you dropped, dined on a plate of lettuce leaves, and where austere, white-cloaked types confiscated any goodies you tried to smuggle in. Today's spas are a place to unwind, to rebalance your mind, body and spirit. Explore holistic therapies, be pampered with luxurious beauty treatments and get into shape. From facials to flotation tanks, Reiki to reflexology, T'ai Chi to Turkish baths – there's every treatment, therapy and activity under the sun. Most spas now offer delicious food and good wine, with a low-calorie option for those who are weight-watching. If you haven't got the time or cash for a long stay – they are not cheap – many spas now cater for day visitors.

Your spa experience should leave you feeling relaxed, revitalized and inspired to keep up your new-found, healthy attitude. 'We find that during their stay people reassess their lives and, when they leave, they carry these thoughts through into their lifestyles,' says Elaine Williams, head of therapies at one of the UK's top spas, Grayshott Hall. 'Their stay here opens up a lot of new possibilities, giving people the chance to try a range of different activities and therapies.'

There are dozens of spas throughout the world here is the pick of the bunch: Givenchy hotel and spa in California, Evian spa and Helianthal in France, Le Sport in St Lucia, Chiva-som in Thailand, Doral Saturnia in Florida, Gleneagles and Turnbury in Scotland, and Grayshot Hall, Chewton Glen, The Dorchester and Champneys in England. There are two types of spa: the health spa and the luxury five-star hotel that has a spa on site. Unfortunately, I only had space to review one of each.

My first visit was to Britain's most famous spa, Champneys – a total health-and-beauty follower's haven. After donning a fluffy, white robe and matching slippers, I had the obligatory, five-minute medical check. With the knowledge I was fit and healthy, I sat down to a cup of coffee with semi-skimmed milk (full fat wasn't on the menu) and studied my timetable. There was almost too much choice. On top of your personalized schedule, there's a jam-packed timetable of daily activities on offer, ranging from all sorts of classes from T'ai Chi to aqua aerobics, talks on subjects as diverse as neuro-linguistic programming (NLP) and an interesting range of general activities. Couple this with the choice of 100 treatments and therapies and no wonder I was in a quandary as to what to do first. It was then that I realized the time had come for my stint in the spa.

After a heat treatment in a steam cabinet, I was led to a dimly lit relaxation room, tucked up in blankets on an extremely comfortable, reclining bed, and left to listen to relaxing sounds. The stress of London life was just beginning to melt away when my peaceful mood was rudely interrupted by the sound of loud snoring. But before I had time to get irritated, I was called for my aromatherapy massage – a half-hour of pummelling away at all those knots. On leaving the spa area I headed to the pool for a swim, but wimped out when I heard the bubbling and gurgling of an enticing Jacuzzi. After 15 minutes

it was time to dress for lunch. I needn't have bothered – almost everyone else was in robes and slippers! After a wholesome, three-course lunch, with an hour to kill I went to a talk on NLP before it was time for my favourite treatment – a facial. An hour of pampering and I was totally relaxed and in the perfect, zombie-like state to join a relaxation class. This time it was I who was doing the snoring!

I ended my day with a swim in the pool (pictured below) and a dip in the outdoor Jacuzzi. Champneys was a place I'd always wanted to visit and it certainly lived up to my expectations.

Chewton Glen, a five-star country retreat, has to be the ultimate place to dine on gourmet food, drink vintage wine, enjoy the countryside and be pampered from head to toe in a first-class spa. The pampering extends to the luxurious rooms in the beautiful surroundings of this splendid stately home. In contrast to Champneys' activity-filled day, my day at Chewton Glen's spa was entirely self-indulgent. There were so many enticing treatments to choose from: algae body wraps, holistic body therapy and mud envelopment were three of many. After plumping for my favourite treatments, I headed to the tranquil pillar-lined pool for a swim and Jacuzzi. During a stroll through the grounds, I discovered an outdoor pool hidden behind trees, where you can swim while breathing in the fresh sea air.

Lunch was held in the spa restaurant. I nibbled on a delicious cold spread followed by a very tasty cheesecake dessert. My treatments kicked off with a vigorous body polish which, in contrast, was followed by a most relaxing full-body massage using aromatherapy oils. Next on the agenda was a seaweed body wrap, where I was covered from head to toe in green gunge, wrapped in a heated blanket, and left to 'boil in the bag'. The treatments were nicely rounded off with an E'SPA facial, which encompassed an incredibly uplifting scalp massage. All the therapists had a sort of spiritual, calm-inducing aura about them which, coupled with such practicalities as soundproofed beauty rooms, prevented anything from ruining my peaceful trance. In fact, the whole atmosphere was one of calm and comfort, with a definite feeling of luxury thrown in. From the towelling robe to the little 'extras' like body lotion in the changing area – nothing had been overlooked. By the end of the day I was utterly relaxed and revitalized. Now it was time to sample the hotel's superb, Michelin-starred cuisine.

Courtesy of Champneys

NUTRITION

Food is the fuel for beauty. Without a healthy, balanced diet – jam-packed with the right nutrients – your body shape, together with the condition of your skin, nails and hair, will suffer.

Bad eating habits are accelerated by today's busy lifestyles and hectic work schedules. Models, who should pay even more attention to eating nourishing food, often skip meals, grabbing little more than a cup of coffee between castings. But many have learnt the hard way. Living off a diet of caffeine, cigarettes and junk food inhibits the uptake of vitamins and minerals, which can result in dull-toned, blemished skin, brittle nails that split and break, and a lacklustre head of hair. Eventually, energy levels and general state of health will also be affected. The basic message for eating to look and feel good is, as Champneys' dietician Priscilla Marmot points out: 'Eat less fat, especially saturated fat, and eat more fibre in the form of vegetables, fruit, cereals and grains, with moderate use of salt and added sugars.'

A BALANCED DIET

A balanced diet is vital for healthy living. As no single item of food contains the 40 different nutrients needed to keep your body in tip-top condition, you'll need to eat a variety of foods from each of the five main food groups: 1. cereals; 2. dairy products; 3. fruit and vegetables; 4. protein; 5. fats and oils. Calorie-counting is now considered archaic, so forget it. Priscilla points out that today's philosophy for keeping trim is to eat a healthy, balanced diet. 'To achieve the correct balance of fat, protein and carbohydrate, it's important to understand the percentage of each that a meal should contain,' explains Priscilla. 'In an ideal eating plan at least 50–55 per cent of energy should be provided by carbohydrate (this includes fibre-containing foods); 30 per cent by fat (10 per cent saturated, 10 per cent or less polyunsaturated and 10 per cent or more mono-unsaturated) and the remaining 15–20 per cent by protein. There is no need to exclude any food completely; each has a contribution to make.'

CHECKLIST FOR HEALTHY EATING

- **Ensure** that everything you eat is of high nutritional value, containing the essential vitamins and minerals.
- **Eat** at least five different portions of fresh fruit and vegetables each day (some of these should be eaten raw). Fruit and vegetables can be eaten in abundance, but remember, they can cause flatulence. It's preferable to eat fruit as a snack, as it takes far less time to digest than if eaten with meals.
- **Juicing** is a great way of getting your full quota of fresh fruit and vegetables, especially for those who are averse to eating them in their raw form. To make a nutritious juice, blend your own mixture of fruit or vegetables.
- **Try** to eat freshly prepared food whenever possible. Cut down on processed, tinned and highly spiced foods, and foods containing additives and preservatives such as so-called convenience foods. Steam, bake or grill food and, when frying, stir fry rather than deep fry.
- **Avoid** refined flour and sugar. Replace refined sugar with honey, raw sugar or fructose (natural sugar found in fruit), and white flour with wholemeal flour. Substitute sugary soft drinks – even diet ones – for naturally sweetened

health drinks or pure, unsweetened fruit juice.

- **Reduce** the amount of salt you use.
- **Because** tea and coffee contain the stimulant caffeine, they can make the skin look sluggish and affect vitamin absorption. Lower your intake of these beverages and substitute them with herbal teas, tisanes or decaffeinated coffee and tea instead.
- **Organic** food is preferable as it is free of pesticides, chemicals and hormones.
- **Alcohol** is okay in moderation. Champneys recommend up to two glasses of red or white wine a day with your evening meal.
- **Include** plenty of fibre-rich foods in your diet. Fibre is high in cereals, especially bran, but is also found in wholemeal flour, brown rice, brown pasta, pulses and oatmeal; vegetables, including cabbage, peas, potatoes, beans; nuts and fruit – almonds, apples, apricots, brazil nuts, dates, figs, raisins, oranges, lemons, plums and prunes. Roughage will aid elimination of waste matter, which is vital to improve conditions such as spots and cellulite.
- **Drink** plenty of water – eight glasses a day if possible. (This does not include the water used to make tea or coffee.) Most models guzzle gallons of the stuff each day. Water helps flush out toxins, hydrates your skin, and thus keeps it clear.
- **Don't** drink too much liquid with meals as it dilutes the intake of nutrients and also causes flatulence.
- **Reduce** fat intake, but, as Priscilla Marmot stresses, do NOT cut fat out of your diet completely. 'Avoid foods which contain bad, "saturated" fats: a diet rich in these can lead to excess weight, cellulite, spots and blemishes. Good, "mono-unsaturated" fats are important in the functioning of your body that leads to healthy teeth and bones, and helps build cell membranes.' Priscilla suggests eating oily fish at least two to three times a week for omega-3 fatty acids. For dressings, use olive oil as well as sunflower, sesame and grapeseed which are all excellent sources of EFAs (essential fatty acids), vital for building cell membranes. Use olive oil for cooking. Those virtually fat-free dieters – who eat bread without any margarine and salad without dressing – will find that their skin becomes dry, and, as they grow older, they will age more rapidly.
- **Don't** be fooled into thinking that cereal bars are less fattening than cakes and sweets; they often contain even more fat.
- **Snack** on fresh fruit, raw vegetables, dried fruit and nuts.
- **Don't** skip meals, especially breakfast.
- **Diuretic** foods: if you suffer from under-eye bags or other water-retention ailments, include melon, strawberries, artichokes and other foods containing potassium and magnesium in your diet.
- **Detoxify** by eating only fruit until lunch; drink fruit juice and herbal teas. Detoxifying foods include raspberries, grapes, apples, citrus fruits, blackcurrants and pineapples.

THE BEAUTY VITAMINS

Vitamin A – tagged the 'beauty vitamin' helps repair body tissue, promote smooth skin and is an antioxidant. Vitamin B complex is good for those with oily skin and also helps nourish hair from the roots. Vitamin C is one of the most important beauty vitamins, an antioxidant that promotes cell renewal. Another antioxidant is vitamin E, which is anti-ageing and great for dry skin. Zinc, being a natural antiseptic, helps fight infection and spots, and is also good for preventing milk spots on nails.

VITAMINS

Here is a list of vitamins and minerals essential to your looks, health and well-being, accompanied by some of the foods which contain them.

Vitamin A – apricots, mangos, plums, dark-green, leafy vegetables, carrots, swedes, butter, cheese, eggs, liver.

Vitamin B1 – wholegrains, wheatgerm, oats, brown rice, brazil nuts, poultry, lamb's liver.

Vitamin B2 – beans, green vegetables, wholegrains, almonds, avocados, brewer's yeast, milk, cheese, eggs, poultry, liver, kidney.

Vitamin B3 – nuts, mushrooms, oily fish, chicken, lamb's liver, kidney, seafood, wholegrains, green vegetables, beans.

Vitamin B5 – broccoli, cabbage, wholegrains, sunflower seeds, corn, bran, nuts, brewer's yeast, egg yolk, kidneys, lamb's liver.

Vitamin B6 – sunflower seeds, wholegrains, nuts, wheatgerm, bananas, green vegetables, carrots, cabbage, poultry, lamb's liver.

Vitamin B9 – wholegrains, green vegetables.

Vitamin B12 – milk, cheese, eggs, fish, soya beans, liver, poultry.

Vitamin C – blackcurrants, citrus fruits, watercress, kiwi fruit, apricots, tomatoes, strawberries, green peppers, cabbage, cauliflower, broccoli, Brussels sprouts.

Vitamin D – oily fish, egg yolk, cheese.

Vitamin E – wholegrains, green vegetables, carrots, cabbage, sunflower seeds, wheatgerm, cereal, brown rice, oats, cheese, eggs.

Vitamin K – cabbage, broccoli, potatoes, wholegrains, eggs, oats, wheatgerm.

MINERALS

Calcium – milk, cheese, sesame seeds, broccoli, almonds, olives, seaweed, molasses.

Chlorine – tomatoes, salt, celery, lettuce, spinach.

Chromium – fruit, nuts, green vegetables, bran, brewer's yeast, poultry.

Cobalt – green vegetables, fruit, wholegrains, meat, cereals.

Copper – nuts, liver, lamb, butter, olive oil, cereals, vegetables, shell fish, poultry, wholegrains.

Fluorine – fish, seafood, tea.

Iodine – seafood, shellfish, seaweed, sea salt.

Iron – kidney, liver, egg yolk, seafood, watercress, green, leafy vegetables, soya, wholegrains, molasses, sunflower seeds.

Magnesium – seafood, sea salt, olives, nuts, wholegrains, green vegetables, cheese, potatoes, dried fruit, tea.

Manganese – nuts, wheatgerm, spinach, cabbage, parsley, watercress, lentils, apricots, kidneys.

Phosphorous – eggs, fish, cheese, meat, wheatgerm, wholegrains.

Potassium – seafood, potatoes, bananas, apricots, figs, soya beans, green vegetables.

Selenium – wholegrains, sesame seeds, mushrooms, seafood, oily fish, brazil nuts, bread, cheese, eggs, cereal.

Sodium – wheatgerm, sea salt, sea food, green vegetables, poultry.

Sulphur – cheese, eggs, milk, poultry, fish, nuts.

Zinc – seafood, eggs, liver, sardines, sunflower seeds, wheatgerm, nuts, bran, lamb, chicken, milk, bread, cereal.

FOOD SUPPLEMENTS

Ideally, a healthy diet should contain all the vitamins and minerals you need. But in practice, the vitamin content is easily destroyed by cooking and preparation. Here a few of the most popular food supplements to promote beauty:

Aloe vera – extracted from the aloe vera plant that grows in warm climates, and, although it is mainly used in beauty products, taken internally it has rejuvenating effects.

Betacarotene – an antioxidant that helps combat the effects of free radicals which damage the structure of cells and tissue.

Echinacea – a herbal supplement from the Echinacea flower that is excellent in preventing spots and blemishes and in strengthening the immune system. It is also known to be anti-ageing and gives skin a healthy glow.

Evening primrose oil – rich in GLA (gamma-linolenic acid), good for dry skin, glossy hair and balancing hormones, thus improving acne.

Fish oil – a rich source of vitamin A and D and omega-3 (a highly beneficial, fatty acid), good for the maintenance of healthy skin, strong nails and glossy hair as well as mobility.

Propolis – a substance produced by bees that has natural antiseptic and antibacterial properties. Good for skin problems such as acne.

Royal jelly – a natural substance provided by bees for their queen bee. It is highly nutritious and promotes general well-being.

Starflower oil – also rich in GLA, and good for skin problems and hormone balance.

DIETING

Over the past 20 years we have been bombarded with various diets, all claiming to be 'The Miracle Diet'. Controversy and conflicting opinion over certain fad diets have led to a general feeling of scepticism. Drastic dieting is now considered by nutritionists and dieticians to have harmful effects on your health and your looks, if not immediately, then in future years. 'The danger of some diets is, that by eliminating certain foods, you end up losing the wrong type of weight – from muscle not fat,' explains dietician Priscilla Marmot. 'In order to maintain muscle tissue, and keep your body functioning correctly, you need a balanced diet including carbohydrates and "good" fats. If you want to go on a strict diet, you should only do so under the supervision of a qualified dietician or nutritionist.'

Slimming tablets, which work by suppressing

your appetite, are used to treat some overweight and obese people, but they can endanger your health. Normal symptoms include aggression and dizziness. However, they have been known to cause far more serious side effects, including heart attacks. Admittedly, slimming pills can have a drastic effect in aiding weight loss but, in many cases, as soon as the patient stops taking the tablets, the weight returns with a vengeance. If you do want to lose weight, eat healthily rather than diet, and combine with regular exercise.

Anorexia is a serious – and sometimes fatal – eating disorder where the victim believes she or he is overweight, even when they are dangerously underweight. Bulimia is another eating disorder. Unlike anorexia, where the victim starves, bulimics binge then vomit. At the opposite end of the spectrum is an obsessive eating disorder which causes obesity.

Models are continuously being reprimanded for supposedly causing a world-wide obsession with being thin. If blame is to be apportioned, it should be to the industry and not the individual models. Contrary to most people's beliefs, neither are models anorexic nor do they have to starve themselves to stay slim. Most models are naturally blessed with size-10 figures in the same way they are blessed with beautiful faces, great bone structure and elongated bodies. Some models, especially in their teens, are pencil thin – the reverse of adolescents who suffer from puppy fat. But as they grow older they fill out. Kate Moss is a perfect example of a model who filled out and developed a more curvaceous and womanly physique by the time she was 20. Jodie Kidd, another teenage model who had the finger wagged at her, has never starved herself. In fact, as her friends, parents and other models confirm, she eats like a horse. Jodie is just an adolescent with a high metabolism.

There will always be a handful of models who take dieting to the extreme. But most models realize these drastic measures can seriously affect their health and even put their lives at risk. The majority of models are lucky to have hungry metabolisms that enable them to eat what they like, when they like. Others eat a healthy, balanced diet of the right foods that are of sufficient nutritional value to keep them in tip-top condition, while giving them the energy required for such a demanding job.

From a more practical point of view, an anorexic or bulimic model just wouldn't work. Firstly, she or he wouldn't have the stamina required to cope with running around town on ten castings a day, travelling from one country to another, or getting up before dawn for a photo shoot, then standing under broiling lights for the rest of the day. Secondly, as anorexia affects the physical appearance by leaving the skin grey and lifeless, causing sunken cheeks and dark rings that look like black eyes, an anorexic model simply wouldn't get booked.

A MODEL MENU

When it comes to healthy eating, one of the UK's leading health spas, Champneys, is the expert. Dietician Priscilla Marmot, in conjunction with Champneys' chef Adam Palmer, have devised four delicious recipes for readers of this book. Each dish is light and highly nutritious without scrimping on the flavour. Enjoy!

TOMATO AND OLIVE SALAD WITH MANGO DRESSING (STARTER)

4 plum tomatoes
4 yellow cherry tomatoes
4 red cherry tomatoes
32 black olives
1 bunch chives cut into batons
Dressing
1 mango
2 dessertspoons white-wine vinegar
2 dessertspoons extra-virgin olive oil
4 basil leaves, shredded
sea salt and freshly milled black pepper

Serves 4

Blanch all the tomatoes together for ten seconds, refresh under cold, running water and remove the skins. To make the dressing, peel the mango and place the flesh into a liquidizer or food-processor with the vinegar. Blend until smooth, then slowly add the olive oil while the machine is running. Pass through a conical strainer and add the shredded basil. Season with a small amount of salt and black pepper and add a little water if the dressing is too thick. To assemble the salad, arrange the tomatoes attractively on a plate with the olives in the centre, season with a little salt and pepper. Sprinkle the chive batons onto the salad and finish with a circle of dressing surrounding the salad. Garnish with four sprigs of purple and green basil.

STUFFED BREAST OF CHICKEN WITH TOMATO VINAIGRETTE

4 x 140g/5oz breasts of corn-fed chicken, skinned, boned and trimmed
2 large carrots, peeled and grated
1 large leek, finely chopped
16 black olives, stoned and roughly chopped
575ml/1pt/$2^1/_2$ cups chicken stock
sea salt and freshly milled black pepper

Vinaigrette

3 large, ripe tomatoes
2 tablespoons extra-virgin olive oil
1 basil leaf
1 tablespoon cider vinegar

Serves 4

Preheat the oven to 220° C/245° F/Gas 7. Make a sharp incision about 2cm long into one side of each chicken breast to form a pocket. Season the grated carrot, chopped leek and the olives with salt and pepper and stuff the chicken breasts with the mixture. Overlap the pocket openings to seal the mixture inside. In an ovenproof dish, bring the chicken stock to the boil on the top of the stove and add the chicken breasts. Place in the oven for approximately ten minutes, until poached. Meanwhile, liquidize all the ingredients for the vinaigrette in a food-processor or blender and pass through a fine sieve. When the chicken is cooked, slice each breast diagonally into five pieces and place on individual plates. Spoon round the vinaigrette and serve immediately.

BANANA EN PAPILLOTE (DESSERT)

4 small, under-ripe bananas
1 cinnamon stick, cut into four pieces
4 star anise
1 vanilla pod, cut into four pieces
1oz/2 tablespoons grated carob
3fl oz/1 cup pineapple juice

Serves 4

Preheat the oven to 230° C/450° F/Gas 8. Lightly grease a piece of aluminium foil large enough to cover one banana and place a banana on top. Arrange a piece of cinnamon stick, one star anise and a piece of vanilla pod around the banana and sprinkle with grated carob and a quarter of the pineapple juice. Fold up the foil to make an airtight pocket. Repeat the process with each banana. Place the sealed bananas on a baking tray and cook in the oven for three to four minutes. Serve immediately.

HERB RISOTTO WITH MARINATED GRILLED VEGETABLES

400g/14oz arborio rice
1 onion, finely chopped
2 cloves garlic, finely chopped
100g/$3^1/_2$oz mushrooms, finely chopped
150g/5oz celery, finely chopped
$1^1/_2$ litres/$2^1/_2$ pints vegetable stock
1 tablespoon olive oil
salt and pepper
2 tablespoons mixed herbs
2 aubergines, sliced
4 courgettes, sliced
4 mixed peppers, cut into eighths
2 fennel bulbs, cut into strips and blanched
2 leeks, cut into 2cm-long rounds

Marinade

basil
olive oil
balsamic vinegar
salt and pepper

Serves 4

In a hot saucepan, sweat the onion, celery and garlic until translucent and add the rice and cook for one minute. Then add the mushrooms. Stirring all the time, add a ladle of hot stock. Do not add any more until the previous ladle has been absorbed. Carry on adding the stock until the rice is cooked and creamy. Next, season well and stir in the fresh herbs. After marinating the vegetables for two hours, grill until browned and tender. Serve the rice in the middle of the plate, surrounding it with the vegetables. Sprinkle with fresh herbs.

Photographed by Richard Lohr courtesy of © Condé Nast PL - British Vogue

PART 4

SO YOU WANT TO BE A MODEL?

WHAT IT TAKES TO MAKE A MODEL

There's no secret formula, but attributes such as determination, personality and professionalism will get you much further than looks alone.

> 'Linda Evangelista is the ultimate role model of someone who studied and perfected her trade,' says model coach Jay Alexander.

PROFESSIONALISM

You may have to stand for hours in extreme conditions – ten degrees below freezing or in sweltering tropical heat – but you *mustn't* complain. The same applies if you're asked to model a hideous outfit, or have your hair styled in a way you simply hate. This is what models are paid *lots* of money to do!

Even at the pinnacle of their careers, supermodels still treat each job with the utmost respect. Yasmin Le Bon helps carry equipment on location, and Linda Evangelista and Christy Turlington are always willing to muck in on shoots. Take a leaf out of their book and you'll get to the top – fast. Professionalism extends to your looks. If you turn up to a casting or job with dirty hair and chewed nails, it's just not good enough. Give 100 per cent at all times.

FIRST IMPRESSIONS

Whether you're at that initial agency appointment, casting, go-see or job interview, you must strive to create a lasting impression. At a casting you may have as little as 30 seconds to sell yourself and build a rapport with the client. Utilize this time. Begin by introducing yourself in a confident, friendly and professional manner. If you're feeling uneasy or are suffering from an attack of nerves, don't avoid speaking: silence only makes the situation more awkward. Smile! Happiness is contagious. Look interested throughout the meeting, and respond with enthusiasm to any questions you are asked. Even if you're suffering from a raging hangover, have just been jilted by your partner, or are coming down with a bad dose of flu – no matter how rough you feel – you must *not* let it show. Finally, never leave without thanking the client or interviewer for their time.

> 'You have to be dispassionate about the whole thing,' says model Emma Noble. 'Think of yourself as a product, and don't take it as a personal attack on your looks when you're rejected.'

'It's all very exciting, but there are the down moments too, like when you spend days just casting and not knowing when your next booking will be,' says model Nina McCann. 'To cope with this you'll need to be determined.'

ATTITUDE

We've heard about supermodels throwing tantrums or storming off the set at a shoot. But this attitude will get you nowhere in modelling nor, for that matter, in any other profession. Big egos are over! The model industry might appear to comprise a bunch of affected egos with attitude, but as you get to know individuals you'll realize that most are genuinely pleasant people who have artistic temperaments. Even if the people you're working for do happen to be stroppy or uncommunicative, you must still be professional. Clients don't take kindly to prima donnas who turn up late and are difficult to work with. Besides, a model with an attitude problem could turn a fun trip to the Bahamas into a complete nightmare.

Good manners are vital. And don't think that airs and graces, or acting as though you are the most wonderful creature on earth, will impress potential clients or agents alike. It won't. Okay – so you need to be sure of yourself, but it should be in a natural, unaffected way. Don't let success go to your head. Even if you've reached the enviable stage where clients send stretch limos to collect you, strive to keep your feet firmly planted on the ground. Remember – no model is indispensable.

Top photographer Nick Knight believes that to be a successful model it takes hard work and an understanding of what the photographer wants.

CONFIDENCE

Modelling will give you the confidence to deal with people from all walks of life. But it's difficult for a model of 16 immediately to gain the self-assurance of a 25-year-old who's been modelling for nearly a decade. An experienced model will naturally be more at ease in most situations because he or she knows what to expect. Nevertheless, most established models have endured – and survived – their fair share of confidence knocks.

Confidence is an asset. Some people are instinctively confident, yet others are naturally insecure.

For those lacking in the confidence department, a little boosting can go along way. Start believing in yourself and confidence will follow. Be positive. If you're sure you will be rejected for every casting you attend, you are doomed to failure. Furthermore, negativity will be picked up by the client. If you have a cheerful, friendly disposition and good poise, you'll undoubtedly come across as confident.

CRITICISM

You must expect some form of criticism from time to time. Perhaps you are too stiff in front of the camera, haven't quite got to grips with the running order at a show, or are just not giving it your best because you're completely exhausted, having worked for hours on end. Maybe your agent feels your image isn't quite right and may make suggestions on how best to alter it. Your agent is the professional, so accept what he or she tells you. Most criticism is constructive. It's simply a professional observation – so try not to take it to heart. It's all character-building stuff!

COPING WITH REJECTION

It's true what they say – if you're going to succeed as a model you will need to be thick skinned. Modelling is a tough business and it takes a certain kind of person with the right attitude to cope with the constant rejection. Even once you are past the first hurdle of having been accepted by an agency, you will still have to face a constant stream of rejections for many of the castings you attend. Most of the time a client will be looking for a particular type, so if you're not chosen you mustn't think it's because you're not good or beautiful enough. Clients tend to have a definite image in mind, and, unless you fit that description, you won't be picked. Don't let it get you down. No model gets every job he or she casts for; if you are going to succeed, rejection is something you will just have to accept.

COMPETITION

One of the most difficult aspects of modelling is that you're constantly surrounded by taller, slimmer, younger or more beautiful models. But you must endeavour to view your fellow models as contemporaries, not rivals. Models are not carbon copies of each other; they are admired and booked for their individuality. You've got something very different to offer the client from the model queuing up in front of you. If the client happens to prefer him/her – never mind – next time it'll probably be you.

DETERMINATION

A would-be model may have all the right attributes, but may lack the motivation and drive required to make a successful model. If you want to make it – you've got to want it badly. To be able to deal with the highs and lows, handle the fast pace, competition, rejection and demanding schedule, not to mention being away from home and missing loved ones, you'll also need to be absolutely determined to succeed. You must persevere – even during days when you have no bookings coming in. At the start of your modelling career you will have to devote weekends and evenings to testing. But without a good selection of photographs for your book, you might as well give up. Eventually, the never-ending treadmill of tests, go-sees and castings will pay off.

STAMINA
Modelling is physically gruelling. Whether you're a supermodel jetting from a Paris show to a New York studio or a new model dashing around town on go-sees, the working life of a model can be exhausting.

> 'It takes more than just beauty to be a model: it takes personality and a natural ability to communicate, get on with people, and to project yourself in front of the camera,' says Richard Habberley of Select Models.

When you see pictures of a model lounging by a Miami pool in a glossy magazine you think: 'Hey, this looks easy'. But it's not. Each photo shoot takes hours of preparation and can be very strenuous for the model. On location, for example, the model is usually up before dawn for hair and make-up, then, after getting into the first outfit of many, he or she must hang around the set while the photographer gets the lighting right and runs off Polaroids. It's not until this point that the shoot actually begins. Shows are equally tiring. In addition to make-up and hair styling, there are lengthy fittings and rehearsals.

PERSONALITY
Modelling is a buyer's market and clients can afford to be selective. A vibrant personality is a great quality and will give you an edge over the competition. Be yourself. On a shoot, photographers and clients want to create a congenial atmosphere, and it's invariably the friendly, down-to-earth models – not the stand-offish, po-faced types – who are popular with the team. If you've gone to see a magazine fashion editor for a trip, and the choice is between you and another model, a good personality will swing the decision in your favour.

When you're still standing in that same spot in the studio three hours later, don't look bored or start yawning. Instead, think about the many jobs that are considerably more mundane than modelling.

PUNCTUALITY
Naomi Campbell may have a reputation for being notoriously late but this doesn't mean you can be. Strolling in late for a job – no matter how good your excuse – starts you off on the wrong foot and could cost you money. In this business time is money. If the photographer, stylist and the rest of the team are being paid by the hour, and you delay the shoot by arriving late, the client may expect you to foot the bill! And besides, it's unlikely you will ever be booked by the same client or photographer again. When you're booked for an assignment, always try to arrive at least 15 minutes early. This way you'll have time to relax, enjoy a cup of coffee (decaffeinated, please!), and get a feel for what's going on.

Time-keeping becomes quite difficult, however, when you've as many as 10 or 12 castings or go-sees to attend in one day. It's inevitable that some will overlap. Even if they pan out nicely, if you're held up by a long wait at your first casting, it could result in you missing the next one altogether. The trick is to juggle your time carefully by prioritizing, and choosing the most important castings and go-sees first. Clients and agents are more tolerant about time-keeping where castings are concerned, as they are aware of the difficulties. Show time is another occasion when models run late. Although designers request that models arrive at least a couple of hours before the show for hair and make-up, some models, who've performed in the previous show, arrive only minutes before the start. Tempers are invariably always strained and models are invariably always late, but somehow the show goes on.

PREPARATION
Be prepared. Invest in a good diary and keep details of every job. Plan each day the night before. If you're off on castings or go-sees, find out where each one is located, then map out your route, making sure that

> 'I always go prepared,' says model Tina Harlow. 'I carry a big bag which consists of my book, composites, a white g-string, swimsuit, my wash bag, make-up, nail kit, lip balm, hand cream, a bottle of water, my diary, a map of the city I'm working in, and a book to read.'

you can feasibly get from one to another in time. Gather together your model kit, with any clothes or accessories you've been asked to bring. If the client has requested a black dress and you don't own such an item, or can't borrow one from a friend, you won't be expected to purchase one especially for the shoot. Nevertheless, you must let your agent or the client know in advance, rather than risk turning up without it. Take your book and composites to every job. And don't forget your make-up kit – you never know if it might come in handy. You should always have shaved body hair, manicured nails, and clean hair. Unless specified, turn up to an assignment free of make-up and hair free of mousse, gel etc. If you're doing lingerie, swimwear or nude work, don't wear constricting garments that could leave marks on your skin.

PERSONAL LIFE

Modelling can radically transform your life. But if you want to succeed as a model, you must be extremely committed and prepared to make the necessary sacrifices. You might find you are constantly travelling,

> 'Every part of a model should look great,' says beauty expert/television presenter Alison Young. 'Models must turn up to every job with manicured nails, an even skin colour, and having shaved or waxed their body hair. I once booked a model for a cellulite demonstration on television only to find she hadn't shaved. I won't be rebooking her.'

for instance. It's particularly difficult for young models who have never been away from home to be suddenly thrust into the big, wide world. In order to cope, you'll need to be emotionally stable. Throughout your career it's extremely important to keep modelling in perspective. You should, therefore, strive to be a well-rounded person, with other interests in your life.

As a model, you will often be required to work long, irregular hours, which can play havoc with your social life. Repeatedly cancelling arrangements will not please even the best of friends. Problems with friends who resent your new-found, glitzy lifestyle are to be expected. But once they realize it's just a job, and not as glamorous as it's cracked up to be, they'll more than likely change their attitude. Your parents or partner might also be averse to you becoming a model. Then again, they might be extremely supportive. Regardless of other peoples' attitudes, if you have been accepted by a good agency, this is a time when you'll need to have great belief in yourself. Aim to fulfil your dream. If you don't try, you'll only regret it later.

> 'An agent can only push a model so much,' says Didier Fernandez of Elite Paris. 'At the end of the day it's down to them.'

TIPS FOR SUCCESS

- **Treat** modelling seriously, but at the same time enjoy it.
- **Don't** give up your studies. If you are still at school or college, you should be able to model in your holidays. If your career suddenly takes off while you're at college or university, only then should you consider deferring your education for a year or taking private tuition.
- **Make** sure you have skills/qualifications to fall back on; modelling can be an unpredictable and short-lived career and should be considered as a career option.
- **Treat** castings and go-sees seriously – without these you will not get work.
- **Don't** get carried away by the whole social whirl of modelling and burn the candle at both ends.
- **Over-indulgence** in drink, drug abuse and late nights will lose you bookings.
- **Be** wise with your money. When you start earning, it's tempting to blow your money on such things as designer clothes and eating out at expensive restaurants. Don't! Follow the business-like attitude of the supermodels and invest some of it. Remember, it's unlikely that you're going to have such a high earning power for the rest of your working life.
- **Remain** level-headed. If you become affected by the whole business you won't last long.
- **Have** respect for your booker. He or she works extremely hard on your behalf. A good agent–model relationship can make a big difference to your modelling career.
- **Don't** take the fashion industry too seriously – it's an insular business. Put modelling into perspective with the rest of your life and the things going on in the world. Get a life!

STARTING OUT

You've read the fairy-tale-style stories of models becoming overnight sensations after having been 'discovered' by chance. Kate Moss was spotted perched on a suitcase at New York's JFK airport, Claudia Schiffer boogieing in one of Düsseldorf's night-clubs, and supermale Marcus Schenkenberg while sunning himself on a Los Angeles beach. These are rare cases, however, and you might spend the rest of your life waiting for fate to pluck you from obscurity. Fortunately for all you budding, would-be models, there are more immediate routes into modelling. You could enter a model contest, or simply take the most direct approach – the agency route.

IS MODELLING RIGHT FOR YOU?

Modelling appears to be the ultimate, enviable career: glamour, money and fame all rolled into one. But before you even consider sending off your favourite snaps, you must ask yourself the following questions, and have read the chapter 'What It Takes to Make a Model' (p.160) thoroughly. For starters, can you handle an unpredictable career, uncertain future, sporadic bookings and a fluctuating income? Modelling offers precious little in the way of security and, as models are booked at such short notice, they often have no idea what the next month, week, or even day holds. So, if you want a secure, nine-

A booker checks a wannabe's vital statistics

to-five job, forget it! Remember – as deeply desirable as it sounds, modelling can be something of a bittersweet career.

Does the idea of travelling alone and working with strangers unnerve or excite you? Are you resilient, or do you have such a fragile ego that you would crumble at the mere thought of rejection? Modelling is extremely competitive, so you'll need sheer determination to make it. If you're considering working in specialist areas such as parts or mature modelling, unless you are exceptionally lucky, it's unlikely to be a full-time vocation. Therefore, have you a career to fall back on, or a flexible job where

you can easily take time off for castings and assignments? Are you willing to put time and effort into trekking to dozens of go-sees and castings? Modelling, in particular the high-fashion field, can turn your world upside down. Could you cope? No matter which area of modelling you choose to enter, without the right attitude you're unlikely to succeed. So, after turning the final page of this book, pause and ask yourself: is modelling really for me?

FINDING THE RIGHT AGENCY

So you think you've got what it takes to storm-troop the world's catwalks, have the perfect hands to be a parts model, or think your child could become the next Gap kid? Your first step is to find a reputable agency. First and foremost choose an agency that specializes in the field of modelling you are interested in and suitable for. If you are only 5'4", there's no point trudging around all the fashion agencies to be told you're too short. Not only will you be wasting the agents' time, but you will lose confidence before you've even begun. Instead, approach glamour, promotional or character agencies that accept models of your height.

Next, consider the size of an agency. You might find a large agency too intimidating and impersonal, whereas a smaller agency might be able to offer you the personal touch you require. If you join a regional agency, it's unlikely there will be as much work available as at a large agency based in one of the major markets.

APPROACHING AN AGENCY

Never walk in off the street and expect to be seen. Agents are extremely busy people and, as they are approached by hundreds of hopefuls each week, they usually allocate certain times to interviewing. Either telephone and make an appointment, or send two recent snapshots (preferably a full-length and head shot), together with details of your age, height and measurements. If you want your photos returned, enclose a stamped, addressed envelope. Applicants who fulfil the basic requirements will be notified by letter and invited for an interview.

THE INTERVIEW

Modelling is a career. Treat the interview seriously: be professional, punctual and prepared. Make sure you take a selection of flattering photographs (snapshots are perfectly acceptable), along with a notepad and pen. If you're under 16, have a parent or guardian accompany you. Do not, however, bring friends along to the interview; this looks most unprofessional. Be resourceful. Before your interview, try to understand how agencies operate (see chapter on model agencies, p.78) and have questions prepared.

You only have one chance to impress an agent, so present yourself in the best possible way. Wear simple yet flattering clothes that accentuate your assets without making you look tarty. See p.110 for how models dress. If you're aiming for fashion modelling, it helps to look as though you are fashion conscious, but this doesn't mean you have to go kitted out in the latest designer labels. Kids can be dressed casually in something they feel comfortable in. Apply a minimal amount of make-up. For interviews with promotional or glamour agencies, you can afford to be a little more generous, but don't slap on so much that you look as though you're heading for a night on the town. Would-be models who have interviews with top fashion agents should turn up as bare-faced as possible. Finally, hair should be clean, loose and natural, not plastered with lacquer.

Once you arrive at an agency, be prepared to wait your turn. If you've come on an open day, there may be a dozen or so people in front of you. The interview will normally only take a few minutes. However, if the agent is interested in you, it might take considerably longer: he or she will probably measure you and will ask you to fill in a form.

REJECTION

Agents can tell at a split-second glance if you've got what it takes to make a model. Most are candid in their assessments: if they don't think you are model material, they'll probably tell you. If you're rejected, your natural instinct is probably to flee through the doors before the agent has had a chance to say 'but...'. Stop! This is a great opportunity to pick the brains of the experts. Just because an agency refuses to sign you up doesn't mean you won't succeed as a model. If you have potential, a good agent will either recommend other agencies they feel you'd be more suited to, or suggest you try another category of modelling altogether. So don't give up. You may have exactly what the next agency on your list is looking for.

You cannot force an agency to take you on its books. Some wannabes are so desperate to become models they dress up in different guises, dye their hair, or turn up wearing wigs. One male wannabe went to such extremes that he actually threatened an agent by pinning him to the wall. Luckily for booking agent Paul Bozchak of The Samantha Bond Agency, the police came to his rescue. Another case of ludicrous behaviour was when a wannabe took Models 1 to court, accusing them of racial discrimination. The agency has models of all origins on its books so, not surprisingly, the case was instantly dismissed.

There are a number of reasons why an agent might not take you on. It could be because there are other models on the books with a similar look.

Alternatively, you might be too short, too tall or have a look that just isn't right for that particular agency. If there is a specific reason, such as weight, hair length or a skin condition that could be remedied, the agent should tell you and may well ask you to return when the problem is resolved. However, unless the agent says so, don't take this as a guarantee you'll be taken on. Three months down the line the agent might still say 'no'. If an agent says your look isn't right for them, as looks change so rapidly it might be worth approaching them six months later. If you've been rejected by every agency, in every field of modelling, you'll just have to come to terms with the fact that you're obviously not cut out to be a model. But this doesn't mean you can't be involved in the industry. Turn to p.98 to find out about other opportunities.

JOINING AN AGENCY

You've been accepted – congratulations! But before you crack open the champagne, remember to ask the agent plenty of questions (see examples below). At this stage you must let your agent know if you have any commitments, such as a part-time job or picking up your children from school. You must also give your booker a list of telephone numbers where you can be contacted. You don't want to miss a booking just because your agent can't get hold of you. If you don't have an answermachine, it will be well worth investing in one.

Here is a list of questions you might want to ask the agent.
- **How** much commission do you take?
- **How** soon will I get work?
- **What** expenses will I incur?
- **How** often will I get paid?
- **Do** you supply a portfolio/book or will I need to buy one?
- **Will** I have to pay for tests? If so, how much?

A NEW FACE

Before you get too excited, remember: the first few months are the toughest part of a model's career. You will need to do a lot of groundwork before you can call yourself a fully-fledged model. When you join an agency, unless you have already modelled, you will be labelled a new face and, if you've been taken on by a fashion agency, you'll be placed on the new faces board. The bookers who supervise débutante models are there to help you through the development stage, from changing your image to sending you on your first test and getting over the most difficult hurdle – your first booking.

Before you arrange your first test shoot, you must work at getting your image right: read Part 3 of this book, together with the chapter on training (p.82). Your booker should recommend a good hairdresser and, as most top fashion agencies have an arrangement with a hair salon, you shouldn't have to pay a penny. You'll also need a selection of decent clothes to wear for test shoots and to wear to castings and go-sees. And for character, mature, extras, kids or commercial models, you'll need to build up a wardrobe of different outfits to wear on assignments where clothes are not provided.

When it comes to getting your book together, your agency will either organize the test shoots for you, or give you a list of photographers to approach direct. In order for you to have a few images in your book, you'll need at least a couple of photo sessions before you can head off to castings and go-sees. (See chapter on models' tools, p.168)

Most female models stay on the new faces board for three to six months before moving on to the main board. If a model is particularly young, and/or still at school, she may remain a new face for considerably longer. Because of various reasons, including the market place and grooming, male models require a shorter development period: the lucky devils only have to spend as little time as a month on the new faces board.

STARTING-UP COSTS

The amount of money you need to fork out at the start of your career largely depends on the category of modelling, and the type of agency you join. Most top fashion agencies advance new models expenses to cover all their starting-up costs, whereas others, such as small, regional agencies, or agencies representing speciality models, expect costs to be borne by the model. Initially, you'll need to pay for tests, prints and a portfolio case, whereas payment for composites or entry into your agency's book normally comes later. Many new models balk at paying start-up costs, but modelling, like most other professions, requires a certain amount of investment which, as long as you're with a reputable agency, will be recuperated from future earnings.

TOOLS
OF THE TRADE

Aside from their looks, models have
several powerful sales tools.

BOOK

A portfolio – more recently labelled a 'book' – is a model's number-one sales tool: a visual résumé which includes a selection of the model's finest photographs. 'Models' books are totally representative of their value as a model,' says Elaine Dugas, head of IMG London, which represents such major names as Niki Taylor, Stephanie Seymour, Tyra Banks and Lauren Hutton.'When it comes to a high-fashion model's book, it's simple: the stronger the editorial and the bigger the photographer, the better the book. And it's this that dictates his or her day rate. The book also reflects the direction the model is taking, i.e. editorial or commercial.'

With the exception of children, extras, lookalikes and promotions models, all models need a portfolio. An established model's book contains roughly 20 images, many of them tearsheets of published work; while a new model might have as few as three or four prints from one his or her first tests. 'Quality is the key; it's better to have a few outstanding photographs than a book crammed with mediocre ones,' says Elaine. 'Clients soon get bored if they have to plough through pages and pages of not-so-hot photographs.'

Versatility and experience should be reflected in the book, along with images that demonstrate the type of work the model does. Containing a mixture of studio and location shots with different backgrounds, the book should also show the model in a variety of looks and poses. Flick through a fashion model's book and you'll see her metamorphose from *femme fatale* to girl next door. A male character model's book might start with a picture of him playing the role of a rugged builder; turn the page and you'll see him pictured as a suave businessman.

If there's an area of work you specialize in, include pictures illustrating this. But watch out that this doesn't typecast you. You may want to edit your book to suit the client's profile. Established models keep copies of all their photographs and tear sheets to hand to be able to interchange them whenever necessary. For example, if you're casting for a swimwear job, dig out a swimsuit shot and pop it into your book.

Generally, most models' books consist of colour photographs, with the occasional black-and-white or toned shot. Variety is essential. A book should never contain work by just one photographer – no matter how much each image differs. Likewise, don't be tempted to use an unflattering tearsheet in place of a strong test shot. Models must constantly update their books, although if one of their strongest pictures is three years old, both the model and agent may decide to keep it in.

The structure of the book must not be overlooked; your booker may well compile it for you. Within each agency there is usually one booker who has a particularly creative eye. 'Kick off with your strongest head shot on the opening page,' explains Elaine Dugas, who possesses such an eye. 'The rest of the images should then flow in some kind of order, rather than be thrown together ad hoc. The two facing pictures don't necessarily have to be from the same shoot or fashion story, but they should complement one another. It's not as simple as saying you can't put a bright-coloured, ski-wear tearsheet next to a natural beauty close-up. Each photograph is like a painting: some work well together and others don't. And when it comes to colour and black-and-white, there was a time when you'd never put a colour shot opposite a black-and-white, now everyone's doing it!'

The standard model's book is a smart, black binder containing plastic sleeves which comfortably hold magazine-size photographs. Portfolio cases can be bought from stationers' or art and design shops. The bigger agencies usually provide models with a book that normally has their logo embossed on the front. As agencies frequently courier books to clients, most models have a second, and sometimes third, book which contains duplicates of all the images in their first book. Original prints and tearsheets are preferred for first books; however, laser copies are normally acceptable for the additional books. Some agencies also like their models to have mini books – a smaller version of their main book. In addition to their regular books, supermodels have press books that contain cuttings of their major press interviews.

TESTS

Testing is where not only the model, but also the photographer, make-up artist, hair and fashion stylists all benefit by having fresh photographs for their books. Confusingly, a test doesn't mean you are testing your skills as a model – it's simply the industry term for an unpaid photo shoot. 'I cannot over-emphasize the importance of testing,' says Elaine Dugas. 'Without good test shots, a model won't get any work.'

Your booker will either set up tests for you, or will recommend certain photographers whom they suggest you test with. Just like new models, photographers starting out need to build up a book. Established photographers also test: they may want to photograph a particular model or, alternatively, they might have a specific idea for a shoot they want to try out. Photographers all have a different style of work, so it may worth seeing their book prior to the shoot. You must also discuss with photographers exactly what you and your agent

Photographed by Rod Howe

want to achieve. If it's fresh-faced, close-up shots you need, you must tell the photographer this in advance; they might need to hire special lighting.

Once the shoot has been arranged, find out if the photographer is organizing hair and make-up. If not, you will either have to arrange this via your agency, or do your own. These days, models, particularly fashion models, rarely test without the full team, complete with make-up artist, hair stylist and fashion stylist. Incidentally, if the photographer has organized a stylist, then he or she should supply clothes and accessories; otherwise you will need to bring along a good selection of your own. Even if clothes are being supplied, it's always a good idea to have a few of your own tucked in your bag, just in case they don't fit.

Not only will it give you material for your book, but from testing you will learn how to act in front of the camera and how to move with ease. However, don't expect to learn the ropes from one shoot. It takes time and, besides, most shoots vary. One photographer might give you direction, while another may just expect you to 'do your thing', regardless of whether it's your first test or not.

Don't think that just because you are not being paid you don't need to give it your all. Treat test shoots as seriously as you would a job: after all it's the photographs from testing that will get you the work in the first place.

The cost of tests differs. Some agencies will arrange test shoots with photographers who do not charge at all. However, many photographers require a small fee to cover the cost of film and processing. In order to build up their books, new models must test frequently. Models with tearsheet-heavy books still need to test from time to time. Fresh photographs may reflect a different look, and, as models are constantly reinventing their look, new tests are necessary to show a change of hairstyle or colour, or a total mage revamp.

TEARSHEETS

A tearsheet is published work, usually from the cover or editorial pages of a magazine. 'We rarely use an advertising tearsheet in models' books,' says Elaine Dugas. 'Generally, advertising is shot in a less artistic way, and the actual advertisement is often covered with text. However, there are always exceptions to the rule. Some of the fashion advertisements are almost indistinguishable from the editorial pages.' Published work instils a client

with confidence. Models use the actual pages from the magazine for two reasons: it is unlikely they will obtain the original photograph and, as most tearsheets have text, or in the case of a cover, title copy, the image is instantly recognizable as work.

Not all editorial tearsheets get pride of place in a model's book, Elaine explains why: 'It's all about prestige. With the teeny magazines, occasionally we use a tearsheet, but the main reason models work for these magazines is to gain experience in front of the camera. The fashion pages of a newspaper don't usually end up in a model's book but, then again, as with advertising, there's always the exception. A Sunday-supplement tearsheet is more akin to a magazine and, as the fashion pages are often a showcase for hot photographers, it's more likely the model will be able to use them. And when it comes to *Vogue*, *Elle*, *Harper's Bazaar*, *Marie Claire*, et al. – need I say any more?'

COMPOSITES

Another powerful promotional tool, the composite – also commonly termed a 'Sed' card, Index card or model card – takes the shape of a black-and-white or colour, A5, printed card. But as Elaine Dugas points out, many agencies, including IMG, now prefer to use laser copies. 'Although there is no difference in the cost, lasers mean we can constantly update the composite and give us the flexibility to print a dozen at a time. With printed cards, you need to have at least 500 printed at once, or it costs a fortune. And being able to change a composite is particularly important for new models who are getting stronger images all the time.'

Composites normally feature a head shot on the front and several full-length images on the flip side. Printed underneath the photographs are such details as the model's name, hair and eye colour, height, dress or suit size, and measurements, along with the agency's logo and address. Composites are vital. They act as a reminder to clients, who usually file them for future use. Carry them at all times. Each time you go to a casting or go-see you must leave a composite behind. Even if you're exactly what the client's looking for, you'll soon be forgotten if they don't have a picture to refer to. And don't expect clients to take photocopies of images from your book. This would look unprofessional on your part and would be time-consuming for the client.

The images selected for your composite should be your strongest. However, if you are having a card printed and don't want it to date, you may want to pick a more timeless image. Published work is preferable to test shots; fashion models quite often have their favourite magazine cover on the front. Models must update their composites regularly, especially if they change their appearance by having a haircut or drastically altering the colour of their hair.

Agencies generally stick to one design so that all their models' composites are of the same style. Some may have elaborate borders around the front picture, while others may bleed the picture off the edge. Elite's composites, for instance, comprise two head shots on the front on a silver background, with their agency logo on the back. The majority of agencies, however, tend to stick to a traditional, white background with a black typeface.

Normally, agencies arrange for the composite to be printed. Agencies usually hang on to a large wad of composites, handing them out to visiting clients, mailing them out and displaying the rest on their shelves. The cost of printed composite cards varies enormously, depending on such factors as whether the card and photographs are in colour or black-and-white, the number of images, and the finish. For example, a four-sided, laminated, coloured card with several images would be far more expensive than a simple, two-sided, black-and-white card.

THE AGENCY BOOK

From the glossy works of art produced by fashion agencies – complete with poetry and transparent paper – to child-model agencies' catalogues of happy snaps, the agency model book is an important promotional tool. As it is frequently referred to by clients, photographers and magazines, it's essential for models to appear within it. Most agencies print a new book each year; although, because children grow so quickly, some child agencies produce books bi-annually. The book may encompass all the agency's divisions or may only include the main board. For example, a fashion agency's book may contain photographs of models from the main board, new faces board, and celebrity or special bookings section.

These type of books are expensive to print, so agencies need to recuperate a large percentage of this cost from their models. The cost depends on such factors as the size of the book, the quality of paper and printing, as well as the number of images each model has within the book.

HEADSHEETS

Some agencies produce headsheets in addition to, or instead of, an agency book. The headsheet is a poster-size sheet dotted with close-up shots of all the agency's models, which includes details of the model's name, height and vital statistics. Agencies send headsheets to their clients, who often pin them to their office or studio wall and use it as a quick reference. As a headsheet is considerably cheaper to produce than a book, the cost to the model is lower. As an alternative to the headsheet, some agencies prefer to print booklets, or small headsheets, which are known as circulation charts.

SHOW REEL/COMPILATION VIDEO

Models who have appeared in three or more commercials and/or videos often compile a video (known as a show reel) of their work to show potential clients.

FUTURE IMAGES

Models' portfolios can now be stored on disc. Each image is scanned and transferred onto a disc format, then entered into a CD-ROM disc drive, thus enabling a client or agency to view the model Imagebase (images in a model's book) on their computer screen. Several of the bigger agencies have a website on the Internet, which means that rather than agencies having the cost and hassle of couriering their models' books, clients can instantly log on to the images of the models they are interested in. Computers and software packages have become so sophisticated that some agencies are now able to produce their own composites and flyers. By scanning the photograph into a design package they can design the copy, add the agency's logo, import the images and print off composites whenever they are needed.

COSTS

Models are expected to cover the cost of the portfolio case/book, composite cards and their entry into the agency book or headsheet. However, many fashion agencies will either give the model an advance or pay the cost on the model's behalf, deducting the amount from his or her future earnings.

Photographed by Dave Foster

A MODEL'S
SCHEDULE

Globetrotting from studios to locations or trekking around town on the casting trail – a model's schedule is gruelling.

It's amazing how the whole model industry operates so successfully at the eleventh hour. Castings are often arranged hours before, and assignments booked at the last minute. You may not find out you're off on a trip abroad until the day before, or even the very same day! This actually happened to top fashion model Joanne Watkins. One minute she was just a wannabe who had casually strolled into Select model agency off the street. The next minute she was booked for a shoot with W magazine which took place in Paris later that day.

CASTINGS

A casting could lead to a £15,000 commercial, a prestigious magazine shoot or might simply end up as yet another rejection. Clients prefer to hold castings when choosing a model for an assignment. With the exception of the supermodels, all models need to cast. Normally, the client will ring several agencies and brief the bookers on the type of model they are looking for. An agency may have a call from a beauty editor requesting girls with amazing blue eyes, or a casting director wanting to audition kids for a toy commercial. If clients ask for a specific look, they will trust the agency to send a selection of models who suitably fit the description.

Castings vary depending on the type of assignment. Commercial castings usually involve a screen test where you might be asked to perform a certain role in front of a video camera. This could mean doing all sorts of things, from dressing in character, to improvizing eating a bar of chocolate. For a speaking part you would be expected to read a few lines from an Autocue or script. Spontaneity is vital: you often have very little – if any – prior knowledge of what the client or casting director wants. I knew one model who had no idea she'd be asked to cry in a screen-test for a jewellery commercial. Fortunately for Helen, she had studied drama, and was able to turn on the tears at the click of a finger; a skill that won her the job. At a show casting the show producer will instruct you to parade up and down the floor as if you were on a runway. You may also be asked to slip on an outfit or two. Castings for photographic work are simpler still: a quick look at your book, a Polaroid, and it's over.

Castings can be daunting and demeaning experiences. There are often a dozen gorgeous models filling every square yard and, with the client picking the choicest contender, the bigger castings – a blanket invitation to every model in town – are a sort of cattle-market-like affair. When it's your turn, the client may flick through your book and say 'next' without even asking your name. This is fairly normal, but a novice often finds this experience leaves them feeling more like an object than an individual. When top model Laura Bailey first started casting, this is how she summed up the experience: 'The first time I went on a casting it was quite embarrassing. The other girls were much more laid back than I'd imagined, but we were all standing there, loads of us in this magazine office, waiting to be seen and inspected. I wanted everyone to know that I had a degree and wasn't as dumb as I must have seemed.'

When taking down your casting details, always try to find out from your booker exactly what the client is looking for. The more you know, the better equipped you'll be. Go prepared. For glamour, body work, hosiery, swimwear or lingerie the client will want to see as much of you as possible, so don't forget to pack that g-string, swimsuit or bikini in your model kit. At a casting for a major hosiery campaign, a client had requested models with good, firm bottoms. Having forgotten her g-string, one of the models came unprepared and was, therefore, unable to display the perfectly formed bottom that could have earned her a lucrative contract. Finally, even if you've had to wait so long you miss your next casting, always smile and be pleasant. You never know – you might just clinch the job!

GO-SEES

A 'go-see' is model-industry jargon for an informal appointment where a model visits photographers, magazine editors, casting directors and other clients. However, agencies often refer to an appointment with a photographer or magazine editor where there is an actual job as a go-see. At the beginning of their careers, new faces fashion models have to attend dozens of go-sees every week. And, until they reach the stage where they are well known, they still need to attend the occasional go-see. Unlike castings, go-sees don't necessarily lead directly to a specific job. Instead, the objective of the go-see is to be seen by as many people in the industry as possible. You may strike it lucky by visiting a photographer who just happens to have a job coming up. On the other hand, you may never work with some of the people you meet. The added benefit of go-sees with photographers is that they may be interested in testing you.

Be pleasant, enthusiastic and lively, but avoid the temptation to ask the client or photographer if they've got any work for you. If you are asked what work you've done, don't be tempted to lie. This is a close-knit industry and the chances are you will be caught out. If the go-see is brief, or the client appears to be rather abrupt, don't worry. This business is full of extremely busy people, and few have time to sit around chit-chatting.

DIRECT BOOKING

Supermodels and other top models are often booked on spec without having to cast for the job. Promotions models, lookalikes, extras, kids and babies, and models who've previously worked with the client are also booked directly. When booking direct, clients make their selection from a model's book, composite, or from the photograph in the agency book.

TRIPS

Models are often whisked off to exotic locations on what is known in the industry as a 'trip'. Clients choose warm climates where sunshine is guaranteed. With its hot sun, sandy beaches and Art Deco buildings, Miami has been the favourite for many years. South Africa, Mexico, the Caribbean, Morocco, Greece, Kenya and Portugal are other locations also popular with clients. During the busy season, long stretches of sand are dotted with location teams all aiming to get that perfect shot.

Trips are a mixture of hard work and fun: you may be in the most heavenly place, but you'll have little time for sight-seeing. The model is usually the first one up – often before dawn – for hair and make-up. An early rise also means having to forget those fun nightspots. Hiccups such as flight delays, sunstroke, sunburn and upset stomachs can cause problems. And, a single difficult or disgruntled member of the team can spoil the whole enjoyment of the trip.

ASSIGNMENT/BOOKING

An assignment could take the form of a catwalk show for Versace, an advertising shoot for Levi's, a showroom season for Cerruti, or a fashion shoot for *Elle*. Commercials and stills are often shot in studios or indoor locations such as villas, châteaux or hotels. Location shoots are the popular alternative to the studio for all kinds of photographic and commercial shoots. You could find yourself by the beach, on safari, lounging around a pool, on a boat, or draped around the pillars of a stately home. Some locations are slightly more challenging. For an advertisement shoot for the retailer Next, a model was photographed standing on an iceberg in Antarctica. And for a magazine fashion shoot, fashion model Tina Harlow was strapped to a harness on top of a two-seater plane. Up among the clouds, the photographer snapped away from the co-pilot's seat. Brave but barmy, Tina loved every minute of it. 'I had always wanted to wing-walk, so it was a bonus to get paid for it.' Those who are scared of heights will be reassured to know that the casting was only attended by four models and, during the test run, only Tina actually managed to do it.

OPTIONS

An option is a sort of provisional booking where the client puts the model on stand-by. If the model is available, the first client to request an option will be granted a 'first'. If another client also wants to option the model for the same day, this client will have to settle for second option. In the event that the second option is for a major advertising campaign, the booker needs to do some clever juggling. When it gets close to the assignment, if the client still hasn't confirmed the first option, the agency puts the pressure on.

TIMETABLES

CASTING AND GO-SEES SCHEDULE

9.30 DROP BY AGENCY TO PICK UP TEARSHEETS

10.30 CASTING FOR HAIR COMMERCIAL

11.00 TIME FOR A QUICK CAPPUCCINO BEFORE NEXT CASTING

11.30 APPOINTMENT TO SEE BOOKINGS EDITOR AT *COSMOPOLITAN*

12.00 CASTING FOR A BEAUTY SHOOT FOR *ELLE*

1.00 APPOINTMENT TO SEE FASHION PHOTOGRAPHER

1.45 GRAB A BITE TO EAT AT NEARBY BRASSERIE

2.30 CASTING FOR A MAIL-ORDER CATALOGUE

3.30 STOP AT CHEMIST TO BUY TIGHTS FOR NEXT DAY'S SHOOT

4.00 SHOW CASTING WITH PRODUCTION COMPANY

5.00 TELEPHONE AGENCY TO FIND OUT DETAILS OF FOLLOWING DAY

5.30 ARRIVE AT PHOTOGRAPHER'S STUDIO FOR TEST SHOOT

5.45 EAT A SANDWICH BEFORE MAKE-UP AND HAIR

7.30 SHOOT BEGINS

10.00 SHOOT ENDS

LOCATION SCHEDULE

5.30 EARLY-MORNING CALL FOLLOWED BY BREAKFAST

6.00 HAIR AND MAKE-UP

8.00 MEET PHOTOGRAPHER AND FASHION TEAM IN HOTEL LOBBY

9.00 AFTER LONG DRIVE IN JEEP, ARRIVE AT BEACH

10.00 SHOOT BEGINS

12.30 BREAK FOR LUNCH

1.30 CHANGE OF CLOTHES AND HAIRSTYLE; MAKE-UP IS RETOUCHED

2.30 START SHOOTING

5.00 ARRIVE BACK AT HOTEL EXHAUSTED

SHOW SCHEDULE

9.00 FITTING FOR SONIA RYKIEL SHOW

10.30 ARRIVE BACKSTAGE FOR JEAN-PAUL GAULTIER SHOW

11.00 MAKE-UP ARTIST GETS TO WORK

11.30 HAIR IS PUT UP IN TOPKNOT

12.30 REHEARSALS

1.00 SHOW IS DUE TO START – WAIT IN WINGS

2.00 SHOW BEGINS

2.45 SHOW IS OVER – DASH BACKSTAGE TO CHANGE AND RUSH OFF TO NEXT SHOW

3.00 NO TIME FOR COMPLETE MAKE-OVER. MAKE-UP ARTIST JUST RETOUCHES MAKE-UP SO IT IS IN KEEPING WITH THE THEME OF THE SHOW

3.15 A QUICK RUN-THROUGH WITH THE SHOW PRODUCER

3.30 ON THE RUNWAY IN VERY HIGH HEELS

4.00 AFTER 15 OUTFIT CHANGES IT'S ALL OVER

4.30 CASTING FOR ONE OF TOMORROW'S SHOWS

5.00 ARRIVE AT THE VENUE FOR NEXT SHOW. STILL TWO MORE TO GO, THEN IT'S PARTY TIME!

FINANCE

A MODEL'S INCOME

Top-league models rake in more money in a day than some people earn in a year. And, with their trickle incomes from modelling spin-offs – books, videos, calendars, etc. – most are set up for life. However, big bucks are only for the lucky few and for every supermodel there are thousands of models struggling to make ends meet.

Models get paid for assignments, but do not earn money for the time spent attending castings and go-sees or testing. Regular pay packets don't exist in this business and, as models are self-employed, they don't get paid for periods of illness or holidays; nor do they earn a penny for those grim days – or even weeks – when there's no work coming in at all. All too often models who've been working continually, suddenly find they hit an unexpected lull. To their horror they find they haven't accounted for this period, and run into financial difficulties. For security, models must spread their earnings to tide them over when work is scarce, rather than blow every penny on a wardrobe full of designer clothes. Supermodel Lisa B advises models to make investments for the future. 'Your looks aren't going to last forever. I know so many models who get paid for job, then just blow the money on a £2,000 Dolce & Gabbana dress they only end up wearing on one occasion.'

Because a considerable amount of models' work is seasonal, their earnings fluctuate throughout the year. Quiet times in the modelling calendar include Christmas, as well as most of August, a time when many of the European model agencies close down and head to the beaches for their summer vacations to take a well-earned rest.

FEES

The supermodels have proved that there is no ceiling on the fees a model can earn. We've all heard them refusing to get out of bed for less than $10,000 a day and holding designers to ransom. The majority of models, however, will leap out of bed for notably less. Because fees vary drastically, from as little as £165 for a day's editorial work to a million-pound contract for a cosmetic campaign, no two models' wages are ever alike.

Factors that influence a model's earning power – which increases his or her day rate – are experience, status and exposure. If a particular model is in demand, clients are prepared to pay considerably more. However, for certain types of work, such as editorial and personal appearances, a fixed amount is paid to models regardless of their day rate.

Other factors that can increase models' fees include overtime and travel. If models are travelling further than a certain radius, they usually get 50 per cent of their hourly fee for travel time. This also extends to travelling on trips. Along with travel fees, if there's a day during a trip when a model is not needed, he or she will get what is known as a 'recreation fee'. For work that runs into evenings or weekends, models are paid overtime (often double their hourly rates).

Fees differ from country to country, model to model and client to client. Advertising pays the fattest cheques, which are determined by the model's day rate, the extent of the usage, and the territories in which the advertisement is to appear. An averagely successful model may earn £2,000 a day working for a national print advertisement. For a world-wide commercial, however, where the model is the main feature, the package, including a 'buy-out', could be in the region of £30,000.

Because of the cachet involved in appearing in glossy fashion magazines, with the exception of superstar models, in the main editorial work is poorly paid. The daily rate for most UK consumer magazines is approximately £165. Mail-order catalogue work is better paid than editorial, as is most calendar work. The fees for show work vary considerably. A British designer who has very little backing will probably only be able to pay a model a few hundred pounds, whereas doing the equivalent show in Paris or Milan can earn a model thousands of pounds. Showroom seasons, shopping-mall or department-store and other run-of-the-mill shows usually pay considerably less than the international designer shows.

BUY-OUT

Instead of paying a model repeat fees each time a commercial is shown, these days most clients prefer to buy the rights to use the image when and where they like. If advertising clients are placing a print campaign or showing a commercial in several countries or regions (known as territories), they will often negotiate a buy-out. The wider the usage, the more profitable the buy-out. Generally, a buy-out can double, or even triple, a model's day rate.

ADDITIONAL USAGE

If a buy-out isn't negotiated, extra usage fees are paid to the model for the rights to use his or her picture for additional purposes other than the original stated use. For example, a hosiery client may decide to use a photograph that was originally shot for an advertisement for point-of-sale showcards and posters, or on the hosiery's packaging itself.

TERRITORIES

If an advertising still or commercial is used in different territories, such as certain regions or several specified countries, models are paid extra fees in addition to their day rate. Alternatively, a buy-out is negotiated.

REPEAT FEES

Fees are paid to the model each time a commercial, video, film or television programme is shown.

VOUCHER/MODEL RELEASE FORM

For most photographic bookings, a model needs to fill in a voucher and get it signed by the client, photographer, editor, etc. The voucher is usually in three parts: a copy for the client, the model and the model's agent.

AGENCY COMMISSION

Model agencies earn money by taking a percentage of their models' earnings. The standard agency commission throughout the world is between 20 and 25 per cent except Japan, where it is between 40 and 50 per cent. The commission deducted by the agency is shown on a model's statement of payment.

PAYMENT

Model agencies are responsible for invoicing clients on behalf of their models. Agencies usually stipulate that clients must pay their invoices within 30 days. But in practice this is rarely adhered to. Agencies are not banks, nor are they legally obliged to pay a model for a job until they have received the payment themselves. Some agencies do, however, advance models money against their earnings, charging interest in return. Once an agency has received payment from the client, they should, by UK law, pay a model no later than ten days after the date of receipt. However, due to accounting reasons, larger agencies usually pay their models at specific times of the month.

AGENCY CONTRACT

Most reputable agencies expect models to sign a contract that outlines terms and conditions. This is perfectly normal. The contract should also specify the percentage of commission the agency takes from its models. Top fashion agencies normally include a clause to prevent their models from working with another agency while on their books. If you are worried about a contract, seek professional advice before signing.

HANDLING ACCOUNTS

Very few agencies advise models on how to handle their accounts. Models are self-employed, which means they are responsible for paying their own tax, national insurance and, if they earn above a certain limit, VAT. And don't think the money you earn abroad is tax free. Your are also liable for tax on your foreign earnings. Child models and models still at school also have to pay tax if their earnings exceed their personal allowance. Listen to supermodel Lisa B's advice: 'Take good care of your accounts and don't avoid the tax situation.'

Accountants: Accountants are hired to do tax returns and help keep tax down to a minimum. They know exactly what expenses models can and cannot claim for. However, their services don't come cheap, so if you've only been modelling for a year or two and your earnings are not very high, you may decide to do your own tax returns.

Keeping accounts: Whether you have an accountant or not, you will need to keep all your receipts and agency payment slips, along with detailed records of your income and expenditure.

Tax-deductible expenses: As a model you can claim various expenses against tax, ranging from day-to-day travel expenses to the cost of prints and portfolio cases. The important thing to remember is that the expenses should be solely for business use. Here is a list of things models are usually able to claim for: test shots, prints, laser copies, composite cards, fashion magazines, portfolio cases, travel, telephone calls, postage, stationery and accountants' fees.

VAT: Once models' earnings reach a certain level, they need to register with customs and excise to pay value added tax. However, this can be set against any VAT paid out for composite cards, prints, etc.

MODEL INDUSTRY LINGO

ADVERTISING – print advertising covers a wide area of work for models, including national press, magazine and billboard. Point-of-sale work such as showcards, posters and packaging also comes under the advertising umbrella.

AGENT – model agent or booker.

ASSIGNMENT – a modelling job/booking.

BEAUTY WORK – varying from a major cosmetic campaign to a commercial for hair or a lip-colour feature in the editorial beauty pages of a magazine.

BOARD – a division of an agency such as the new faces board or main board.

BOOK – new word for a model's portfolio which comprises prints and tearsheets.

BOOKER – a member of the model agency staff who handles models' careers, also known as a booking agent or agent.

BOOKING – a modelling job/assignment.

BOOKING OUT – a term used whenever a model takes time off or is unavailable for work.

BOOKING TABLE – bookers sit around this large, circular table, which comprises either a rotating filing system of models' charts or computers.

BUY-OUT – when a client buys the rights to use a photograph in certain media and/or in particular territories.

CALENDAR – Pirelli, Unipart and Mintex are just three of the many different companies which produce yearly pin-up calendars and hire glamour or fashion models to appear in them.

CALL BACK – a second casting.

CAMPAIGN – print or commercial advertising that appears in different media such as magazines, billboards and television.

CASTING – where models audition for a specific job.

CATALOGUE – encompasses all types of catalogue work, from the run-of-the-mill, mail-order catalogues to glossy brochures for fashion stores. Models use catalogue work as a way of earning bread-and-butter money. As the client usually books each model for a few days, the work is financially viable. Many catalogues are shot on location, so this type of work often results in a trip abroad.

CATWALK – the ramp used for models to walk down at fashion shows.

CHARTS – details of models' schedules kept by their agency bookers.

CIRCULATION CHART – a smaller form of promotional material than a headsheet.

CLIENT – the person who hires the model, i.e. the photographer, magazine bookings editor, PR, designer, casting director etc.

COMMERCIALS – the advertisements that appear on television or the big screen.

COMMERCIAL WORK – advertising, catalogue or other work which involves selling a product. Whether it's a job for the fashion pages of a catalogue or a product-advertising campaign, commercial-style work is usually photographed in a more salesy and less creative way than editorial-style photography. A 'commerical' model has more of a girl-next-door look.

COMPOSITE – an A5-size card or laser copy with one or more pictures of the model, together with the agency's details and the model's statistics.

CONTACT SHEETS – a photographic sheet of small prints that are easier to choose from than negatives.

DAY RATE – the fee that a model commands for a full day's work.

EDITORIAL – refers to the covers, fashion and beauty pages of magazines, as well as newspapers and supplements. Highly prestigious yet poorly paid, once a model has a cover or fashion tearsheet from a top magazine such as *Vogue*, *Marie Claire* or *Elle*, it can lead to major advertising campaigns. Magazines also hire models to illustrate their features or short stories.

EDITORIAL STYLE – this style of photography is generally far more spontaneous and looser than that used for catalogue or advertising. A model who is termed 'editorial' is a high-fashion model, who has a stronger, more directional image than a commercial-looking model.

EXHIBITIONS – wholesalers exhibit their clothes on stands in large exhibition halls, partly as a promotional exercise, and partly to take orders. Aside from fashion exhibitions, there are bridal, lingerie, shoe, swimwear and hosiery exhibitions.

FITTINGS AND SIZINGS – fashion manufacturers, retailers or designers hire standard-size models to act as mannequins while they size up samples of their collection. If a child is booked for catalogue, brochure or any other work involving clothing, they will usually be needed for a fitting prior to the shoot. This saves time and problems with sizes, and the client can be sure that the clothes suitably fit the child before the shoot takes place.

GO-SEES – informal appointments where models visit a photographer or magazine editor to introduce themselves and show their book.

HEADSHEET – a large sheet produced by agencies which includes small pictures of all their models.

HEAD SHOT – a close-up photograph of a model's face or head and shoulders.

IMAGE – a photograph.

INFORMAL MODELLING – where clothes are modelled without a runway. Also known as 'couture style'. Usually done in a showroom or on an exhibition stand.

LOCATION – a job that takes place anywhere outside a studio.

MODEL AGENCY BOOK – a yearly book that includes one or more pictures of all the agency's models along with their statistics.

MODEL RELEASE FORM – also called voucher. A form that should be signed after each photographic job by the model, photographer and client.

MOTHER AGENT – the agency a model first joins.

OPTION – a sort of provisional booking which places a model on stand-by.

PARTS MODELLING – work for hands, legs, feet and other body parts.

PHOTO SESSION – a photographic shoot.

POINT OF SALE – photographs that are used on display in a shop, such as posters and showcards, to help promote the clothes or product.

PORTFOLIO – a model's book of photographs.

PRINTS – individual photographs.

RUNWAY – the more up-to-date term for catwalk.

SCOUT – a person hired by an agency to search for new talent.

SHOOT – a photographic session.

SHOW FITTINGS – hand-in-hand with each catwalk show goes the fitting. During a fitting, the designer ensures that each model fits the clothes like a glove, and, if not, the necessary alterations are made. A loose waistband at a show, for example, could mean a catwalk disaster!

SHOWROOM – fashion companies and designers which work on a wholesale basis often operate from showrooms. Some of these companies hire permanent 'house models', while others may only require models during the buying season. Full-time showroom work is not usually booked through a model agency. Fashion companies often advertise for house models in newspapers, via recruitment agencies which specialize in fashion, or else by sticking a notice in their showroom window.

SHOWROOM SEASON – the buying season which can be anything from two to eight weeks and takes place twice a year.

SHOWS – the international designers' twice-yearly fashion shows, also referred to as 'collections'. The glitz of the catwalk show is no longer exclusively for the fashion trade, however: nowadays the general public has access to shows, too. Shopping malls, department and chain stores regularly stage catwalk shows for their customers. Fashion shows are also becoming popular at special events, conventions, fashion-trade exhibitions and live magazine shows.

SNAPSHOTS – photographs such as holiday pictures.

STATISTICS – a model's body measurements, height, eye and hair colour.

TEARSHEET – a published page from a magazine or newspaper.

TESTS – an unpaid photo shoot. The purpose is for the model to get photographs for his or her book. Photographers, make-up artists, fashion and hair stylists also need to test.

TRANSPARENCY – a colour negative from a shoot where colour film was used.

TRIP – an assignment abroad.

VIDEO – models are often used to add that touch of glamour to videos. Aside from music videos, different model types are hired by companies producing corporate, demonstration, promotional and in-house sales videos.

VOUCHER – another term for model release form.

Photographed by Neil Kirk courtesy of © Condé Nast PL - British Vogue

PART 5

MODELLING AROUND THE WORLD

THE INTERNATIONAL MODELLING WORLD

Model fever has swept the globe.

A MODEL WORLD

Siberia's Eskimo model, Irina Pantaeva, along with the Czech Republic's most famous export, Eva Herzigova; Kiara Kabukura, who hails from Uganda and Dinka tribeswoman Alek Wek, are some of modelling's hottest properties. Today, models of diverse origins are enjoying successful careers in what was traditionally a very limited market. And, as a result, a profession once frowned upon by non-western cultures is attracting models on a universal scale. Because clients now recognize that modelling has developed into a multi-cultural industry – no longer dominated by western ideals – models of every nationality are in demand.

WORLD MARKETS

Nowadays, you no longer need to live in Paris, New York, Milan or London to join a top agency. To reach previously untapped markets, agency networks such as Elite's and Ford's are enlarging the modelling map by setting up offices in far-flung places. Independent agencies are also springing up in all corners of the world. So, wherever you live, the chances are you won't be too far away from a model agency. And, once on an agency's books, you'll have the choice of either working in your own country, or modelling internationally in one or more of the many foreign markets now open to you.

High-fashion work is the passport to international modelling. Nowadays, to be a successful high-fashion model, it's essential to work internationally, and be represented by agencies in the key modelling markets – Paris, New York, Milan and London. But these four cities are not the only modelling arenas. Other busy markets on the international circuit include Japan, Germany, Amsterdam, Switzerland, Canada, South Africa, Los Angeles and Miami. Most model agencies are centred around big cities, although these cities are not necessarily the capital of a country, two examples being New York and Milan. If you join a regional model agency – an agency based outside the prime modelling centre – the work is more likely to be local, rather than international.

WORKING ABROAD

Travel is one of the highlights of a model's career. You certainly get to see the world. Throughout her career, Jerry Hall has modelled in no less than 68 countries. To be booked directly by a client for an assignment abroad – particularly on a trip to an exotic location – is a perk of the job. In addition to your fee, the client pays all expenses, including travel, accommodation and food. Fashion, child, glamour and character models are some of the model types who are booked for the multitude of catalogues, magazines, calendars and advertisements photographed overseas.

Besides travelling abroad for specific bookings, some models, especially fashion models, spend a few weeks or even several months working with an agency in a foreign market. For example, a model from Eastern models in Poland will come to London to spend a couple of months with Models 1, which is the London agency representing her. Similarly, a model from Storm may spend a couple of months with Riccardo Gay in Milan. This opportunity gives models the chance to work for clients or magazines in different markets, which results in tearsheets and, if they're lucky, earns them money. Some markets, including London, Milan and Tokyo are easier for new models with no more than a handful of test shots to break into, while others, like Germany, Paris and New York, require a strong book of tearsheets.

Both the agency networks and independents work with a number of agencies in each foreign market. Some may be associated with or affiliated to one another, while others will have set up a simple working agreement: a sort of informal trading system whereby they send models to each other. As the agencies receive a percentage of the a model's commission, both agents benefit from the arrangement.

One method of finding a foreign agency to represent you is for your agent to send a selection of photographs (laser copies are perfectly adequate) or your composite to an agency in a market they feel your look would be suitable for. For example, a fresh-faced, blue-eyed blonde might find she works non-stop in

Eskimo supermodel Irina Pantaeva left the icy plains of Siberia for the international catwalk.

Japan, whereas a raven-haired, pale-skinned model might find it difficult to get a Japanese agency even to consider representing her.

Another way of being recruited by an overseas agency is to be introduced to a scout or representative who has visited your agency. Scouts from the major international agencies are continually travelling to foreign agencies. Storm's Jessica Hallet travels to both the big agencies in the modelling centres, as well as the small, regional agencies. And a scout from international agency Pauline's discovered Guess? model Lonneke Engel at a small child agency in the little town of Eindhoven in Holland.

COSTS OF WORKING WITH AN OVERSEAS AGENCY

Once an overseas agency agrees for you come over, they may pay your air fare and advance you money for accommodation and living expenses. However, not all agencies are prepared to take the risk, and may expect you to contribute to, if not fund, the full cost yourself. This differs from one agency to another, and is often determined by the size of agency, how established a model you are, or simply the market place.

THE PROBLEMS

Spending time in another country can be lonely and problematic. First of all there's the culture shock which, for a model who has hardly ever stepped foot out of her native country, is magnified. Modelling in Japan, for example, is fairly regimented and quite different to working in Europe. Then, there's the language barrier, unless, like Eva Herzigova or Karen Mulder, you speak several languages.

Travelling to and from your destination can also be a daunting experience. For young models, or models who have never flown before, a long-haul flight coupled with a transfer can be terrifying – especially if they miss the flight. One young model was returning from a two-month contract in Tokyo when, busy shopping in duty free, she failed to listen out for the flight call. As a result, a petrified 16-year-old girl was stranded at Tokyo airport.

The positive side of working overseas is that you can have fun, broaden your horizons, see beautiful parts of the world and meet a wide variety of interesting people from many different cultures.

INTERNATIONAL MODEL AGENCY
DIRECTORY

Types: includes characters, families, commercial models
Talent: includes extras, actors
Fashion: includes women and men

Argentina
FORD
IST AND SECOND FLOOR
AVENUE SANTE FE
BUENOS AIRES 1060
TEL: 00 541 815 0489
Fashion

Australia
CAMERONS
EDGECLIFFE COURT
2 McLEAN STREET
EDGECLIFFE
SYDNEY
NSW 2027
TEL: 00 61 2 362 0100
Fashion • Petites • Plus sizes

CAMERONS
3/402 CHAPEL STREET
SOUTH YARRA
MELBOURNE
VIC 3141
TEL: 00 61 3 9827 1687
Fashion • Petites • Plus sizes

CHADWICKS
32A OXFORD STREET
DARUNGHURST
SYDNEY
NSW 2010
TEL: 00 61 2 9332 4177
Fashion

CHADWICKS
37-39 ALBERT ROAD
SOUTH MELBOURNE
VIC 3004
TEL: 00 61 3 9866 3231
Fashion

CHIC MODELS
44 ROSLYN GARDENS
ELIZABETH BAY
SYDNEY
NSW 2011
TEL: 00 61 2 9326 9488
Fashion • Talent

Austria
ELITE
PASSAUER PLATZ 1
VIENNA 1010
TEL: 00 43 1 533 5816
Fashion

NEXT COMPANY MODEL MANAGEMENT
WERDERTORGASSE 12
VIENNA 1010
TEL: 00 43 1 535 9669
Fashion

Belgium
DOMINIQUE MODEL AGENCY
93 AVENUE DE TERVUERENIN
BRUSSELS 1040
TEL: 00 32 2 734 9405
Fashion • Character

MODEL TEAM
20 RUE BUCHHOLTZ
BRUSSELS 1050
TEL: 00 32 2 646 3540
Fashion • Parts • Character

MODELS OFFICE
34 RUE ST ANNE
BRUSSELS 1000
TEL: 00 32 2 511 4141
Fashion

Brazil
ELITE
RUA SAMPALO VIDAL 1096
SAO PAULO 01443
TEL: 00 5511 8164355
Fashion

FORD
RUA JACQUES FELIX 19
SAO PAULO CEP 04309
TEL: 00 55 11 816 4355
Fashion

Canada
DISTINCT LOOK AGENCY
783 LAWRENCE AVENUE WEST 12B
TORONTO
ONTARIO M6A 1C2
TEL: 00 1 416 767 6423
Character • Talent • Extras • Children

ELEANOR FULCHER MODEL AGENCY AND SCHOOL
615 YONGE STREET SUITE 200
TORONTO
ONTARIO M4Y 1Z5
TEL: 00 1 416 922 1945
Fashion • Children • Petites • Mature

ELITE
477 RICHMOND STREET WEST
SUITE 301
TORONTO
ONTARIO M5V 3E7
TEL: 00 1 416 369 9995
Fashion

FOLIO
295 DE LA COMMUNE OUEST
MONTREAL
QUEBEC H2Y 2E1
TEL: 00 1 514 288 8080
Fashion • Mature • Children

FORD
3 SULTAN STREET
TORONTO
ONTARIO M55 116
TEL: 00 1 416 962 6500
Fashion

GIOVANNI MODEL MGMT
291 PLACE D'YOUVILLE
MONTREAL
QUEBEC H2Y 285
TEL: 00 1 514 845 1278
Fashion • Mature

RICHARDS MODEL AGENCY
1450 WEST GEORGIA #PH
VANCOUVER BC V6B 2T8
TEL: 00 1 604 683 7485
Fashion • Talent • Children

SUTHERLAND MODELS
20 EGLINGTON AVENUE EAST
TORONTO
ONTARIO M4P 1A9
TEL: 00 1 416 488 0900
Fashion • Talent • Children

VHM MODELS
200-1311 HOWE STREET
VANCOUVER BC V6Z 2P3
TEL: 00 1 604 687 4682
Fashion • Talent • Extras • Petites

Czech republic

BOHEMIA MODELS
SENOVAZNE NAMESTI 21
PRAGUE 11000
TEL: 00 420 2 2414 2945
Fashion

DONNA MODEL MGMT
1 GORAZDOVA
PRAGUE 2 18600
TEL: 00 420 2 294 635
Fashion • Character • Children

Denmark

ELITE
MAGSTRAODE 10
1204 COPENHAGEN
TEL: 00 45 3315 1414
Fashion

SCANDINAVIAN MODELS
MAGSTRAODE 10
1204 COPENHAGEN
TEL: 00 45 33 93 2424
Fashion

UNIQUE MODELS
3 NY OSTERGADE
K 1107 COPENHAGEN
TEL: 00 45 3312 0055
Fashion • Mature

Egypt

TALENTS CASTING AGENCY
15 ABDEL RAHMAN EL RAFAEY STR
CAIRO
TEL: 00 20 2 335 4335
Fashion • Types

Finland

AZZURRO
MUSEOKATU 11
HELSINKI 00100
TEL: 00 358 9 5494 8800
Fashion • Character • Children • Mature

BOOM
PURSIMIEHENKATU
HELSINKI 00150
TEL: 00 358 9 626 055
Fashion

FONDI
UNIONKATU 45A
HELSINKI 00170
TEL: 00 358 9 135 2100
Fashion

PAPARAZZI
SALOMONKATU 17 B 30
HELSINKI 00100
TEL: 00 358 9 686 6410
Fashion

France

ABSOLU/PH1
50 RUE ETIENNNE MARCEL
PARIS 75002
TEL: 00 33 144 76 58 90
Fashion

ALLIX AGENCY
80 RUE VANEAU
PARIS 75007
TEL: 00 33 1 4284 0303
Babies • Children • Teenagers

AMAZONE INTERNATIONAL
120 BOULEVARD PERIER
MARSEILLES 13008
TEL: 00 33 4 9137 6161
Fashion • Children • Character

BANANAS
217 RUE DE FG SAINT HONORÉ
PARIS 75008
TEL: 00 33 1 4289 4209
Fashion – men

CITY MODELS
21 RUE JEAN MERMOZ
PARIS 75008
TEL: 00 33 1 5393 3333
Fashion – women

COMPANY
26 RUE DE LA TREMOILLE
PARIS 75008
TEL: 00 33 1 5367 7700
Fashion – women

ELITE MODEL MANAGEMENT
8 BIS RUE LECUIROT
PARIS 75014
TEL: 00 33 1 4044 3222
Fashion – women

FAM INTERNATIONAL
30 BOULEVARD VITAL BOUHOT
92521 NIUILLY
PARIS
TEL: 00 33 1 4192 0650
Fashion – women

FORD MODELS EUROPE
9 RUE SCRIBE
PARIS 75009
TEL: 00 33 1 5305 2525
Fashion

IMG MODELS
2 RUE DUFRENOY
PARIS 75116
TEL: 00 33 1 4503 8500
Fashion – women

KARINS MODELS
9 AVENUE HOCHE
PARIS 75008
TEL: 00 33 1 4563 0823
Fashion

THE MARYLIN AGENCY
4 RUE DE LA PAIX
PARIS 75002
TEL: 00 33 1 4277 0404
Fashion – women

METROPOLITAN
7 BOULEVARD DES CAPUCINES
PARIS 75002
TEL: 00 33 1 4266 5285
Fashion – women

NATHALLE MODEL AGENCY
10 RUE DAUBIGNY
PARIS 75017
TEL 33 1 4429 0710
Fashion – women

PAULINES
21 BIS RUE MOLIERE
PARIS75001
TEL: 00 33 1 4260 5252
Fashion – women

PRIVILEGE
5 RUE DE LONGCHAMPS
NICE 06000
TEL: 00 33 1 49387 5212
Fashion • Children

VIVA MODELS
15 RUE DUHPOT
PARIS 75001
TEL: 00 33 1 4455 1260
Fashion – women

Germany

BERLIN MODELS
ROSENTHALER STRASSE 3
BERLIN 1054
TEL: 00 49 30 280 5126
Fashion • Talent

D'SELECTION
CECILIEN ALLEE 66
DÜSSELDORF 40474
TEL: 00 49 211 84 555
Fashion

E MODELS
CORNELIUS STRASSE 71
DÜSSELDORF 40215
TEL: 00 49 211 386 100
Fashion • Plus sizes

HARRYS MODEL MGT
VIRCHON STRASSE 2
MUNICH 80805
TEL: 00 49 89 360 0000
Fashion

LOUISA MODELS
EBERSBERGER STRASSE 9
MUNICH 81679
TEL: 00 49 89 9210 9620
Fashion • Plus sizes

MEGA
WEXSTRASSE 26
HAMBURG 20355
TEL: 00 49 40 343 009
Fashion

MODEL MANAGEMENT
HARTUNGSTRASSE 5
HAMBURG 20146
TEL: 00 49 40 440 555
Fashion

MODEL TEAM
SCHLUTER STRASSE 60
HAMBURG 20146
TEL: 00 49 40 414 1037
Fashion

MUNICH MODELS
KARL THEODOR STRASSE 18A
MUNICH 80803
TEL: 00 49 89 341 336
Fashion – female

NO TOYS
SCHWANENMARKT
DÜSSELDORF 40213
TEL: 00 49 211 322 100
Fashion

PEOPLE
GRUNDEL STRASSE 14
MUNICH 81825
TEL: 00 49 89 422 896
Character

TALENTS MODEL AGENCY
MUEHLENKAMP 31 2000
HAMBURG 22303
TEL: 00 49 40 271 047
Fashion

Greece

ACTION MODELS
PATRIACHOU LOAKIM 11
ATHENS 10675
TEL: 00 30 1 721 1075
Fashion – women

FASHION CULT MODEL AGENCY
5 IPERIDOU STR & NIKIS
ATHENS 10558
TEL: 00 30 1 322 1301
Fashion • Types • Children

UNIQUE MODELS
15 KARNEADOU STR
ATHENS 10675
TEL: 00 30 1 729 2611 14
Fashion • Talent • Children

Hong Kong

ELITE
SUITE 901 WORKINGTON TOWER
78 BONHAM STRAND
SHEUNG WAN
TEL: 00 85 2 2850 5550
Fashion

Ireland

EDDIE SHAHAHAN, THE AGENCY
38 CLARENDON STREET
DUBLIN 2
TEL: 00 353 1 679 3929
Fashion

Italy

CASTING
31 VIA CAVOUR
FLORENCE 50129
TEL: 00 39 55 238 1348
Fashion

ELITE MODEL MGMT
40 VIA SAN VITTORE
MILAN 20123
TEL: 00 39 2 481 4704
Fashion

EYE FOR I
29 VIA ARELIO SAFFI
MILAN 20123
TEL: 00 39 2 480 12877
Fashion

FASHION MODEL MGMT
80 VIA MONTE ROSA
MILAN 20149
TEL: 00 39 2 4808 6222
Fashion

FUNNY TYPE 2 TROVAROBE
11 VIA AURELIO SAFFI
MILAN 21023
TEL: 00 39 2 4390672
Character

PETIT MODEL
25 VIA ALBERTO MARIO
MILAN 20149
TEL: 00 39 2 498 3678
Babies • Children • Teenagers

RICCARDO GAY
8 VIA REVERE
MILAN 20123
TEL: 00 39 2 4800 2713
Fashion

WHY NOT
2 VIA GIOBERTI
MILAN 20123
TEL: 00 39 2 481 8341
Fashion – women

Japan

CHIC
ISUGURI MANSION
4-18-6 JINGUMAE
SHIBUYA-KU
TOKYO 150
TEL: 00 81 3 478 5867
Fashion

CINQ DEUX UN
9-6-28 AKASAKA
MINATO-KU
TOKYO 107
TEL: 00 81 3 3402 8445
Fashion

COSMOPOLITAN
ASAHI PLAZA UMEDA #714
4-11 TSURUNO-CHO
KITA-KU
OSAKA 530
TEL: 00 81 6 359 5067
Fashion

ELITE/FOLIO
1-10-10 AZABUJUBAN
MINATO-KU
TOKYO 106
TEL: 00 81 3 3586 6481
Fashion

EVE MODELS
12-2-200 UMEDA
KITA-KU
OSAKA
TEL: 00 81 6 344 6346
Fashion

SATORU/GEM
BELAIRE GARDENS
4-2-11 JINGUMAE
SHIBUYA-KU
TOKYO 150
TEL: 00 81 3 3475 0555
Fashion

VISAGE
1-2-2-200 UMEDA
KITA-KU
OSAKA
TEL: 00 81 6 348 1855
Fashion

YOSHIE INC.
40-30-22 TAISHIDO
SETAGAYA-KU
TOKYO 154
TEL: 00 81 3 3486 7291
Fashion – women

Netherlands

CORINE'S
PRINSENGRACHT 678
1017 KX AMSTERDAM
TEL: 00 31 20 622 6755
Fashion

DE BOEKERS
HERENGRACHT 407
1017 BP AMSTERDAM
TEL: 00 31 20 627 2760
Fashion

ELITE
KEIZERSGRACHT 448
1016 GD AMSTERDAM
TEL: 00 31 20 627 9929
Fashion

TOUCHE
284 SINGEL
1016 AD AMSTERDAM
TEL: 00 31 20 625 0254
Fashion

New Zealand

MAYSIE BESTALL-COHEN MODEL MANAGEMENT
THE REGENT AUCKLAND
SWANSON STREET
AUCKLAND 1
TEL: 00 649 309 9408
Fashion

NOVA MODEL AND TALENT
79 ANZAC AVENUE
AUCKLAND
TEL: 00 649 309 6405
Fashion • Talent • Character
• Children • Types

VISAGE
171 PARNELL ROAD
PARNELL
AUCKLAND 1
TEL: 00 649 309 6405
Fashion

Norway

ELITE
RIDDERVOLDSGT 3
0258 OSLO 2
TEL: 00 47 2244 4811
Fashion

TEAM
18 BALDERSGT
0263 OSLO 0263
TEL: 00 47 2255 8850
Fashion • Children • Character

Poland

EASTERN MODELS
UL SMOLNA 34/1
WARSAW 00375
TEL: 00 48 22 827 8729
Fashion

Portugal

L'AGENCIE
RUA COELHO DA ROCHA 69
1300 LISBON
TEL: 00 35 11 397 4207
Fashion • Types

LOOK/ELITE
RUA JOAO NEPOMMUCENO 32B
1200 LISBON
TEL: 00 35 11 386 2421
Fashion

Russia

RED STARS
DEVIATKIN PER 2-7
MOSCOW 101000
TEL: 00 7 095 924 2055
Fashion • Types

Singapore

CARRIE MODELS
273A SOUTH BRIDGE ROAD
SINGAPORE 0105
TEL: 00 65 2239 289
Fashion

Slovakia

SLOVAK MODELS
PANENSKA 3
81103 BRATISLAVA
TEL: 00 421 7 531 8296
Fashion • Types

South Africa

G3 MODELS
G3 HOUSE
111 A DE SMIDT STREET
CAPE TOWN 8001
TEL: 00 27 21 419 1101
Fashion • Character • Children

G3 MODELS
PO BOX 7227
JOHANNESBURG 2000
TEL: 00 27 11 484 3317
Fashion • Character • Children

ICE MODELS
DARTONS ROAD GARDENS
CAPE TOWN 8001
TEL: 00 27 21 232 244
Fashion

THE MODEL COMPANY
20 WANDEL STREET GARDENS
CAPE TOWN 8001
TEL: 00 27 21 462 2461
Fashion • Character • Children

MODEL TEAM
11A BELLEVUE STREET
TAMBOERSKLOOF
CAPE TOWN 8001
TEL: 00 27 21 262 410
Fashion

MULLIGAN'S MODELS
15 VARNEYS ROAD
GREENPOINT
CAPE TOWN 8001
TEL: 00 27 21 439 0304
Fashion • Mature

STUDIO 001
1 WOLFGANG AVENUE NORWOOD
JOHANNESBURG 2000
TEL: 00 27 11 728 3868
Fashion

Spain

ATLANTIC MODELS
LUIS MUNTA DAS 2
BARCELONA 08035
TEL: 00 34 3 418 8099
Fashion • Children • Character

ELITE
CALLE FORTUNY 37
5 DERECHA B
MADRID 28010
TEL: 00 34 1 310 27777
Fashion

ELITE
AVENIDA TIBIDABO 56 BAJOS TORRE
08035 BARCELONA
TEL: 00 34 3 418 8099
Fashion

ISASI MODEL AGENCY & SCHOOL
ENCARNACION 10
MADRID 28013
TEL: 00 34 1 541 6007
Fashion • Talent

LA AGENCIA
3RD FLOOR
AVENIDA DIAGONAL 40049
BARCELONA 08021
TEL: 00 34 3 444 3000
Fashion

NATASHA'S MODELS
AVENIDA DIAGONAL 469 6 2A
BARCELONA 08036
TEL: 00 34 3 405 3435
Fashion

STARS
SAGASTA 4 2ND FLOOR
MADRID 28004
TEL: 00 34 1 521 1111
Fashion

Sweden

FACE IT
GREVGATAN 22
11453 STOCKHOLM
TEL: 00 46 8 662 7296
Fashion

MIKA'S
14 RAGVALDSGATAN
STOCKHOLM
TEL: 00 46 8 641 0807
Fashion • Children • Character

SWEDEN MODELS
SKOMAKAREGATAN 2
MALMO 21134
TEL: 00 46 40 978401
*Fashion • Children • Character •
Plus sizes*

Switzerland

ELITE MODEL MANAGEMENT SA
15 ROUTE DES ARSENAUX
1700 FRIBOURG
TEL: 00 41 37 224815
Fashion – women

PMS FOTOMODELL SERVICE
RIETERSTRASSE 21
8002 ZURICH
TEL: 00 41 1 202 3744
Fashion

TIME MODEL AGENCY
SPITALGASSE 4
8001 ZURICH
TEL: 00 411 261 6040
Fashion • Children

Taiwan

FACE MODELS
2F NO 11 LANES 26
CHUNG-SHAN N ROAD SECTION 2
TAIPEI
TEL: 00 886 2 567 7002
Fashion

MAD MODEL
4F NO 17 LANE 16
CHUNG-SHAN N ROAD SECTION 2
TAIPEI
TEL: 00 886 2 523 0222
Fashion

UK

BOSS
HALF MOON CHAMBERS
CHAPEL WALKS
MANCHESTER M2 1HN
TEL: 00 44 161 834 3403
Fashion • Child

BOSS MODELS
7 BERNERS MEWS
LONDON W1
TEL: 00 44 171 580 2444
Fashion

CRAWFORDS
2 CONDUIT STREET
LONDON W1R 9TG
TEL: 00 44 171 629 6464
Types

THE DAVID AGENCY
153 BATTERSEA RISE
LONDON SW11 1HP
TEL: 00 44 171 223 7720
Extras

DERRICKS
153 BATTERSEA RISE
LONDON SW11 1HP
TEL: 00 44 171 223 7720
Parts

ELITE PREMIER
40-42 PARKER STREET
LONDON WC2B 5PH
TEL: 00 44 171 333 0888
Fashion

ELIZABETH SMITH
81 HEADSTONE ROAD
HARROW
MIDDLESEX
TEL: 00 44 181 863 2331
*Babies • Children • Teenagers •
Families*

EXCEL
THE WORX
16-18 UNDERWOOD STREET
LONDON N1
TEL: 00 44 171 336 6373
Plus sizes – women

FREDDIES
THE CLOCK HOUSE
ST CATHERINE'S MEWS
MILNER STREET
LONDON SW3 2PX
TEL: 00 44 171 225 1355
Fashion

HIRED HANDS
12 CRESSY ROAD
LONDON NW3 2LY
TEL: 00 44 171 267 9212
Hands

HUGHES MODELS
67 FRANCISCAN ROAD
LONDON SW17
TEL: 00 44 181 672 8494
Plus sizes • Petites – women

IMG
13/16 JACOB'S WELL MEWS
GEORGE STREET
LONDON W1H 5PO
TEL: 00 44 171 486 8011
Fashion – women

LOUISE DYSON
95 SPENCER STREET
BIRMINGHAM B18 6DA
TEL: 00 44 121 554 7878
Fashion • Child • Character/types

MODELS 1
OMEGA HOUSE
471-473 KINGS ROAD
LONDON SW10 0LU
TEL: 00 44 171 351 1195
Fashion • Mature

MODELS PLUS
82A BELSIZE ROAD
LONDON NW6
TEL: 00 44 171 624 5045
Promotions • Fashion

THE MODEL TEAM
180 HOPE STREET
GLASGOW G2
TEL: 00 44 141 332 1915
Fashion • Children

NEVS
REGAL HOUSE
198 KINGS ROAD
LONDON SW3 5XX
TEL: 00 44 171 352 9496
Fashion

NORRIE CARR
30 FRYENT WAY
LONDON NW9 9SB
TEL: 00 44 181 204 2241
*Babies • Children • Teenagers •
Families*

PROFILE
12/13 HENRIETTA STREET
LONDON WC2E 8LH
TEL: 00 44 171 836 5282
Fashion – women

RESPECT
PARSONAGE CHAMBERS
3 THE PARSONAGE
MANCHESTER M3 2HB
TEL: 00 44 161 832 5543
Fashion • Children

SAMANTHA BOND
199 KINGS ROAD
LONDON SW3 5ED
TEL: 00 44 171 352 3767
Glamour

SELECT
3RD FLOOR
43 KINGS STREET
LONDON WC2
TEL: 00 44 171 470 5200
Fashion

SPIRIT MANAGEMENT
1ST FLOOR
50 HANS CRESCENT
LONDON SW1X 0NA
TEL: 00 44 171 838 1838
Celebrity models

STORM
1ST FLOOR
JUBILEE PLACE
LONDON SW3
TEL: 00 44 171 376 7764
Fashion

SUSAN SCOTT LOOKALIKES
24A LYNDALE AVENUE
LONDON NW2
TEL: 00 44 171 387 9245
Lookalikes

TOP MODELS
3RD FLOOR
21/25 GOLDHAWK ROAD
LONDON W12
TEL: 00 44 181 743 0640
Mature • Types

UGLY
265 EDGWARE ROAD
LONDON W2
TEL: 00 44 171 402 5564
Character • Types

USA

ARIA MODEL AND TALENT
1017 WEST WASHINGTON SUITE 2A
CHICAGO
ILLINOIS 60607
TEL: 00 1 312 243 9400
Fashion

ARLENE WILSON
887 WEST MARIETTA STREET
ATLANTA
GEORGIA30318
TEL: 00 1 404 876 8555
Fashion • Child

ARLINE SOULIERS
121 MADISON AVENUE
NEW YORK
NEW YORK 10016
TEL: 00 1 212 213 4937
Fashion

BOSS MODELS
1 GAVENSOORT STREET
NEW YORK
NEW YORK 10014
TEL: 00 1 212 242 2444
Fashion – men

CITY MODELS
123 TOWNSEND #510
SAN FRANCISCO
CALIFORNIA 94107
TEL: 00 1 415 546 3160
Fashion

CLICK
CARNEGIE HALL STUDIO 1013
881 SEVENTH AVENUE
NEW YORK
NEW YORK 10019
TEL: 00 1 212 315 2200
Fashion

COMPANY
270 LAFAYETTE STREET
SUITE 1400
NEW YORK
NEW YORK 10012
TEL: 00 1 212 226 9190
Fashion – women

ELITE ATLANTA
181 14TH STREET
ATLANTA
30309 GEORGIA
TEL: 00 1 404 872 7444
Fashion

ELITE CHICAGO
212 WEST SUPERIOR
CHICAGO
ILLINOIS 60610
TEL: 00 1 312 943 3226
Fashion

ELITE LA
345 NORTH MAPLE DRIVE
SUITE 397
BEVERLY HILLS
CALIFORNIA 90210
TEL: 00 1 310 274 9395
Fashion

ELITE MIAMI
1200 COLLINS AVENUE
MIAMI BEACH
FLORIDA 33139
TEL: 00 1 305 674 9500
Fashion

ELITE NEW YORK
111 EAST 22ND STREET
NEW YORK
NEW YORK 10010
TEL: 00 1 212 529 9700
Fashion

FORD CALIFORNIA
8826 BURTON WAY
BEVERLY HILLS
CALIFORNIA 90211
TEL: 00 1 310 276 8100
Fashion

FORD FLORIDA
826 OCEAN DRIVE
MIAMI BEACH
FLORIDA 33139
TEL: 00 1 305 534 7200
Fashion

FORD/ROBERT BLACK
7525 E CAMELBACK ROAD
SCOTTSDALE
ARIZONA 85251
TEL: 00 1 602 966 2537
Fashion

THE FORDS
344 EAST 59TH STREET
NEW YORK
NEW YORK 10022
TEL: 00 1 212 546 9296
Fashion • Mature • Petite • Plus sizes

IMG
170 FIFTH AVENUE
NEW YORK
NEW YORK 10010
TEL: 00 1 212 627 0400
Fashion

IRENE MARIE
728 OCEAN DRIVE
MIAMI BEACH
FLORIDA 333139
TEL: 00 1 305 672 2929
Fashion

L'AGENCE
5901 C PEACHTREE DUNWOODY
ROAD
ATLANTA
GEORGIA 30328
TEL: 00 1 770 396 9015
Fashion • Children • Talent

LOOK MODELS/LOOK TALENT
166 GEARY STREET 14TH FLOOR
SAN FRANCISCO
CALIFORNIA 94108
TEL: 00 1 415 781 2822
Fashion • Talent • Extras • Mature • Children

METROPOLITAN
5 UNION SQUARE WEST
NEW YORK
NEW YORK 10003
TEL: 00 1 212 989 0100
Fashion – women

MICHELLE POMMIER MODELS
81 WASHINGTON AVENUE
MIAMI BEACH
FLORIDA 33139
TEL: 00 1 305 672 9344
Fashion • Talent • Children

NEXT
23 WATTS STREET
NEW YORK
NEW YORK 10013
TEL: 00 1 212 925 5100
Fashion

PAGE PARKS
763 COLLINS AVENUE
MIAMI BEACH
FLORIDA 33139
TEL: 00 1 305 672 4869
Fashion

PARTS MODELS
PO BOX 7529
FDR STATION
NEW YORK
NEW YORK 10150
TEL: 00 1 212 744 6123
Parts

PAULINES
379 WEST BROADWAY
NEW YORK
NEW YORK 10012
TEL: 00 1 212 941 6000
Fashion – women

PLAYBOY MODELS
9242 BEVERLY BOULEVARD
BEVERLY HILLS
CALIFORNIA 91210
TEL: 00 1 310 246 4000
Glamour

PLUS MODELS
1400 OCEAN DRIVE
MIAMI BEACH
FLORIDA 33139
TEL: 00 1 305 672 9882
Plus sizes • Petites

PRIMA/OMARS MGMT
6855 SANTA MONICA BOULEVARD
#406
LOS ANGELES 90038
TEL: 00 1 213 468 2255
Fashion

STARS
777 DAVIS STREET
SAN FRANCISCO
CALIFORNIA 94111
TEL: 00 1 415 421 6272
Fashion • Talent • Children

SUSAN JOHNSON TALENT
108 WEST OAK STREET
CHICAGO
ILLINOIS 60610
TEL: 00 1 312 943 8315
Fashion • Children

SWIFT KIDS
1400 OCEAN DRIVE
MIAMI BEACH
FLORIDA 33139
TEL: 00 1 305 672 9882
Babies • Children • Teenagers

WILHELMINA
300 PARK AVENUE SOUTH
NEW YORK
NEW YORK 10010
TEL: 00 1 212 4730700
Fashion • Children • Mature • Plus sizes

WILHELMINA WEST
8383 WILSHIRE BOULEVARD
BEVERLY HILLS
CALIFORNIA 90211
TEL: 00 1 213 655 0909
Fashion

WOMEN
103 GREENE STREET
NEW YORK
NEW YORK 110012
TEL: 00 1 212 334 7480
Fashion – women

CONTRIBUTORS' DIRECTORY

As a special thank-you to all the experts who contributed to the image section, here is a list of all those who have products, salons or services to offer the public.

CHAMPNEYS
HEALTH SPA
HERTFORDSHIRE, ENGLAND
TEL: 00 44 1442 863351

CHEWTON GLEN
HOTEL & SPA
HAMPSHIRE, ENGLAND
TEL: 00 44 1425 275341

NICKY CLARKE
LONDON SALON
TEL: 00 44 171 491 4700
HAIROMATHERAPY HAIR PRODUCTS
WIDELY AVAILABLE

E'SPA
MAIL ORDER AND INFORMATION LINE
TEL: 00 44 1483 454444

SUSIE FAUX
WARDROBE
LONDON
TEL: 00 44 171 494 1131

STEPHEN GLASS
LONDON
TEL: 00 44 171 935 8478

GRAYSHOTT HALL
HEALTH SPA
SURREY, ENGLAND
TEL 00 44 1428 604331

MARY GREENWELL
PREMIER
TEL : 00 44 171 221 2333

RUBY HAMMER
MAKE-UP ATRIST
DEBBIE WALTERS
TEL: 00 44 171 266 2600

RUBY HAMMER'S MASTERCLASS
LONDON AESTHETIC
TEL: 00 44 171 636 1893

JO HANSFORD
COLOURIST
LONDON SALON
TEL: 00 44 171 495 7747

DOUGLAS HARRISON
PLASTIC SURGEON
LONDON CONSULTING ROOMS
TEL: 00 44 171 935 6184

MAGGIE HUNT
JOY GOODMAN
TEL: 00 44 181 968 6887
MAGGIE HUNT'S MAKE-UP BRUSHES
(MAIL ORDER)
TEL: 00 44 191 268 2288

INTERNATIONAL MODEL AND TALENT ASSOCIATION
USA
TEL: 00 602 997 4907

PHILIP KINGSLEY
TRICHOLOGIST
NEW YORK CLINIC
TEL: 00 212 753 9608
LONDON CLINIC
TEL: 00 44 171 629 4004

ROB LANDER
FITNESS TRAINER
TEL: 00 44 171 554 9026

EVE LOM
LONDON SALON
TEL: 00 44 171 935 9988
PRODUCTS AVAILABLE
AT DICKINS & JONES

OR MAIL ORDER
TEL: 00 44 181 661 7991

SAM MCKNIGHT
RANGE OF HAIR PRODUCTS AVAILABLE
AT BOOTS THE CHEMIST

PRISCILLA MARMOT
DIETICIAN
CHAMPNEYS
TEL: 00 44 1442 863351

ANTHONY MASCOLA
TONY & GUY HAIR SALONS
H/O TEL: 00 44 171 629 8348

ORLANDO PITA
JOHN FRIEDA
RANGE OF PRODUCTS AVAILABLE
AT CHEMISTS

ARIANNE POOLE
MAKE-UP ARTISTS'
COSMETIC COUNSELLING
JOY GOODMAN
TEL: 00 44 181 968 6887

NIGEL SAPSED
FITNESS TRAINER
THE CONRAD HOTEL
LONDON
TEL: 00 44 171 823 3000

CHARLES WORTHINGTON
WORTHINGTON'S SALON
TEL: 00 44 171 831 5303

ALISON YOUNG/AVEDA
NATURAL-BASED PRODUCTS
MAIL ORDER
TEL: 00 44 171 636 7911

PHOTO CREDITS AND ACKNOWLEDGEMENTS

1, 6, 8, 14, 51, 55, 72, 74, 76, 77, 82, 86, 122, 183 courtesy of © Niall McInerney. 2 & 3 Nick Knight courtesy of © Condé Nast PL - British *Vogue*. 5 courtesy of Rod Howe, also with thanks to Elite Premier. 11 Jacques Olivar courtesy of © Condé Nast PL - British *Vogue*. 13 Patrick Demarchelier courtesy of © Condé Nast PL - British *Vogue*. 16 courtesy of Rod Howe with thanks to Elite Premier. 19 courtesy of Rod Howe with thanks to Howard Daniels and *Cosmopolitan*. 20 Catherine Rowlands courtesy of Rod Howe with thanks to Howard Daniels and *Cosmopolitan*. 21 Howard Daniels courtesy of *Cosmopolitan*. 23 Marco Palumbo courtesy of Spirit Management/*Tatler*. 24 & 25 courtesy of Richard Bradbury, also with thanks to the Ugly agency. 27 courtesy of Advertising Archives. 29 courtesy of Rankin, also with thanks to *Dazed & Confused*. 30 courtesy of Richard Bradbury, also with thanks to the Ugly agency. 36 & 37 courtesy of Stephen Perry, also with thanks to the Samantha Bond agency. 39 courtesy of Stephen Perry, also with thanks to *Loaded* and the Samantha Bond agency. 40 courtesy of Stephen Perry, also with thanks to Samantha Bond. 42 courtesy of Rod Howe. 45 courtesy of Martyn Elford. 47 courtesy of Advertising Archives. 48 courtesy of Darleine Honey. 49 courtesy of Rod Howe, also with thanks to Daniel Pangborne. 61 courtesy of Derek Lee. 64 courtesy of Trevor Hurst. 68 & 69 courtesy of Rod Howe, also with thanks to Models 1. 71 courtesy of Elite. 87 courtesy of Rod Howe, also with thanks to Models 1. 85 courtesy of Elite. 88, 89 & 91 courtesy of Elite. 92 Tony McGee courtesy of *Cosmopolitan*. 102 & 103 John Swannell courtesy of © Condé Nast PL – *Tatler*. 106 & 107 Nick Knight courtesy of © Condé Nast PL - British *Vogue*. 111 Miles Aldridge courtesy of © Condé Nast PL - British *Vogue*. 116 & 117 illustrations courtesy of Maggie Hunt. 118 Sante D'Orazio courtesy of © Condé Nast PL - British *Vogue*. 128 Kim Knott courtesy of © Condé Nast PL - British *Vogue*. 135 Andrea Blanche courtesy of © Conde Nast PL - British *Vogue*. 140 Michael Thompson courtesy of © Condé Nast PL - British *Vogue*. 145 Arthur Elgort courtesy of © Condé Nast PL - British *Vogue*. 149 courtesy of Champneys. 153 Neil Kirk courtesy of © Condé Nast PL – British *Vogue*. 158 & 159 Richard Lohr courtesy of © Condé Nast PL - British *Vogue*. 165 courtesy of Rod Howe, also with thanks to Models 1. 169 courtesy of Rod Howe and Models 1. 172 Dave Foster courtesy of Rod Howe, also with thanks to Ian Forster. 180 & 181 Neil Kirk courtesy of © Condé Nast PL – British *Vogue*. Author picture courtesy of Universal.

ACKNOWLEDGEMENTS

The author would like to say a big thank-you to everyone who helped with the book. She would like to say a special thank-you to the following people who kindly gave their time, information and help with this book: Miranda Denoff, Gareth Roberts, Stephanie Pierre at Elite Premier; Didier Fernandez at Elite Paris; Paula Karaiskos, Jessica Hallet, Marie Soulier and Sarah Doukas at Storm; April Ducksbury, Jose Fonseca and Jane Wood at Models 1; Richard Habberley at Select Models; Elaine Dugas at IMG; Jonathan Phang at Spirit Management; Elizabeth Smith at Elizabeth Smith; Cheryl Hughes at Hughes Models; Pat Swift at Swift Kids and Plus Models; Susan Scott at Susan Scott Lookalikes; Joan Dewar-Spangler at Look Talent; Lalia Debs at The David Agency; Steve Barker at Hired Hands; Marc French at Ugly; Samantha Bond and Paul Bozchac at Samantha Bond; Bill Fairly at the Playboy agency; Stevie Walters at Models Plus; Allison Bramwell at Excel; Danny Korwin at Parts Models, Susan Georget at Wilhelmina; Karen Long at Boss Models; Carmel Allen and Georgina Knight at *Vogue* UK; Elaine Deed and Byrony Toogood at *Cosmopolitan*; Nick Knight and Charlotte Wheeler; Sarah Walters at *Marie Claire*; Maggie Hunt; Ruby Hammer; Mary Greenwell; Arianne Poole; Stephen Glass; Sam McKnight; Colin Gold; Nicky Clarke; Charles Worthington; Philip Kingsley; Jo Hansford; Orlando Pita; Anthony Mascola; Jay Alexander; Rankin; Daniel Pangborne; Rod Howe; Howard Daniels; Richard Bradbury; Nigel Sapsed; Rod Lander; Christina Thomas; Priscilla Marmot; Adam Palmer and Kathryn Paling at Champneys, Philippa Roberts at Chewton Glen; Elaine Williams at Grayshott Hall; Eve Lom, Susan Harmsworth at ESPA; George Hammer at Aveda; Mina Kuhera at Millie Kendal PR; Alison Young, June Marsh, Susie Faux at Wardrobe; Anna Scholz. The author would like to extend her thanks to the models – Lisa Barbuscia, Tina Harlow, Rachel Roberts, Nina McCann, Philip Philmar, Margot Dillon, Alex Cameron, Nicky Lilly, Joanne Guest, Emma Noble, Nancy Sorell, Gemma Dunn, Jack Davies, The Ellison family, Lesley Lowe, Vicky Hoskins, Sarah Paterson, Simone Ive, Helen Slaymaker and Sarah Clive. Sandra would like to say a special thank-you to her agent Fiona Batty at Peters, Fraser and Dunlop and the team at Weidenfeld & Nicolson for giving her the opportunity to write and produce *The Model Manual*. Sandra has dedicated this book to her sister. The publisher and author are not responsible for any injuries caused by those attempting the exercises in this book or any allergies or problems whatsoever arising from beauty treatments recommended. Every effort has been made to ensure that the credits, directory and information are accurate. However, if any errors are brought to the attention of the publishers, they will be more than happy to make any corrections in the event of a reprint.